THE PRACTICAL ENCYCLOPEDIA OF
MAGIC

Whether your aim is to become a full-time professional magician or simply a competent hobbiest ready to entertain your friends at your next party, the following pages will teach you the basics of this wonderful art – and much more besides. Prepare to enjoy over 120 magic tricks that will keep you and your audiences amused for hours.

THE PRACTICAL ENCYCLOPEDIA OF
MAGIC

NICHOLAS EINHORN

PHOTOGRAPHY BY JOHN FREEMAN

HERMES
HOUSE

*To Hilary, Stanley and Francine
for their never-ending support,
And to my wife Joanne for the magic
she gives me every single day*

This edition is published by Hermes House

Hermes House is an imprint of
Anness Publishing Ltd
Hermes House, 88–89 Blackfriars Road,
London SE1 8HA
tel. 020 7401 2077; fax 020 7633 9499;
info@anness.com

© Anness Publishing Ltd 2002, 2003

A CIP catalogue record for this book is
available from the British Library.

Publisher: Joanna Lorenz
Managing Editor: Judith Simons
Project Editor: Felicity Forster
Art Manager: Clare Reynolds
Editor: Judy Cox
Photography: John Freeman, assisted by
    Alex Dow
Hand Model: Jennifer Schofield
Designer: Steve West
Jacket Design: Peter Ridley
Editorial Reader: Penelope Goodare
Production Controller: Steve Lang

Previously published as *The Art of Magic*

10 9 8 7 6 5 4 3 2 1

The author and publishers have made
every effort to ensure that all instructions
contained within this book are accurate
and safe, and cannot accept liability for any
resulting injury, damage or loss to persons
or property, however it may arise. Matches
and rope should be used with caution.

contents

introduction

If you have never before had an interest in learning the art of magic, then be warned. You are at the beginning of a journey that could and often does last a lifetime!

I became interested in magic while watching a magician on my fourth birthday and knew at that very moment what I was going to do for the rest of my life. That was 22 years ago and I have been performing, creating and learning ever since.

Those of you who have already learnt a few magic tricks know how much fun it is to amaze and amuse people. Magic as a hobby is unique in that it not only fascinates the person studying it, but family and friends also. This is one reason why magic is such a wonderful pastime. Another is the sense of achievement from mastering any of the skills you undertake to learn.

Magic is also universally recognized as a wonderful form of entertainment. If you ever get the opportunity to visit one of the many magic conventions that take place all over the world, you will see a wide mixture of people. Every ethnic background is represented – young and old, amateurs and professionals, students and people in every career imaginable – but all of them share one thing in common. They all love magic.

Many of the routines and magic tricks in this book can be performed at a moment's notice with whatever objects happen to be lying around. You may want to break the ice at a meeting in the office, entertain at a dinner party or show a few tricks to your children. Whatever the situation, you will be in a position to perform something amazing.

Within this book you will find over 120 miracles to learn and perform. Many are very simple and are what magicians call "self-working tricks". Despite this term, do not expect that the tricks will work themselves. However simple a trick may appear to be, practice and rehearsal are always required to enable the performer and performance to look polished and professional. You may only wish to learn one or two of these magic tricks, but if you perform them with confidence you will be amazed at the reaction you will receive, and may well be inspired to learn more.

As you progress though the book, you will be introduced to a number of moves and sleight-of-hand techniques. Many of these are not particularly difficult to learn, but again require practice in order to reach a point where you will feel comfortable using them.

If you learn everything in this book, you will have an excellent grounding in the basics of the art of magic. If you want to learn more, you will find details of your nearest magic shop at the back of the book.

Above: Many hours of practice and rehearsal are necessary in order for you to attain a level of ability that will leave your audiences speechless at your skill and stunned by your magic.

The methods for all the tricks are clearly explained, with photographs showing each step. For convenience, the explanations are from a right-handed person's point of view; left-handed readers can reverse the left and right hands, as necessary.

Professional magicians use many of the tricks in this book, and very soon you will be performing them too. You may be surprised at just how simple some of these tricks are to perform, but do not be disappointed. The easier the method the less there is to go wrong.

Remember how you felt the first time you saw a magician make a coin vanish right before your eyes? Or that time your card was found, even though you shuffled the deck and told no one what it was? Well, in learning magic you are about to give up some of that sense of wonder in order to allow others to experience and appreciate the art. This brings us on to a very important point.

keeping the secret

A magician's golden rule is always to keep the secret. There are several reasons for this. You are investing time and effort in learning the magic tricks in this

Left: For centuries audiences have marvelled and puzzled over how a woman can be sawn in half. If the audience saw how the illusion was achieved, they would be far from impressed. Luckily for professional illusionists there is more than one method to saw someone in two! Guarding your secrets is fundamental to your success.

Below: Magicians are a regular feature at children's parties, and many of the world's greatest magic stars were inspired from a very early age.

book. When you perform them properly, the first thing people will say is "How did you do that?" which is the ultimate compliment because it means that they were amazed. Some of the tricks are very simple to perform, so you would disappoint people by letting them in on the secret. If you tell your friends how a trick works you become nothing more than a presenter of clever puzzles and they will no longer give you the credit you deserve. If they are amazed, baffled and entertained, they will want to see you perform over and over again.

People often think the secret to a trick is very complicated and involves mirrors, wires and trapdoors. Allow their amazement to continue. To take this sense of wonder away is like telling someone how a film ends before they have watched it. Keeping the secret is also fundamental to the continuing success of magic as an art form. If everyone knew all of the secrets, then magic could eventually cease to exist.

Learning magic has long been a "chicken-and-egg" scenario because if magicians do not tell people their secrets, how is it possible to learn? You are holding the answer in your hands. This book has been written to introduce you to the basics of the art of magic, and a little beyond. Whether you choose to continue further is entirely up to you.

You are taking the time to learn something that can make you memorable and popular for all the right reasons. If you keep the secrets, the secrets will keep you.

We hope that regardless of whether you learn or perform any of the magic inside this book, you will respect the art of magic by keeping the secrets to yourself.

fooling people

There is a big difference between fooling someone and making someone look a fool. Some people will feel threatened when they realize that you are going to be "doing a trick on them". They may respond with a line such as "Oh! Please don't pick on me."

They assume that you are going to make them feel silly or make them look foolish. Always be aware of this. There is a fine line between amazing someone and frustrating or offending them. The best route to success is to win your audience over by creating a rapport with them – a feeling of mutual respect. This will become second nature if you are aware of it from the outset.

"Magic" is created by the magician, not by the trick. What does this mean? Simply that a trick with a poor performance is merely a puzzle. Combine a fun presentation with a great performance and you can create miracles.

misdirection

Paris
in the
the spring

Read the sentence in the triangle. Read it again. Did you notice that the word "the" is printed twice? Chances are you did not. This is an example of how you can look directly at something and yet fail to see the whole picture.

Misdirection is a very important part of magic and is in itself a subject that could fill the whole of this book. All you need to know for now is that misdirection is the name given to the technique of directing someone's attention away from what you don't want to be seen. This may mean diverting their eyesight away from your right hand as it secretly places an object in your pocket, or making them think something is going to happen to a coin when it was the glass they should have been watching.

There is an art to making misdirection subtle and difficult to detect. When used correctly, it becomes invisible. Later on in the book we will be discussing the basics of misdirection in more detail, with particular relevance to some of the tricks you will learn. As you begin to use this psychological tool with confidence, you will be amazed at how much you can get away with!

Above: Practising can sometimes be very frustrating, especially when you are attempting some of the effects that require manual dexterity. Do not give up. Just like learning to ride a bicycle, the more you practise, the better you will get.

practice, patter and style

It is vital to practise if you wish to succeed with any of the tricks in this book. The best way to learn is to read through the instructions of a trick from beginning to end and then try it out step-by-step, as shown.

Once you have learnt the order of the moves, put the book to one side and practise by talking out loud and looking at yourself performing the trick in a mirror. You may feel silly doing this initially, but a mirror is the perfect way to see what your audience will see. Often you can correct your own mistakes by following this technique.

Patter is the term used to define the words that will accompany the trick. It is a very important aspect of your overall presentation and should be considered carefully. Plan everything you will say and how you will say it, even if the words seem obvious. You will create a more polished performance by doing this. Some tricks require you to talk through what you are doing; others may need a simple story to accompany the routine. Remember to put your personality into the performance.

Think about the kind of style you wish to create. Do you want it to be fun and comical, or serious? If you make the style an extension of your personality, you will find this easier.

magic shops

There are shops dedicated to selling magic all over the world, in places you would never imagine. Have a look in your local business directory to find out where your nearest shop is located. Magic shops usually keep fairly quiet about their existence, and only a few of them advertise widely in order to stop the merely curious from learning too many secrets.

Some magic shops are like Aladdin's cave – small, dark and mysterious. Others are modern, bright and spacious. There will be experienced demonstrators behind the counter ready to show you what each trick does, and they will be able to recommend certain tricks to you, depending on your ability. As well as individual tricks, you will see magic books not to be found on the shelves of your local bookstore. Many of the books written by leading experts in the field of magic will be too advanced for a beginner, but there are others written for the aspiring amateur. Videos and DVDs are the latest way of learning magic.

You will find all of these things and more inside a magic shop. You may also be surprised at who you meet in such places. I have often bumped into famous magicians who I recognized from their performances on television.

watch and learn

Next time you watch a professional magician, even if you know the secrets of each trick, admire the performance and try to see beyond the trick in order to understand what really makes the magic work. By now you will have realized that there is far more to being a good magician than you first thought, but many of the things we have discussed will eventually become second nature.

If this book inspires and encourages you to learn more about the art of magic, you will find a hobby that will fascinate you for the rest of your life. You are already on your way to learning some of the greatest secrets ever kept, and to creating moments of happiness and amazement for people everywhere. Your journey is just beginning…enjoy!

Below: The audience here is seen waiting to watch a magic show. It is often difficult for a lay person to appreciate how much time has been spent on planning and rehearsal in order to put together such a performance. In a theatre, atmospheric music and carefully designed lighting can change the mood and help to add drama to the performance. These theatrical tools are a vital ingredient for a full show of magic, where a variety of performance styles can often make the whole experience far more dynamic and therefore more enjoyable to watch.

magicians' equipment

Most of the magic tricks in this book require very little in terms of special props. Nearly all of the items needed will be found at home, and the special props that are required for certain effects can be made very easily, as will become apparent.

books

If you intend to perform magic seriously, however, it is advisable that you visit a local magic shop and invest in a few essential items. In a shop you will be able to talk to the experienced demonstrators behind the counter, and find out about tricks that involve the use of specially made props. Magic shops are also a good source for books, videos and DVDs about magic.

There are hundreds of magic shops all over the world that you may wish to visit in person or on the Internet; you will find some of these listed at the back of the book. If your area is not listed, take a look in your local business directory.

playing cards

These are available in many shapes and sizes. The two most common sizes are bridge size, approximately 56 x 87mm (2 x 3½in), which tend to be more popular in Europe, and poker size, approximately 63 x 88mm (2½ x 3½in), which are fairly standard in casinos and throughout the USA. It is essential that you purchase a good deck of playing cards. In several of the routines in this book you will require more than one deck, and to make the special gimmicks you will be required to destroy a number of duplicate cards.

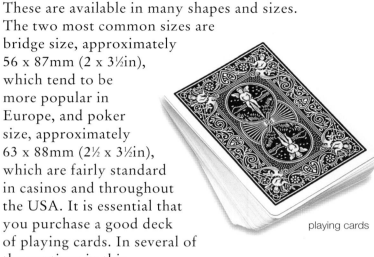

playing cards

close-up mat

close-up mat

Your first purchase might be a close-up mat. This is basically like a large computer mouse pad with a rubber base and a spongy felt top which makes spreading cards and picking up objects much easier than other surfaces such as a wooden table. Close-up mats are available in a range of different colours and sizes. Once you have a close-up mat, you can perform magic anywhere and will not have to worry about finding a nice surface on which to work. In the event that a close-up mat cannot be found, then it is advisable to work on a soft surface such as a tablecloth.

silks, cups and balls

Colourful silk handkerchiefs, together with attractive props such as the Cups and Balls, may be worth your serious consideration. The aluminium cups shown here are specially manufactured for this one trick, and there are many different styles and sizes available.

brightly coloured silks

cups and balls

rope and string

For the magic tricks in this book, most types of rope or string will suffice. If you would like a more professional rope, magic shops will be able to supply you with hanks of specially made soft "magicians' rope". This is relatively inexpensive, and available in a wide range of colours. Try to find a rope that has a high cotton content, and one that is soft and flexible.

blue and white rope
and ball of string

stationery

In order to make some of the special props, you will need a few items of stationery, such as envelopes, paper, scissors, a scalpel, pen and pencils, and adhesives. Professional equipment is always available from your local magic shop, but it is fun to make up the various props. Also, constructing props yourself can often help you to understand how they operate.

envelopes, post-it notes, scissors,
scalpel, pencil, pen, glue stick,
reusable adhesive and adhesive tape

household items

General household items – such as silverware, napkins, glasses, matches, dice, thimbles and sugar cubes – are useful for many magic tricks. They are especially suited to "impromptu magic" because performances can be off-the-cuff, with little or no preparation necessary.

silverware, napkin, glass, matches,
dice, thimbles and sugar cubes

money

Banknotes and coins are props that are easy to find, and can be used for an enormous range of magic tricks. You do not need to have new banknotes – many routines require folding or even gluing them – but shiny new coins create the best impression and are easier to see than old coins.

banknotes
and coins

history of mystery

The history of magic is so long and interesting it could easily fill every page in this book. This is not intended as a definitive account but as a brief introduction to some of the most important events and names in magic's rich history, showing how they helped to move the art forward.

magic and magicians through the ages

It is difficult to pinpoint with accuracy exactly when magic began. To start with, we need to define what we mean by "magic". Man's ability to create fire could be described as a "magical" happening, but we are only concerning ourselves here with the type of magic used as a form of entertainment.

The earliest documented evidence to suggest a performance of magic was found in the Westcar Papyrus, written about 1700BC, which tells a story that goes back to about 2600BC. Dedi, an Egyptian magician, was summoned to entertain King Cheops. One of his tricks involved cutting off an animal's head and then bringing it back to life unscathed. Dedi was asked to do the trick again using a prisoner. Much to the king's disappointment, he declined to do so, but repeated the effect with an ox instead.

The Cups and Balls is often mistakenly considered to be the earliest magic trick. It features in what was once thought to be the earliest known illustration of a magical performance. Egyptologists have dated a painting on a wall at an Egyptian tomb at Beni Hasan as being between 2500BC and 2200BC. It depicts two people playing with four cups. Recently there has been much speculation whether the absence of balls in the painting nullifies the claim that it is indeed the Cups and Balls. It certainly is an ancient trick, however, and is still popular today. There are many variations, but the basic effect is that of balls magically passing from cup to cup, appearing and disappearing at the magician's

Above right: *Le Joueur de Gobelets* is an early engraving which suggests that the Cups and Balls has been a popular trick for street performers for a very long time.

Right: This late fifteenth-century painting by Hieronymus Bosch is called *The Juggler*. It is another example which highlights the popularity of the famous Cups and Balls. Magicians were often referred to as "jugglers", which explains the title of the painting. Did you notice the man in the back row stealing the purse of the person in front of him?

successful wherever he appeared, and is known to have frequently performed for royalty. In 1783, while he was performing in Paris, Henri Decremps, a Parisian lawyer and amateur magician, exposed Pinetti's methods in a book. Ironically, the exposure only helped Pinetti's fame to spread, and he became even more popular. In 1784 he performed at the Haymarket Theatre in London, an important event because it marked the move of magic from the streets and fairgrounds to the theatre, inspiring a whole new generation of performers.

John Henry Anderson (1814–74) was a Scottish magician, often known as "The Wizard of the North". He was very successful throughout Europe, America and Australia and was, prior to Harry Houdini, the most successful publicist in magic. Anderson was known for his large props, which were often made of solid silver. He amassed a fortune but lost it after several theatres in which he was working burnt to the ground, leaving him bankrupt.

By now, society had recognized magic as an art form. Its popularity and success continued fruitfully into the next century as a steadily increasing number of magicians performed to larger audiences. In the days before motion pictures and television, magic was one of the most popular forms of live entertainment and performers such as those mentioned here generated enthusiastic responses wherever they performed.

Above: The incredibly successful Isaac Fawkes was a regular performer at London's annual Bartholomew Fair. He is seen here producing many objects from an apparently empty bag.

Below right: John Henry Anderson became known as "The Wizard of the North". His daughter Louise accompanied him on stage.

will. The trick often finishes with the surprise production of large objects from beneath the cups – sometimes even live chicks and mice! HRH Prince Charles became a member of The Magic Circle in London in 1975 after visiting the society and performing this classic trick.

By the eighteenth century magic was a very popular form of entertainment. Isaac Fawkes (1675–1731) was responsible for generating much of the interest in Britain. He worked at large fairgrounds and gathered huge crowds for his incredible tricks, many of which relied on spectacular mechanical principles that were well ahead of their time. One of these mechanical marvels was an apple tree which blossomed and bore fruit in less than a minute. He became very famous, amassing a fortune before his death.

Giuseppe Pinetti (1750–1800), born in Italy, was another of the most important figures in the history of magic. Inspired by the success of Isaac Fawkes, he also displayed mechanical marvels. He was hugely

magical inventors

Inventors are vital to the continuation of the art of magic and their revolutionary ideas often bring about great changes. Some inventors are also great performers, but many take a back seat and prefer to watch someone else breathe life into their creations. Here we take a look at some of the most important inventors in magic's history and those who are leading the field today.

Jean-Eugène Robert (1805–71) was born in France. He later added his wife's name to his own, becoming Robert-Houdin, and will forever be known as "The Father of Modern Magic". Robert-Houdin was a pioneer and innovator who opened his own Theatre of Magic in Paris in 1845, where he performed and thrilled audiences with his original work and amazing automata, including a version of Isaac Fawkes's tree that grew and bore fruit. He also wrote several books on magic, which were undoubtedly the best available at the time. His style and ideas were often copied by others but never equalled.

A century after Robert-Houdin's death, the French government issued a commemorative postage stamp to celebrate the life of their most famous magician.

Another French inventor was Buatier De Kolta (1847–1903). Although he performed frequently, his real strength was his ability to create and invent. He was responsible for some of the most incredible illusions of the time, some of which are still being used today. One example is the Vanishing Lady, or the

Above: Jean-Eugène Robert-Houdin was a mechanical genius and successful performer whose literary works inspired the young Harry Houdini.

Above left: This postage stamp was commissioned by the French government 100 years after Robert-Houdin's death in recognition of his achievements and as France's finest magician.

De Kolta Chair, as it is now known. A woman would sit on a chair in the centre of the stage. A sheet of newspaper was laid on the floor to show there was no trapdoor, and the woman was covered with a large cloth. As the cloth was whipped away, she vanished. This remains one of the most beautiful illusions to watch. Another of De Kolta's famous tricks was the Vanishing Bird Cage, in which a small cage containing a bird would be made to disappear without a trace. This particular trick was performed by illusionist Carl Hertz in 1921, who created a sensation when he vanished a bird cage for members of the House of Commons in England.

Servais Le Roy (1865–1953) was born in Belgium but moved to England at an early age. He was well known for his rendition of the classic Cups and Balls trick, and even more so for some of his inventions. These were revolutionary at the time, and are still used in one form or another by many large illusion acts all over the world. If one had to single out a particular illusion, it would have to be the Asrah Levitation. An assistant is

Right: Buatier De Kolta, one of magic's greatest inventors and also a fine sleight-of-hand magician. Many of his creations are used to this very day by the world's leading illusionists.

covered in a thin sheet and made to levitate slowly from the ground to a position high in the air. The sheet is pulled away and the assistant melts away in mid-air.

The English magician Percy Tibbles (1881–1938) spelt his family name backwards, leaving out one "b", to become known as Selbit. He created many superb and widely used illusions. In about 1921 he performed a new invention of his that started a wave of excitement which was to spread around the globe. Sawing Through a Woman became the most famous illusion of all time. Selbit's American contemporary Horace Goldin was inspired by this illusion and quickly developed a variation called Sawing a Woman in Half. Since then, countless versions have been invented with a surprising number of different methods – with or without boxes, using large or small saws, and most recently using lasers.

Guy Jarett (1881–1972), born in Ohio, USA, was one of the most important inventors of the twentieth century. He was an odd man with many antisocial habits, but his knowledge of magic and his ability to create new and fresh methods for illusions remain unmatched. His 21-person cabinet became legendary. A small cabinet, barely large enough to hold five people, was

shown empty. Despite the cabinet being isolated in the centre of the stage and off the floor, 21 people were made to appear from within. As a special effects consultant, Jarett provided illusions for several Broadway shows and for the most popular magicians of the time, who were thankful for fresh ideas. It was his idea to make an elephant appear on stage, and a similar method is still being used today by superstars Siegfried and Roy. In fact, many of today's illusions work on principles devised and developed by this genius in magic.

Robert Harbin (1910–78) was born Ned Williams in South Africa. He moved to England and created a huge impact with his numerous inventions. Harbin is perhaps best known for the incredible Zig-Zag Girl illusion. An assistant stands inside a small cabinet, which is then divided into three sections by two large, imposing blades. The middle section of the box is pushed over to one side, creating a sight that simply defies explanation. This is still one of the most popular illusions among performing magicians. Harbin was also a busy cabaret performer, working on cruise ships all over the world and at private events in London hotels.

Magicians today are as inventive as ever. Pat Page, Ali Bongo, Jim Steinmeyer, John Gaughan, Paul Osborne, Tommy Wonder, Juan Tamariz, Eugene Burger, Max Maven, Paul Harris and Michael Ammar are just a few of those who have helped to move the art of magic forward thanks to their incredible knowledge and sheer originality.

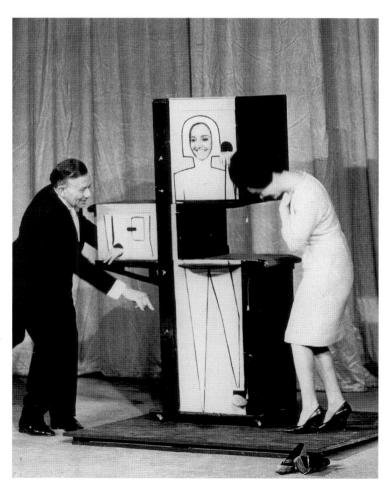

Left: Robert Harbin presenting his most famous illusion, the Zig-Zag Girl. It was to become one of the most popular and most performed illusions of all time. The original cabinet is currently on display at The Magic Circle Museum, London.

literary experts

Until the relatively recent introduction of videos and DVDs, magicians relied heavily on books for information about the art of magic. The first English book to include magic was published in 1584 and since then tens of thousands of books have been written covering every aspect of this ancient art. A plethora of new material continues to appear at an almost daunting rate, but a few literary works stand out as being particularly important to magicians of their time and to today's students and performers.

During the sixteenth and seventeenth centuries people who performed magic were often feared to be working in league with the Devil. As history books tell us, witchcraft was heavily frowned upon and was considered a crime punishable by death. In 1584 Reginald Scot published *The Discoverie of Witchcraft*, the first English book to expose the methods of magicians and to reveal how they used sleight of hand rather than evil powers to perform their magic. The book even contained the method used for decapitating animals as performed in Egypt by Dedi in about 2600BC. It caused huge controversy, and King James I ordered it to be publicly destroyed.

In the same year, 1584, a less well-known French book was published – *Clever and Pleasant Inventions* by J. Prevost. Unlike *The Discoverie of Witchcraft*, this book completely focused on the performance of magic as entertainment rather than denouncing witchcraft.

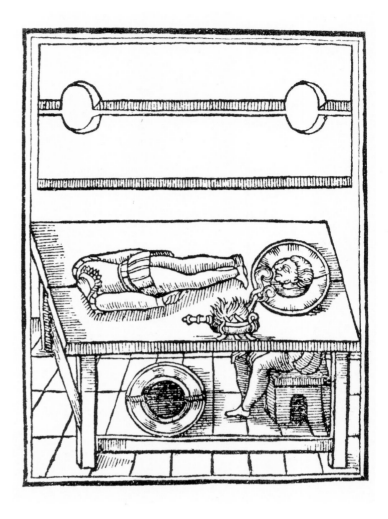

Above right: This diagram, taken from Reginald Scot's *The Discoverie of Witchcraft*, clearly shows the workings of a decapitation illusion. When the trick was performed, a curtain would cover the trestlework to hide the secret. It is just one of the many illusions exposed within this famous book.

Right: The original title page of Reginald Scot's book, which was fiercely condemned during the reign of King James I.

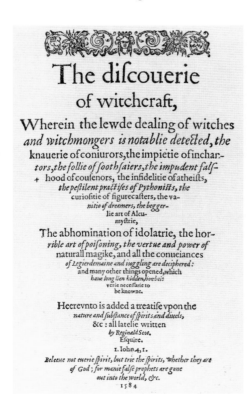

Between 1876 and 1911 Professor Louis Hoffmann (1839–1919) wrote numerous books. These included *Modern Magic*, *More Magic* and *Later Magic*, as well as English translations of earlier books by Robert-Houdin. It is said that Hoffmann's books have had more influence on the art of magic than any others. They revealed many secrets and were responsible for a whole new wave of magicians. His English translation of the *Memoires of Robert-Houdin* captured the imagination of a young man who was later to become the most famous magician of all time and whose name is synonymous with magic – Harry Houdini.

S.W. Erdnase wrote *The Expert at the Card Table*, published in 1902. This exposed the underhand methods of card cheats and introduced many of the sleight-of-hand techniques that today's card sleights are based on. His name spelt backwards is E.S. Andrews but the true identity of Erdnase still remains a mystery.

In 1910 the French magician J.B. Bobo wrote *Modern Coin Magic*, which is still regarded as one of the best reference books concerning this branch of the

Ricky Jay and Edwin A. Dawes, together with the late Milbourne Christopher and Walter B. Gibson, are all recognized for their important literary works which unveil many interesting and significant facts about magic's history. These names represent some of the leading experts in the field of magic history. Gibson was also known for having written a vast number of magic books for the amateur.

Many other magicians have written books and essays discussing the psychology of magic and "misdirection". They include Dariel Fitzkee, Eugene Burger, Tommy Wonder, Michael Ammar and Darwin Ortiz. With the exception of Fitzkee, who died in 1977, they continue to be major authorities in magic.

Today there is a steady stream of new magic books being published. Most of these can only be bought at magic shops and will not be found on the shelves of your local bookstore. Reading the ideas, philosophy and psychology of respected magicians is a rewarding experience, and a great opportunity to increase your knowledge and develop your skills.

Left: British-born Professor Louis Hoffmann wrote many books on the subject of magic, several of which became legendary.

Below: Harlan Tarbell was thought by many to be the most influential writer on the subject of magic after Professor Hoffmann. His huge *Course in Magic* continues to be recognized as one of the finest sets of books available.

art. The American Harlan Tarbell (1890–1960) was the author of *The Tarbell Course in Magic*. Originally designed as individual lessons which were sent regularly to subscribers, they were eventually bound in six volumes. The contents form one of the most comprehensive references to magical effects and methods, and include every type of magic imaginable. This huge set of books is highly regarded among professionals and amateurs alike. After Tarbell's death more volumes were added, and there are now eight volumes in total.

In 1949 Jean Hugard and Frederick Braue published *The Royal Road to Card Magic*. This book teaches a huge range of card techniques and an array of card tricks that would be received as well now as when they were written. It was considered to be the foremost book on basic card magic, though it has now been superseded by the work of the Swiss, Roberto Giobbi. Giobbi expertly documented advances in modern card handling in a later set of books, *Card College Volumes 1–4*, published from 1998 onwards.

magical venues

In 1873 the Egyptian Hall in London was the venue for regular performances by John Nevil Maskalyne (1839–1917) and George Alfred Cooke (1825–1905). These performers were known for their ability to weave their magic into short plays, which gave their tricks and illusions meaning and helped to provide a context for the magic. This clever concept can be seen in the work of some of today's great illusionists such as David Copperfield, who brings together music, dance, theatre and magic to incredible effect.

Maskalyne and Cooke's original show was due to last for three months, but Maskalyne went on to become a regular fixture at the Egyptian Hall for some 30 years, during which time he became part manager. Many of the world's great magicians had performed at this venue before him, but during this period it became synonymous with magic. He would invite singers, pianists and jugglers as well as other magicians to perform, thus making every show unique and therefore watchable over and over again. The Egyptian Hall became known as "England's Home of Mystery". It closed in 1905 but Maskalyne's success enabled him to buy a new theatre in which to continue his shows. St George's Hall, only a few minutes away from the old site, became "The New Home of Mystery". Shortly after the new venue opened, Cooke died and Maskalyne found a new partner, David Devant (1868–1941). Devant was considered one of the best magicians of the time and the duo became an even more successful team than Maskalyne and Cooke. After Maskalyne's death the theatre remained a magical showcase for the greatest performers of the day. St George's Hall was finally sold in 1933. It is now a hotel.

In 1905 a group of 23 magicians decided to start a magic club in London. The Magic Circle is now one of the world's most exclusive and famous magic societies. Early meetings took place in a room above St George's Hall, with David Devant as the society's first president. Its Latin motto "Indocilis Privata Loqui" roughly translates as "Not apt to disclose secrets", and any member who breaks this rule stands to lose their membership.

Above: The Egyptian Hall in London was originally a museum. It was built in 1812 and later became known as "England's Home of Mystery" when Maskalyne and Cooke became regular performers. It was a popular venue for many of the leading magicians of the time, until its demolition in 1905.

Left: The enchanting and awe-inspiring spiral staircase at The Centre for the Magic Arts, London. This is The Magic Circle headquarters, one of the most prestigious magic societies in the world. It houses a library, museum and theatre.

In 1998 The Magic Circle bought an old office block near London's Euston Station and transformed it into The Centre for the Magic Arts. Meetings are held every Monday evening, and the facilities include a library which boasts Europe's largest collection of books on the subject and a museum that houses some of the most important artefacts in magical history. The theatre is used regularly and often features shows that are open to the general public.

In 1963 the Academy of Magical Arts was established in Hollywood by William Larsen Snr. The Magic Castle, erected as its headquarters, is possibly the foremost magic building in the world today. It remains a private members' club and showcases leading magicians from around the world, who perform nightly. Soon after its opening, the Magic Castle became a mecca of magic and many of the great magicians relocated just to be near this home of mystery. More than a few of today's magic stars owe a great deal to the Larsen family, who continue to run this incredible club and to promote the good name of magic.

comedy magicians

Arthur Carlton Philps (1881–1942), known simply as Carlton, performed mostly in London's music halls in the early 1900s. He developed a unique style which made him a hit with his audiences. Carlton was incredibly skinny and his skin-tight black tights made him look even thinner; he also wore a bald wig and increased his height with platform shoes. He was known as the "Human Matchstick" and later as the "Human Hairpin". His very presence on stage was enough to set the audience laughing, and his comical throwaway lines made him into a commercial act that would be received as well in today's theatres as then. When the music halls began to close during the late 1930s and trade became slack, Carlton put on a lot of weight, which destroyed the very thing that made him so funny. Sadly his final years contained little to laugh about and he died having lost everything he once had.

Tommy Cooper (1922–84) was without doubt one of England's funniest men. After discovering early on in his career that his audiences found him more entertaining when he made mistakes, he created a character that will never be forgotten. Like Carlton before him, Cooper could make an audience howl with laughter without saying a word. The fact that he was a big, tall man with a face made for comedy probably helped. Always wearing his trademark fez, Cooper was a superb comedian who wrote some of the funniest lines and sketches, for example:

> I went to the dentist. He said, "Say aaah."
> I said, "Why?" He said, "My dog died!"

On 15 April 1984 Cooper collapsed on stage at Her Majesty's Theatre, London, and soon afterwards he died of a massive heart attack. The show was being broadcast live to viewers all over Britain. Most of the audience thought it was part of an elaborate joke and bellowed with laughter until the curtain dropped and it became clear something was very wrong. It was perhaps how he would have liked to have died – in front of his adoring fans. Britain, however, had lost an incredible comedian and magician.

American comedy magician Carl Ballantine (born 1922) became a well-known actor and magician throughout the United States after television catapulted his name across the nation in the 1950s. "The Great Ballantine", as he is known, performed on many of the top shows of the time including "The Ed Sullivan Show", "The Steve Allen Show" and "The Johnny Carson Show". Like Tommy Cooper, Ballantine realized early on in his career that his magic and style was best suited to comedy, and his act is a catalogue of disasters from start to finish. His superb timing and hysterical sight gags have made him a legend among comedy magicians.

The well-known American duo Penn and Teller (born 1955 and 1948 respectively) have been together since 1975. After ten years performing on and off Broadway, they shot to fame following many television appearances. They became known within the industry as "the bad boys of magic" due to their offbeat brand of humour and their apparent exposure of magical methods. Although their style would not be to everyone's taste, they have extended the boundaries of magic and comedy, and their numerous television specials have won several industry awards. Penn and Teller's busy schedule of live shows continues to amaze and amuse huge audiences wherever they perform.

Above: Tommy Cooper was one of Britain's funniest magicians and best-loved comedians. His trademark fez and recognizable laugh, together with many hysterical routines and sketches, left his audiences bellowing with laughter.

close-up magicians

The term "close-up" is used to describe the type of magic performed intimately for small groups of people. Compared to the other areas of the art, it is a fairly recent branch of magic which has become hugely popular and has seen a sharp increase in bookings for magicians at private parties, banquets and corporate events. Its popularity among magicians is probably due to the fact that expensive props are not necessary and there is no need for a stage or particular lighting. The beauty of "close-up" is that it can be performed anywhere and with virtually anything.

Nate Leipzig (1873–1939) was a Swedish-born magician who moved to America and became an important authority in close-up magic. Perhaps best known for tearing up a cigarette paper and restoring it in a very magical way, his techniques and effects are still studied today and remain in constant use.

The great Max Malini (1873–1942) was of Polish-Austrian descent but moved to America at a young age, where he became a wonderful performer of intimate magic. He was also very highly paid for his larger shows and became famous throughout the world during the 1920s when he gave many prestigious performances for royalty and heads of state. His astounding magic is still talked about and there is much to be learnt from his methods and philosophy. There is more information about Malini and his magic in the introduction to the chapter on Dinner Table Magic.

Fred Kaps (1926–80) was an outstanding Dutch magician who became famous within the magic fraternity in the 1950s. He was a role model for many future magicians – his skill and style were impeccable and his ability to change his performance to suit his audience was outstanding. As well as performing wonderful close-up magic, Kaps was known as a superb manipulator with a great sense of humour. His incredible sleight of hand ensured a faultless act that was enjoyed by millions of people all over the world.

Canadian Dai Vernon (1894–1992), famous for his rendition of the Cups and Balls, was a legend of magic affectionately known among his peers as "The Professor". He was quite simply regarded

Above: The great Max Malini performed for some of the most important people of his time. Several US Presidents, as well as royalty throughout Europe, enjoyed his magic. Many of Malini's tricks are still talked about, and even today one wonders how he could make such large objects appear from under his hat without anyone seeing how it was done.

as the absolute master. His close-up magic, at which he excelled, was of a quality rarely seen, and it is doubtful whether the close-up magic of today would be where it is without this wonderfully talented man, whose influence on magicians everywhere was substantial. Another of the most influential magicians of the twentieth century was Tony Slydini (1901–91). Originally from Italy, Slydini lived in New York and was the East Coast's answer to Vernon. Magicians would travel from all over the world to see him and to persuade him to teach them his techniques for "misdirection", which are still largely recognized and used to this day.

American Albert Goshman (1920–91) should be noted for two reasons. He was an exceptional performer who understood "misdirection" in a way very few people do. To watch a performance of his legendary coin under the salt shaker routine was an unforgettable experience. Despite two people watching as closely as they could, Goshman made coins continually vanish and reappear under the salt shakers, which were right in front of the spectators. He also built a factory which manufactured sponge balls for magicians. Sponge balls have become incredibly popular because of the interest they generate with audiences, and more importantly because of their ease of manipulation. The development of sponge-ball magic owes a great deal to Albert Goshman, but sadly it is believed that constant exposure to the fumes of the factory contributed to his death.

Today the field of close-up magic is led by the likes of Eugene Burger, Paul Harris, Juan Tamariz, Michael Close, Guy Hollingworth, Lennart Green, Daryl Martinez, David Williamson, Michael Ammar, Tommy Wonder, Ricky Jay, John Carney, Harry Lorayne and many more wonderful performers.

Left: Nate Leipzig, a true master of sleight of hand, travelled the world with his act. Leipzig would perform only for a small crowd he had invited upon the stage. The reactions of this lucky few were apparently enough to delight the rest of the audience – only a true showman could manage that.

illusionists

As well as illusionists such as De Kolta, Selbit and Servais Le Roy, there are others who were known predominantly for their incredible showmanship and dramatic presentations.

Born in France, Alexander Herrmann (1844–96) was the youngest of 16 children. His father Samuel and his brother Compers were both magicians, and by the time Alexander decided to build a career in magic, his brother Compers was already known as one of the best magicians of the day. However, the style Alexander adopted was well ahead of his time. Instead of the usual presentations associated with magicians, he injected a great deal of humour and fun into his shows. He quickly became the foremost magician of the mid- to late nineteenth century. "Herrmann the Great", as he became known, worked extensively in America, and later in England he performed large illusions regularly at the Egyptian Hall. By the time of his death he was so famous that he was regarded as a living legend.

The American Harry Kellar (1849–1922) belonged to the same era as Herrmann, and there was a bitter rivalry between them. Kellar filled the gap in the market after Herrmann died, touring his show all over the world. He was heavily influenced by England's master magician Maskalyne, and tried to purchase the method and rights to perform Maskalyne's levitation illusion. Maskalyne declined to sell, but this was the first of many effects to appear suddenly in Kellar's repertoire with remarkable similarities to Maskalyne's creations. After Kellar's retirement in 1908, he announced Howard Thurston as his successor. Thus Howard

Above: Alexander Herrmann had a huge family and a background steeped in entertainment. He was the most famous of the Herrmanns, and created a sensation with his act. He toured successfully around the globe, often performing for royalty.

Above: Harry Kellar was regarded by many as America's leading magician. He toured his illusion show all over the world.

Right: Howard Thurston's impressive illusion show assured him of rapid success.

Thurston (1869–1936) became America's leading magician. He updated Kellar's show and added fresh illusions, including the vanish of a motor car. He was a huge success, and his repertoire became so extensive that it took ten railway carriages to transport all of the necessary props and scenery.

William Ellsworth Robinson (1861–1918) was born in New York. After a fairly uneventful beginning to his magical career he decided to create a Chinese act, influenced by the famous Chinese magician of the time, Ching Ling Foo. Robinson chose the "oriental" name Hop Sing Loo but soon changed it to Chung Ling Soo, the name that was to make him famous. Soo's act was as colourful and visual as it was entertaining, and proved very successful with his audiences. He made bowls full of goldfish materialize from nowhere and caused money to appear in abundance. Although he was considered a competent illusionist, it is not this for which he is famous. The one trick that will forever be associated with Chung Ling Soo is the notorious Bullet Catch. A bullet is marked for later identification and shot from a gun aimed at the magician. The marked bullet is, incredibly, caught before it has a chance to do any harm and the markings are verified. On 23 March 1918 at the Wood Green Empire in London, Chung Ling Soo was shot on stage after the gun misfired. He was rushed to hospital but died the following

Above: A poster depicting Chung Ling Soo performing the famous Bullet Catch which finally killed him after the gun misfired.

morning. He was not the first magician to lose his life performing the Bullet Catch, but he was certainly the most famous.

German-born Sigmund Neuberger (1872–1911), later known as "The Great Lafayette", was a superb and very dramatic performer who worked all over the world. He was famous for incorporating large animals into his illusions. The scale of these shows had never been seen before and he was one of the highest-paid performers. Beauty, one of the dogs he used in his act, was a gift from Houdini. Lafayette's love for his animals, especially Beauty, was obsessive and frequently mocked. He died on 4 May 1911 when the Edinburgh theatre he was performing in burnt to the ground during a performance.

Horace Goldin (1873–1939) was born Hyman Goldstein in Poland. He moved to America in his teens and became known as "The Whirlwind Illusionist" because of the speed at which he rushed through his repertoire. Goldin's most famous illusion was Sawing a Lady in Half. In his first version, his assistant was placed inside a box which was then sawn in half and split down the middle before being reassembled. In 1931 he presented a new version which disposed of the boxes and gave the audience a clear view of a huge circular saw ripping through the lady's midriff. The publicity generated by this spectacular illusion was incredible, and Goldin travelled the world with his show. He died suddenly after a performance at the Wood Green Empire in London, on the same stage where 21 years earlier Chung Ling Soo had been shot dead during his bullet-catching routine.

Above: The Great Lafayette, one of the highest-paid performers of his time, with his beloved dog Beauty, a gift from his friend Harry Houdini.

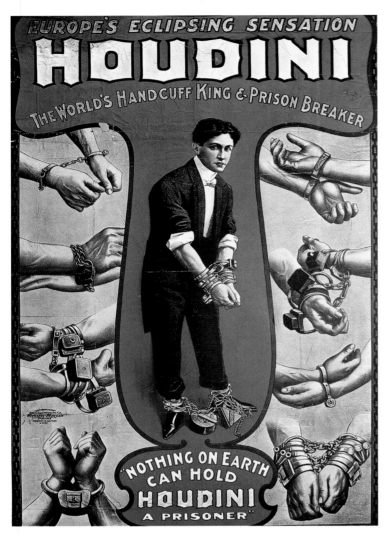

Bess, tied and bound. It was, as you can imagine, a staggering illusion and one that has stood the test of time. Modern versions of it are still performed frequently by many of today's illusionists. One particular act, The Pendragons, are able to effect the change faster than anyone else in the world, in under half a second!

Before long Houdini was known specifically for his escapology, and often offered large monetary rewards to anyone who could produce a pair of cuffs from which he could not escape. His escapes from milk cans, safes and prison cells excited, amazed and thrilled audiences the world over. Another of his most famous illusions was the Chinese Water Torture Cell, in which he was shackled and placed upside down inside a tall glass-walled cabinet filled with water. Despite the impossibility of the situation, Houdini was able to escape from the confines of the tiny cabinet. The publicity he generated was huge, and he sustained a continued and successful performing career until 22 October 1926. One of his incredible abilities was to withstand punches to the stomach without discomfort, but on this occasion he was struck without warning and suffered a ruptured appendix. Houdini bravely continued his engagements until he could no longer stand the pain. Peritonitis had set in and a week after being punched, at the age of 52, one of the greatest showmen on earth passed away. In death he became even more famous.

Harry Houdini (1874–1926) was born Ehrich Weiss in Budapest. Soon after his birth the Weiss family moved to Appleton, Wisconsin, USA, and it was here during his teens that Ehrich developed a keen interest in magic after reading the *Memoires of Robert-Houdin*. Adding an "i" to the end of this great magician's name, he changed his name to become Houdini. He married Wilhelmina Beatrice Rahner, known to all as Bess, and together they toured Europe with an act that quickly established Houdini as a sensation wherever he went. One of the illusions most associated with Houdini is Metamorphosis. Houdini would be handcuffed and tied up inside a sack, then placed in a large trunk which was locked shut. A curtain would be pulled around the trunk and Bess would tell everyone to watch carefully as she entered the curtained enclosure. Within seconds the curtains would open and Houdini would be seen standing free of the shackles, ropes and cuffs that had bound him only moments earlier. The trunk was unlocked, the sack opened and there inside would be

Above left: An early Houdini poster showing the master escapologist bound by chains. He was possibly the greatest publicist in the history of magic. Almost a century after his death, he remains famous all over the world.

Right: Harry Blackstone Snr was a popular illusionist whose name became synonymous with magic throughout the USA during his lifetime and continued to remain known as a result of the highly successful career of his son, Harry Blackstone Jnr.

In 1918 Henri Boughton (1885–1965) changed his name to Harry Blackstone. He was America's next greatest illusionist after Thurston. As his show grew so did his repertoire, which included the incredible vanish of a horse and Sawing a Lady in Half with a huge circular saw (similar to Goldin). He was also a master of more intimate magic, which he would perform in front of the stage curtains while the next big illusion was being set up. Two of the smaller illusions associated with him were the Dancing Handkerchief, in which a borrowed handkerchief was caused to come to life, bouncing, squiggling, squirming and floating across the stage before being handed back to its startled owner, and the vanish of a canary from a bird cage held by several children from the audience.

The name Blackstone continued to be associated with magic for many years thanks to his son, Harry Blackstone Jnr (1934–97). Harry toured a smaller show in the 1960s and 70s before reproducing his father's show with some new illusions and touring it across America. He became a prominent magician on American television and a well-known and respected celebrity. He is remembered for his incredible Floating Light Bulb, which glowed, levitated and floated across the stage before sailing out just above the heads of the audience.

Few dispute the assertion that American Channing Pollock (born 1926) was one of the greatest manipulators of the mid-1900s. This suave, handsome man handled cards, coins, billiard balls and doves with a style and panache never seen before. His incredible production of doves started a whole line of copycat acts, but although many magicians strive to reach the standard of Pollock's dove productions, few succeed. It is Channing Pollock we have to thank for one of today's top manipulators and illusionists. Lance Burton (born 1960) was inspired by the work of Pollock, and is one of the few magicians who have managed to equal his incredible skill. Burton's shows in the theatre built especially for him at the Monte Carlo in Las Vegas continue to astound audiences twice daily. His repertoire includes a version of the act that won him the FISM Grand Prix in 1982. FISM is the biggest and most important magic convention in the world and the enormous competition held every three years is the Olympics of magic. Burton's illusion show enables a modern audience to appreciate what audiences in the days of Thurston, Kellar, Goldin and Blackstone Snr must have felt. He is one of the leading showmen of magic today.

Siegfried and Roy (born 1939 and 1944 respectively) are perhaps the most successful megastars and illusionists in the history of magic. Their incredible show is the main attraction at the Mirage, one of the biggest hotels in Las Vegas, and their performances are constantly sold out. At one time it was the most expensive show ever to be produced, with a cast of hundreds. The two German-born magicians met in the early 1960s and worked on cruise ships around the world before landing their very own show in Vegas in the mid-70s. Their sensational illusions use large white tigers and there is no shortage of lions, elephants, cheetahs and other exotic animals, which are made to appear and vanish close to and often directly above the audience. Together with David Copperfield, Siegfried and Roy are one of the highest-paid acts in the world, and are contracted to continue their run at the Mirage for the remainder of their career.

television magicians

David Nixon (1919–78) became Britain's first regular television magician. He was a kind, gentle and popular man whose weekly show made him famous throughout Britain from the 1950s to the 70s. Meanwhile, across the Atlantic the American Mark Wilson (born 1929) also became a television legend. His show "The Magic World of Allakazam" featured many top magicians, and ensured a future of stardom and fame which continues to this day.

Doug Henning (1947–2000) was born in Canada and became a magical superstar of the 1970s and 80s. Having studied under the greatest (Dai Vernon and Slydini), he developed several stage shows that changed the face of magic with a style never before seen. He did not look like the typical magician; in fact he looked as if he had just stepped out of the 60s in full Woodstock regalia, including tie-dyed tops and flared trousers. His journey in magic began to take off when he appeared in the 1974 Broadway show "The Magic Man" and he followed this debut with eight television specials which were, and still are, among the greatest shows ever caught on camera. The fact that the shows were filmed live is testimony to Henning

Above right: Master illusionist David Copperfield, whose television specials and live shows make him one of the world's best-paid and most recognized modern-day magicians.

Below: David Nixon became Britain's first successful resident television magician. His show "It's Magic" featured many top magical acts from around the world.

and his team's incredible skill. Doug Henning became a sensation in America, touring with an awesome illusion show until he decided to leave his life of showbiz to live in India, where his religious studies became the focus of his life. He had begun work on designing a transcendental meditation theme park in Ontario, but sadly died before his dream could be realized.

David Copperfield (born 1956) was born David Seth Kotkin in New Jersey. After developing an interest in magic at the age of ten, he knew there was only one thing he ever wanted to do. He started his career on stage in the Chicago version of "The Magic Man" and was soon signed up for his own television special, the first of many which catapulted him to fame. His sensational style and incredible stage presence, together with his groundbreaking illusions, keep audiences on the edge of their seats. He is one of the world's highest-paid entertainers and also one of the busiest, performing over 500 shows a year. Copperfield made a name for himself by performing illusions that captured the world's imagination. In 1981 he vanished a Lear jet and two years later he caused the Statue of Liberty to disappear. This illusion was the biggest ever performed at the time and attracted huge television audiences, causing a worldwide sensation. These grand-scale illusions became a necessity to Copperfield's television specials and fans were eager to see what he would do next. Among other stunts, he walked through the Great Wall of China and levitated

and vanished an Orient Express railway carriage. David Copperfield has become one of the most important icons in magic and will always be regarded as a leader in the field.

Paul Daniels (born 1938) became Britain's most famous magician shortly after he hit the television screen in 1970. His cheeky banter was a huge contrast to the style of David Nixon, and his catchphrase "You'll like it, not a lot but you'll like it!" was an instant success with the public. In 1979 he appeared in the Royal Variety Show and his weekly television slot "The Paul Daniels Magic Show" pulled in huge viewing figures for over ten years, winning many industry awards including the Golden Rose of Montreux. He later married his long-term assistant Debbie McGee and the husband-and-wife team became a celebrity couple recognized all over Britain. Daniels was without doubt one of the most talented magicians of the late twentieth century and a major influence on British magic.

Although not publicly famous worldwide, Luis de Matos of Portugal, Juan Tamariz of Spain and Silvan of Italy are all superb magicians, well known in their own countries for their television shows. De Matos is a suave and elegant performer of close-up magic and larger illusions, often creating mini-playlets complete with incredibly designed sets comparable in style to David Copperfield's. Tamariz is one of the most talented card magicians in the world today. His regular television shows are popular with his audiences, who recognize him as one of Spain's top television personalities. Silvan, like Luis de Matos, is an all-rounder, performing huge illusions as well as incredible close-up magic.

David Blaine (born 1974) represents a new wave of magicians. Breaking with tradition, he successfully stripped magic of its glamour and pretentiousness,

showing the world that magicians do not need a stage with trapdoors, expensive sets and careful lighting to perform miracles. Blaine takes his magic on to the streets and performs for unsuspecting members of the public. The television crew captures the surprise and awe of his spectators, and this unique approach has made him immensely successful in a relatively short time. He is currently creating the kind of publicity and awareness that has not been seen since the likes of Houdini. Blaine is known around the world thanks to the power of international media and repeats of his television specials, which are aired frequently on channels across the globe. He is known for his ability to read people's minds, for levitating himself off the ground and for bizarre publicity stunts such as standing in a block of ice for over 60 hours, being buried alive for five days, and standing on top of a pole above the streets of New York for 35 hours. One thing is certain – his image is fresh and his style unique. Trends in magic will change, and another star will one day take the world by storm, but for now David Blaine is one of the most talked-about magicians of our time.

Above left: Paul Daniels is one of Britain's most successful television magicians, and was undoubtedly responsible for inspiring a whole new generation of conjurors during the 1980s and 90s.

Below: American street magician David Blaine froze himself inside a block of ice for over 60 hours as one of his feats of endurance.

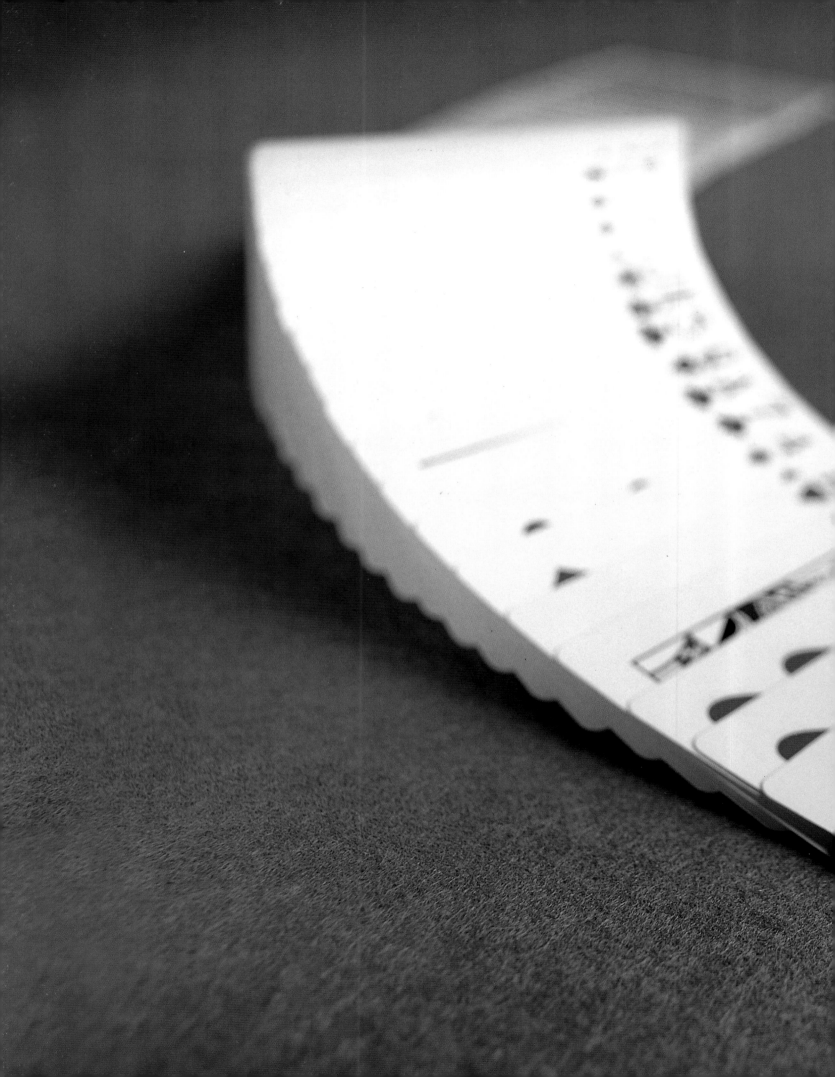

card magic

Why are card tricks so popular? One reason could be that playing cards are internationally recognized symbols. Over the centuries magicians from the East shared their ideas and card tricks with magicians in the West, resulting in a universal familiarity with cards. Perhaps this explains why there are more card tricks published than any other type of magic. The scope for creating illusions with a deck of cards is huge. As you will learn in the following pages, they can be made to appear, disappear, change colour, multiply, defy gravity and a lot more besides.

- basic card techniques
- shuffling cards
- self-working card tricks
- controlling a card
- card tricks requiring skill
- forcing a card
- special gimmicks
- advanced flourishes

introduction

Playing cards have a rich history of their own. The origins of the playing card are as mysterious as the beginnings of magic itself, and much of their history can only be speculated because of lack of evidence.

The first playing cards are thought to have been invented in the twelfth century in China, and from there their popularity spread quickly throughout the East. Playing cards probably began to appear in Europe at the end of the fourteenth century. They changed drastically as the original Eastern designs were replaced by European designs, which evolved as they passed from country to country.

It seems it was some time before it occurred to anyone that playing cards could be used for magic. A Spanish magician by the name of Dalmau performed card tricks for Emperor Charles V in Milan at the turn of the sixteenth century, and there is evidence to suggest that by the seventeenth century card magic was a popular form of entertainment. Queen Elizabeth I apparently enjoyed watching card tricks, and in 1602 paid an Italian magician 200 crowns to perform for her.

One of the greatest playing-card manipulators of the twentieth century was the Welshman Richard Pitchford (1894–1973), known as Cardini. His act involved the incredible manipulation of playing cards, billiard balls and cigarettes. The character he chose to adopt was that of a very elegant, well-dressed but slightly drunk English gentleman to whom strange things tended to happen. With his trademark monocle, Cardini acted as if he were as amazed at his antics as his audience. His act relied heavily on the Back Palm, which can be found at the end of this chapter. However, rather than producing just a single card, Cardini was able to produce a seemingly endless supply, one by one, several at once and in beautiful fans – even while wearing gloves.

Playing cards are available in many shapes and sizes. The two most common sizes are bridge size, approximately 56 x 87mm (2 x 3½in), which tend to be more popular in Europe, and poker size, approximately 63 x 88mm (2½ x 3½in), which are pretty much standard in casinos and throughout the USA. The other variant is the quality of the card itself. Different boards are used by different manufacturers – some are very hard-wearing and long-lasting, but others can be ruined in a matter of minutes. A poor-quality card will crack if you bend it; a good-quality card will bend out of shape but can usually be bent back again. It is recommended that before you begin this chapter you purchase several good-quality decks of cards.

Top: Cardini shown here with his wife Swan, who became part of his act. Many tried to imitate Cardini's style and repertoire but no one could equal the artistry of this master magician.

Above: Playing cards and tarot cards are universally recognized, but designs differ from country to country.

As well as the "you pick a card, I'll find it" type of effect, many illusions can be created using cards. You can predict which card will be chosen (Magic Time, Face Value), vanish cards (Back Palm, Card through Tablecloth), change cards (Changing Card, Card under Glass, Card to Matchbox, Find the Lady) and move cards without any visible means (Rising Card from Box, Versions 1 and 2).

Playing cards can generally be found in most homes and in many public places. It always pays to know a few card tricks so that when the opportunity arises you can be ready to spring into action!

Above: Croupiers are trained to handle cards with incredible manual dexterity. Some of their skills are similar to those of a magician.
Right: A specially printed deck of magicians' fanning cards. The designs are bold and colourful, and every time the deck is fanned in a different way the pattern changes. Cardini used a similar deck for a sequence within his card act.

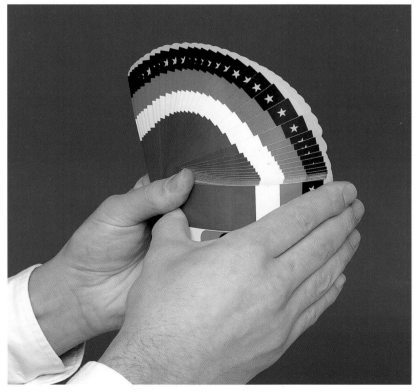

basic card techniques

For many of the techniques you will learn in the following pages it is important for you to hold the deck in the correct way so that you can accomplish the moves with ease and success. The grips shown below *are simple to master and should feel very very natural after just a little practice. Do not let the names of the various grips worry you. They sound more complicated than they really are!*

the hand

In order to fully understand how to handle a deck of cards, it is vital that you know which part of the hand is which.

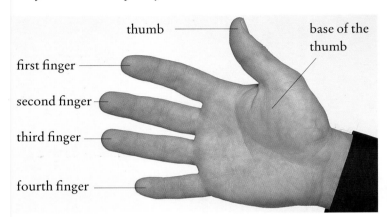

thumb

base of the thumb

first finger

second finger

third finger

fourth finger

Although mostly self-explanatory, you may find that some of the terms used to describe the parts of the hand are unfamiliar to you. Therefore, before you continue, take a moment to check that you know which part of the hand is which.

dealing grip

In most instances you will be holding the deck as shown below. It is likely that you would hold a deck of cards like this instinctively.

The deck is clipped by the thumb in the left hand. All the fingers are located along the other long edge. Notice how the thumb is positioned on the top of the deck and how the cards bevel slightly. In this position it is possible for the thumb to push off cards singly from the top of the deck in readiness to be dealt to the table.

mechanics' grip

This variation of the Dealing Grip will allow certain moves to become possible. However, in most cases these two grips are interchangeable.

The difference between this and the Dealing Grip is that the cards are held more firmly, with the left first finger curled round the top short edge of the deck and the thumb positioned straight along the left edge of the deck.

biddle grip

This is another simple grip that you will need to become familiar with in order to perform many of the sleights in this book.

Hold the deck from above in the right hand. The thumb holds the deck at the short edge nearest you. The first finger is curled gently on top of the deck and the second and third fingers hold the deck at the short edge furthest from you.

dribbling cards

This is a simple flourish with a deck of cards. Learning to dribble will help you to become familiar with handling a deck comfortably. Aside from a simple flourish, the dribble can also be used to help make controlling a card more deceptive (see In-Jog Dribble Control).

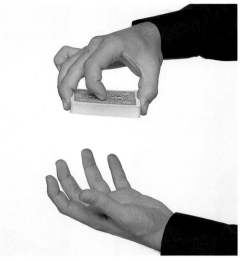

1 Hold the deck in the right-hand Biddle Grip position with the left hand in an open position below.

2 With the right first finger (curled on top of the deck), apply pressure as the right fingers and thumb simultaneously release pressure, allowing the cards to fall rapidly, one after the other, into the waiting left hand. Try experimenting with varying distances between your hands.

3 Cradle the cards in the left hand and square them to complete the flourish.

two-handed spread

This is simply a neat way to offer cards for a selection. It is a very basic technique, but one with which you should become familiar from the outset. A nice spread of cards can be an early indication to your spectators that you are a polished performer.

1 Hold the cards using the left-hand Dealing Grip or Mechanics' Grip. The left thumb pushes the top few cards to the right.

2 The right hand approaches, gripping the spread of cards in the crotch between the thumb and base of the fingers. The left fingers and thumb begin to push several more cards over to the right, the right fingers providing support from beneath.

3 Continue to push the cards with the left thumb as your hands stretch into an arc. The result is a neat and uniform spread of cards.

4 From underneath the spread, you can see how the cards are supported by the outstretched fingers of both hands.

squaring the cards

This is a simple procedure to ensure that the cards are neat, tidy and perfectly square. Very often working with a deck of cards that have *been neatly squared will make the learning process easier and facilitate general card handling.*

1 Hold the untidy deck in the left hand. Start to square the cards so that you hold the deck in a loose Mechanics' Grip.

2 Approach the deck from above in the right-hand Biddle Grip position. Squeeze the short ends of the deck together. Slide the right hand back and forth along the short edges, then support the deck in the Biddle Grip position while your left hand moves up and down.

3 The result is a deck of cards squared neatly in the left hand.

swing cut

This is a very useful cut that is simple to learn and is referred to in many of the routines in this book. The top card of the deck has *been marked with a black border so that you can follow the sequence of the cut more clearly.*

1 Hold the deck in the right-hand Biddle Grip position.

2 Extend the first finger so that it rests near the corner of the deck furthest from you.

3 With your first finger, lift half of the cards and pivot them out to the left. (Your right thumb is the pivot point.)

4 With your left hand, pinch the top half of the deck in the crotch of the thumb.

5 With your right hand, place the original bottom half on top of the left-hand cards. Square the deck to complete the cut.

charlier cut

This is a pretty, one-handed cut. It is relatively easy to master with just a little practice. If you experience difficulty with it, try altering *your grip at the first stage. Through trial and error, the Charlier Cut will become second nature to you.*

1 Hold the deck high up at the left fingertips. Notice how the deck is held from all sides.

2 Releasing pressure from your thumb, allow approximately half of the deck to fall down towards the palm of your hand.

3 Your first finger should now curl under the deck and push the bottom stock of cards towards the thumb.

4 Let the bottom stock clear the top stock, which drops on to the curled first finger.

5 Close your thumb and fingers together to complete the cut. You can now use your right hand to help square the cards.

the glimpse

It is often necessary to secretly look at and remember a particular card in the deck. This secret move is known as a "glimpse". There are many ways to do this, depending on how the cards are being held.

Two "glimpses" are explained here, enabling you to learn the bottom card of the deck secretly, in an unsuspicious fashion. You may be able to think of other subtle ways too.

out of the box glimpse

An ideal time to "glimpse" a card occurs when you are removing the cards from the card box. Simply ensure that the deck is orientated so that it is pulled out of the box face up. Absolutely no attention should be drawn to the deck at this stage. If required, a casual Overhand Shuffle gives you an extra opportunity to move the "glimpsed" card to another location such as the top of the deck.

square and glimpse

This is another way to secretly look at the bottom card of the deck while handling the cards in a natural way. The "glimpse" takes place during the innocent action of squaring the deck. All the movements

occur in one smooth action. Essentially you are squaring the deck while turning it from end to end. It is so subtle, your audience will never suspect a thing!

1 Hold the deck face down in the left hand, with the right hand supporting the deck in the Biddle Grip. The deck is squared.

2 With the right hand, lift the deck and turn it palm up by twisting at the wrist. Simultaneously turn the left hand palm down so that it can continue the squaring action along the long sides of the deck. The bottom card of the deck will now be facing you, and this is when you "glimpse" the card.

3 Almost immediately, lift the deck with the left hand and turn it palm up again as the right hand turns palm down, back to the start position. The hands square the cards one final time.

the braue reversal

A magician called Frederick Braue created this simple way to reverse a card in the centre of the deck. It is assumed the top card is to be reversed. Performed at speed, the Braue Reversal simply looks like a series of quick cuts and should not arouse any suspicion.

1 Hold the deck in right-hand Biddle Grip with a Thumb Break under the top card. For ease of explanation, there is a black border on the top card.

2 With the left hand, take the bottom half of the deck and turn it face up, flipping it on top of the right-hand cards.

3 Allow all the remaining cards below the break to fall into the left hand. These are again reversed and replaced under the right-hand cards.

4 Spread the deck between your hands. The result will be that the top card of the deck has been reversed in the centre.

tip *This method of reversing a card can also be used to reveal a selected card. Have a card returned to the deck and controlled to the top. Now perform the Braue Reversal and spread the deck on to the table to display one card reversed. It will be the one selected.*

the glide

This is a useful move, creating the illusion that the bottom card of the deck has been removed when in reality the second from bottom card is removed. This simple procedure is worth learning if only for Gliding Home, which is a wonderful trick.

1 Hold the deck in the left hand from above. The deck should be held by the long edges, thumb on the right side and fingers on the left. Ensure the cards are held high enough to allow the first joints of the fingers to bend around the deck and rest on the bottom card.

2 This view from underneath shows how the extreme tips of the fingers are positioned on the face of the card.

3 Drag the bottom card back about 5–10mm (¼–½in) by pulling the second, third and fourth fingers backwards. (The first finger remains stationary.) The bottom card remains aligned against the left thumb.

4 The right hand approaches palm up and reaches under the deck to supposedly remove the bottom card. What actually happens is that the second card is removed instead. The tips of the right fingers drag the second card forward, facilitated by the overlap created by the Glide.

tip *The Glide is not seen from the front. It is a secret move that remains hidden under the deck. An alternative method is to approach the deck with the right hand and push the bottom card back a fraction of a second before the second card is pulled forward.*

double lift and turnover

The Double Lift and Turnover is another essential sleight to master if you wish to become a competent cardician. Theoretically the procedure is simple, but to put the theory into effect will take plenty of practice. In theory a "double lift" is the name given to the concept of lifting two cards and displaying them as one. The technique is used to achieve many results, a few of which are explored in the explanations that follow.

There are enough techniques and variations to the turning of two cards as one to fill this entire book. The truth is, every individual finds a technique that is comfortable for them and sticks with it. Further reading will enable you to explore different options, and with time you will find small changes that suit you. As long as your Double Lift is convincing, it does not really matter which technique you choose.

There a few important points to be aware of. The "get-ready" should remain unseen. The turning of the two cards should look natural and arouse no suspicion. In other words, don't say "Here is the top card of the deck", because as soon as you say that people will start to wonder if it really is the top card of the deck. If you just show it, perhaps saying the card's name out loud, people will just assume it is the top card. You must create a reason for placing the card back on to the deck after the first display.

1 The Double Lift requires a "get-ready". It is necessary to separate the top two cards from the rest of the deck. In order to achieve this, hold the deck in left-hand Mechanics' Grip. The left thumb pushes off the top few cards, to the right, in a spread.

secret view

2 While the first finger is curled around the end of the deck furthest from you, the second and third fingers stretch out and begin to pull the cards flush again, but as this happens the fourth finger separates the top two cards of the deck.

secret view

3 The deck should now be held, squared, in the left hand with a Finger Break, as shown, under the top two cards.

4 The view from the front reveals nothing. The cards are simply held in the Mechanics' Grip with a Finger Break below the top two cards.

secret view

5 The right hand approaches the deck in Biddle Grip position. The gap created by the Finger Break enables the top two cards only to be lifted. The right first finger pushes gently on the back of the card(s) to keep them aligned.

6 The right hand turns at the wrist to reveal the face of the card. It is mistaken for the top card of the deck but in reality is the second card from the top.

7 After the display, turn the wrist once again and replace the card(s) back on to the top of the deck. Snap your fingers or make a magical gesture and pick up the real top card of the deck, turning it over to reveal the card has mysteriously changed.

snap change

This is a visually stunning sleight, which takes only a little practice to perfect. With a snap of the fingers one card instantly changes to another. It is recommended that you learn this sleight so that if ever a card trick goes wrong you can simply ask which card was chosen and spread through the deck, cutting the selector's card second from the top. Show the top card as an indifferent card, perform the Snap Change and magically change the indifferent card into the one selected. Magicians call these types of scenarios "outs", that is, they can get the magician out of trouble if a trick goes wrong.

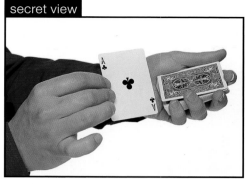
secret view

1 Show the top card of the deck (in this example the Ace of Clubs). Secretly obtain a Finger Break under the top card in the left hand.

secret view

2 Lay the Ace of Clubs face up and square on to the deck.

3 The Finger Break will enable you to pick up the top two cards with ease. The two cards are held together as one between the right thumb and second finger at the extreme end. The first finger is bent on top.

4 Move the card(s) under your elbow and temporarily out of sight.

5 Squeeze the two cards, allowing them to flick off the second finger so that the cards flip over and are pinched at the lower right corner by the thumb and first finger. The cards should still be perfectly aligned.

6 Immediately bring the cards into sight and place them back on to the top of the deck where they can be squared. The card will be seen to have changed.

7 Turn the top card face down to complete the sleight. This is a speedy and highly visual piece of magic.

ribbon spread and turnover

This is a lovely flourish, pretty to watch and a sign of a magician who can handle a deck of cards. The cards are spread and displayed in a neat face-down line, then caused to flip face up "domino-style". You will find it easier to perform with a deck of cards in good condition and on a soft surface such as a tablecloth or close-up mat. You will also need a clear space to ensure a smooth spread.

1 Hold the deck face down in the right-hand Biddle Grip. Place the deck flat on the table at your far left.

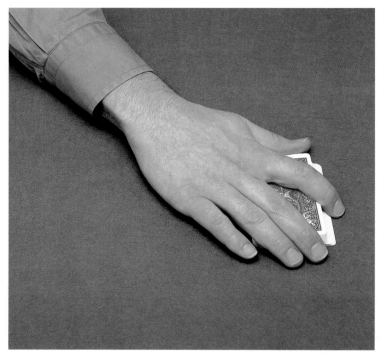

2 Stretch out your first finger so that it rests on the long edge of the deck and just brushes the surface of the table. Pull the deck to the right a fraction, and the deck will naturally bevel.

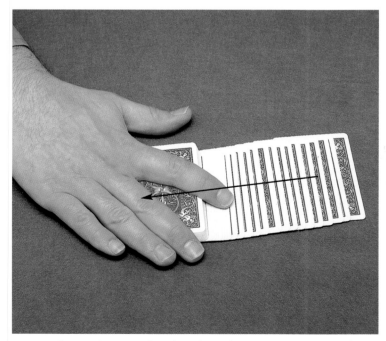

3 Begin moving your hand to the right at an even pace with even pressure. With the first finger, regulate the distance between each card as you continue to spread the deck in a straight line until all the cards are spread out.

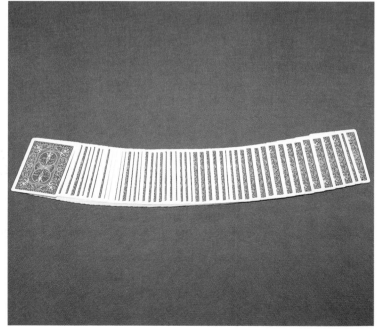

4 The result is an even spread of cards in a relatively straight line. With practice you will be able to spread the cards instantly, in under a second, and with absolute precision.

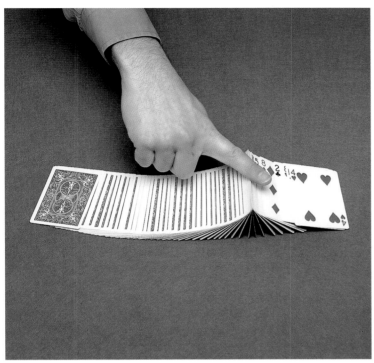

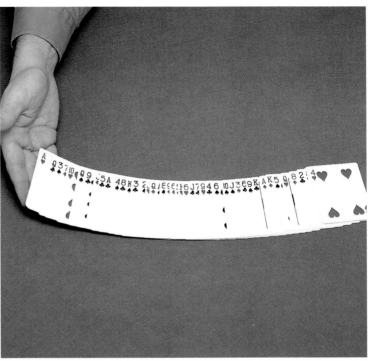

5 To turn the cards face up, lift the edge of the cards at the far left of the spread and run your first finger along the edges so that the spread begins to turn face up "domino-style".

6 When you reach the end of the spread, allow the last cards to drop face up on to your palm in preparation for the final stage. Do not let the cards fall flat on to the table.

7 Now move the right hand to the left, scooping up the deck into one pile. Lift this pile off the table.

8 Finish the sequence by squaring the cards with both hands and continue with your next card trick or flourish.

shuffling cards

Very often you can impress your audience before you even begin a single trick by handling the cards in a way that suggests you have spent considerable time and effort practising. Apart from the Weave

Shuffle and Waterfall, these shuffles are not too difficult to master. Indeed, you may be familiar with them already. Often several shuffles are required to thoroughly mix the deck.

overhand shuffle

This is arguably the most commonly used and easiest shuffle. These moves are repeated over and over with varying amounts of cards until you are satisfied the deck has been shuffled.

Due to the fact that the cards are being mixed in small packets, it will take a lot of shuffling to ensure a very thorough disruption of the sequence of cards.

1 Hold the deck with one of its long edges along the crease lines at the base of the left fingers. The thumb naturally rests on the back of the deck, and the fingers do likewise on the front.

2 With the right hand, approach from above and pick up approximately the bottom three-quarters of the deck.

3 In a chopping motion, bring the right hand back to the deck and deposit half the cards on top of the deck. Then bring the right hand away with the other half.

4 Finally, with one more chop, deposit the remainder of the cards on the top.

table riffle shuffle

This is an effective and professional way to shuffle a deck of cards. By controlling the cards as they fall, you can ensure that the last group of cards are "riffled" off the right thumb. Any cards within this group (which was on the top of the deck at the beginning) will be on top of the deck at the end of the shuffle. The Riffle Shuffle can thus be used as a false shuffle, allowing you to retain cards at the top of the deck.

1 The deck should be squared and lying on the table, long side towards you. With the right hand, cut off approximately half of the cards.

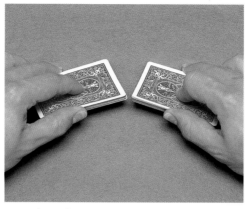

2 Place this packet to the right of the bottom half and mirror your grip with the left hand. With the thumbs of both hands, lift up the back edges. Notice how the corners almost touch. The front edges of the deck rest on the table.

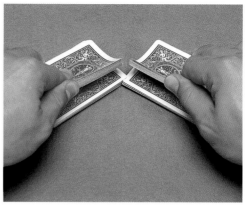

3 Slowly allow the cards to riffle off both thumbs. As this happens, nudge both packets together.

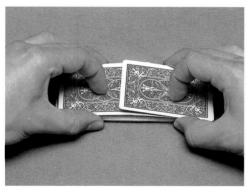

4 When this riffle is complete, push each packet into the other about halfway.

5 Change your grip so that you can push both packets together completely by applying pressure along the short sides of the deck with both first fingers while simultaneously squaring the cards with your thumbs on the long edge nearest you.

6 The result is a shuffled, squared deck which is then ready for your next miracle.

weave shuffle and waterfall

This shuffle looks fantastic when it is performed smoothly. It creates the impression that you are a master card sharp! You must use a deck of cards in perfect condition because you are relying on the corners of the deck to ensure a good weave. If the edges of the individual cards are split or damaged you will find this shuffle very difficult indeed. With enough practice, you will be able to split the cards into exactly two packets of 26 and shuffle them so accurately that every card will be woven in the opposite direction to its neighbour. Professional magicians know this as the Perfect Faro shuffle. If you can achieve this degree of accuracy every time, you will be able to master almost any card sleight-of-hand trick you may come across in the future. The end result is well worth the effort you need to put in.

1 Make sure the cards are perfectly square. Hold them high up at the tips of the left fingers, as shown here.

2 With the right hand, approach the deck from above. The first finger is held straight out and rests on the short edge of the deck furthest from you.

3 With the right thumb, second and third fingers cut and lift half of the deck up and away from the lower packet.

4 Tap this top half gently against the short edge of the bottom half, to ensure that the edges of both packets are perfectly square.

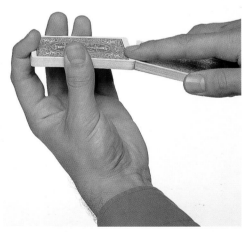

5 Place the corners nearest you against each other. Notice at this stage how only the corners at the front touch, and how the first finger of the right hand keeps the packets perfectly level with each other.

6 Gently push the corners together, and the cards will begin to weave, as shown here. (You may find that a slight back-and-forth motion will ease the cards into the weave.)

7 Push the packets together so that approximately one-quarter of the cards are overlapped.

8 Adjust the left hand's grip by moving your thumb, third and fourth fingers down to the woven section. This gives you the ability to hold the deck in one hand.

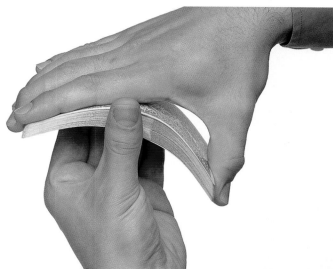

9 Stretch the right hand wide open and approach the deck from above. Your thumb should grip the short edge nearest you, with the fingers on the short edge furthest away.

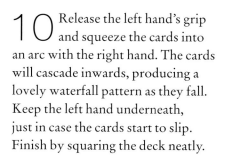

10 Release the left hand's grip and squeeze the cards into an arc with the right hand. The cards will cascade inwards, producing a lovely waterfall pattern as they fall. Keep the left hand underneath, just in case the cards start to slip. Finish by squaring the deck neatly.

self-working card tricks

It is important to realize that although self-working card tricks are relatively easy to perform, they do require a certain amount of human input and will not work unless the various stages are followed *correctly. The advantage of self-working tricks is that you can spend less time learning the mechanics of the trick and more time working on an entertaining presentation.*

sense of touch

After performing a few card tricks, state that it is possible to develop super-sensitivity in your fingertips. As a demonstration, shuffle the cards and hold them face down. The top card is held with its back *towards the magician, yet by feeling its face it is possible to identify the card every time. Explain that your sensitive fingers allow you to know whether the card is black or red, and how many pips are on it.*

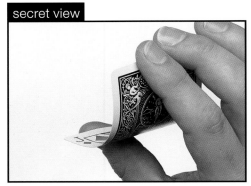

secret view

1 From a shuffled deck, deal one card face down into your right hand and hold it in front of you at about neck level. Hold it by the thumb at the bottom edge and the fingers at the top edge, with its back towards you. Your left first finger moves up to touch the face of the card.

2 This shows the view from behind. As the finger touches the face of the card for the first time, gently squeeze your right fingers and thumb. This will begin to bend or bow the card backwards.

3 The left finger is omitted here so that you can clearly see what happens. The card is bowed just enough for you to glimpse the lower left index.

the four burglars

This classic trick is accompanied by a story. Four Jacks are shown to be at the top of the deck, and one by one they are placed separately into different positions. The four Jacks magically return to the top. Read through the steps with your cards in hand until you are familiar *with the order of the steps. Then learn the patter and match up the words to the moves. When learnt and performed confidently, this will become a charming addition to your repertoire, and is sure to get a great reaction every time it is performed.*

1 Secretly remove any three cards plus the four Jacks.

2 Hold the Jacks in a fan, with the extra three cards squared neatly below the lowest one.

3 Begin by displaying the four Jacks to the audience. (They should be unaware of the extra cards.)

4 Neatly square the cards in the left hand, being careful to hide the extra thickness along the edge of the cards.

5 Turn the packet of cards face down and place them on top of the deck.

6 Take the top card of the deck and, without showing its face, push it into the deck approximately ten cards from the bottom. Leave it protruding half its length.

7 Take the new top card and push it into the deck at the halfway point. Leave it protruding as before.

8 Repeat with the new top card, inserting it about ten cards from the top of the deck.

9 Turn the top card face up to show a Jack, then replace it face down, but protruding from the top of the deck.

10 Slowly push all four cards neatly and squarely into the deck.

11 Dribble the cards from hand to hand, matching your actions to your patter.

12 Deal the top four cards face up to show that the Jacks have returned.

the story *(the numbers correspond to the above steps):*

"There were four burglars named Jack who decided to try to burgle a house (3, 4, 5). The first burglar broke into the basement (6), the second managed to enter the kitchen (7), and the third burglar climbed through an open window in a bedroom (8).

The last burglar stayed on the roof to look out for the police (9). As each of the burglars entered the house (10), the lookout on the roof saw a police car driving towards them. He called his three friends (11), who immediately ran up to the roof, slid down the drainpipe, and made their escape (12)."

hocus pocus

Twenty-one cards are dealt on to the table and one is thought of by the spectator. After a short process of dealing the cards, the magic words "Hocus Pocus" are used to find the selection. This is one of the best-known card tricks, but it still amazes everyone who sees it.

Although the principle and method are mathematical, it requires no skill or mathematics on the part of the magician. Better still, it works every single time as long as the steps are followed in the correct order. Try this out with the cards in hand and you may even amaze yourself!

1 Deal three cards face up from left to right (as if you were dealing a round of cards to three people).

2 Deal another three cards in exactly the same way. Continue until you have three columns of seven cards – 21 cards in total. Ask the spectator to remember any one of the cards. In our example the chosen card is the Queen of Diamonds.

3 Ask the spectator to tell you which column the chosen card is in. (In our example it is in column number three.) Pick up one of the other piles, then pick up the chosen pile and place it on top.

4 Finally pick up the last pile, adding it to the others. Remember the golden rule: the chosen column must be placed in the middle of the other two.

5 Deal three cards from the top of the packet as you did at the beginning, but holding the packet face up.

6 Continue dealing until all the cards have once again been dealt.

7 Ask the spectator to confirm which column their card is in this time. As before, pick up all three columns, ensuring that the chosen column goes between the other two.

8 Re-deal the cards in exactly the same fashion as before. Ask the spectator one final time which column contains their card. Collect the cards as before.

9 Turn the cards face down and explain that to find the selected card you need to use the ancient magic words "Hocus Pocus". Deal the cards on to the table, spelling out loud one letter for each card.

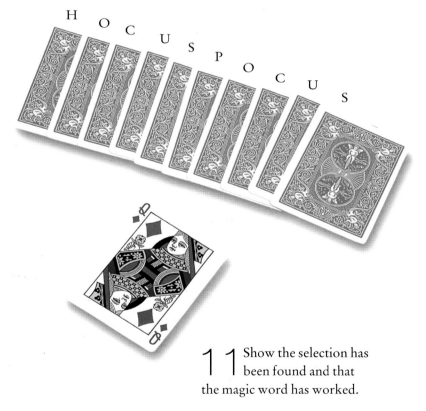

10 The very next card will be the one selected. Ask for the name of the chosen card and turn the top card over.

11 Show the selection has been found and that the magic word has worked.

tip *After the process of dealing has been repeated three times, the mentally selected card will automatically be the eleventh card down from the top of the face-down packet. This means you could use any word with ten or eleven letters to find the selection, so with a little thought you can personalize this trick. You may be able to use your name, your spectator's name or the name of your company.*

reversed

A card is chosen and inserted back into the deck. You explain that you will demonstrate the fastest trick in the world. You then place the cards behind your back for a split second. When they are brought to the front again, you spread the cards and one is seen reversed in the centre. It is the card selected.

This is a typical example of a very simple method used to accomplish what seems like a miracle. Performed well, this effect cannot fail to win over an audience.

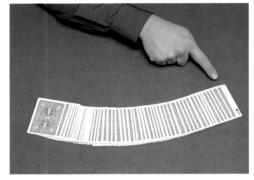

1 The set-up is simple and will take one second to accomplish. Secretly reverse the bottom card face up under the face-down deck.

2 Spread the face-down deck between your hands and ask for a card to be selected. Take care that the bottom card is not seen to be reversed.

3 While the card selected is being looked at and remembered by the spectator, secretly turn the deck upside down. To make this easier, you could explain that you will turn your back so that you cannot see the selected card. When your back is turned, reverse the deck.

4 Because of the card reversed earlier, the deck will still appear to be face down. Make sure the deck is perfectly squared, then ask the spectator to push their card somewhere into the middle of the deck.

secret view

5 Announce that you will demonstrate the world's fastest trick. Move the cards behind your back. As soon as they are out of sight, push the top card off the deck and turn the whole deck over on top of this card.

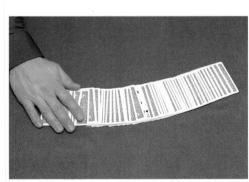

6 Bring the deck to the front again and it will look as if nothing has changed. The deck will still appear face down. Spread the cards between your hands or ribbon-spread them across a table to show that there is one card reversed.

7 The reversed card will be the one selected. Turn it face down again and continue with another trick.

face value

The magician removes a card from the deck and places it to one side as a prediction for later on. A random number of cards are dealt on to the table by a spectator and two piles are made. The top card of each *pile is turned over and the suit of one together with the value of another are combined and found to match the earlier prediction. This is a simple but very baffling card trick.*

1 Ask a spectator to shuffle the cards and then hand the deck to you. Fan the cards towards yourself and take note of the top two cards – simply remember the value of the first card and the suit of the second. This combined card will become your prediction. In our example, the prediction would be the Four of Clubs. Remove it and place it to one side, but in full view.

2 Give the deck back to the spectator and ask them to deal the cards on to a table, one on top of the other until they wish to stop dealing. The original top two cards of the deck are now at the bottom of this pile. In order to get them to the top again, the cards must be dealt once more.

3 Discard the rest of the deck and have the pile of cards on the table dealt alternately into two piles. Notice which pile the final card is placed on.

4 Turn over whichever card was dealt last, explaining that you will use the card's value only and ignore the suit. (In our example it is the *Four* of Hearts.)

5 Turn over the top card of the other pile and explain that you will use the suit, but not the value (the Two of *Clubs*).

6 Reveal that your earlier prediction matches the combination of the cards randomly shuffled to the top of the two piles.

tip *On a rare occasion you may find that the first two cards of the deck will not produce a usable prediction. For example, if the Six of Clubs were next to the Six of Spades the prediction should be the* *Six of Spades, but that card cannot be removed from the deck. If this happens, cut the deck, positioning two new cards at the top. Unless you are very unlucky, these new top cards should be usable.*

the indicator

A card is chosen and returned to the deck. The deck is spread and one card is found reversed. Although it is not the card selected, it acts as an indicator and helps to find it.

This is a good example of how a key card is used to achieve a certain goal, that is, finding the selection. Once you understand the principle involved, you can use any card as the "indicator" and simply adjust the set-up accordingly. For example, if the Five of Hearts was used, the reversed card would need to be set five cards from the bottom.

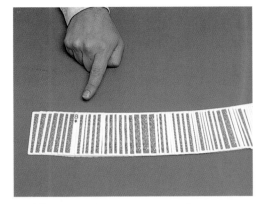

1 The set-up is easy to remember. Reverse any Eight and position it eight cards from the bottom of the deck. This is a secret set-up, so the reversed card should remain hidden.

2 Fan the cards for a selection, but do not spread them too far in case the reversed card is prematurely exposed. With a small amount of practice, the cards can be handled relatively freely.

3 While the card is being looked at, swing-cut the top half of the deck into the left hand.

4 Have the selected card replaced on top of the left-hand cards, then place the right-hand cards on top of it.

5 Riffle the end of the deck, explaining that one card will reverse itself.

6 Spread the deck and show the Eight reversed in the centre. Cut the deck at this point, bringing the Eight to the top of the deck. The selector will be quick to tell you it is the wrong card.

7 Explain that the Eight is merely an indicator card and indicates to you that the chosen card is in fact eight cards down from the top.

8 Place the Eight to one side and count off seven cards one at a time, out loud. Turn over the eighth card. It will be the card selected.

you find it!

The deck is given to a spectator – the magician never touches it throughout the trick. A card is chosen and returned to the deck, which is then cut a number of times. The magician merely glances at the side of the deck and tells the spectator the exact position of the selected card.

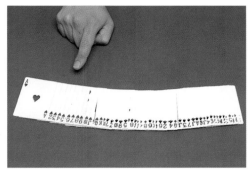

1 To set up the deck, sort all the Hearts into numerical order, Ace through to King. Place this stack on the bottom of the deck, with the Ace lowermost.

2 Set the deck face down in front of a spectator and instruct them to cut off half the cards.

3 Ask them to look at the card they cut to and to remember it.

4 Have the card replaced on the opposite pile (on top of the original top card).

5 Instruct them to complete the cut and square the cards neatly.

6 Now ask them to turn the deck face up.

7 Instruct the spectator to cut and complete the cut. What you need them to do is to cut to one of the cards in the stack which you set up earlier (that is, any Heart). If you are lucky they will do this first time; if not simply ask them to cut the deck again, and again if necessary. Eventually they will cut somewhere into the stack of Hearts. In our example it is the Four of Hearts. Just remember "four".

8 Have the deck turned face down and stare at the edge of the deck as if making some difficult calculations. State their selection is "four" cards down from the top of the deck. After all the cutting, this seems quite a bold statement to make – even the spectator has lost track of the card. Ask them to deal three cards face down and turn over the fourth. It will be the card selected.

tip *A Jack counts as 11, a Queen as 12 and a King as 13.*

instant card revelation

A card is chosen and returned to the deck in the fairest of manners. Without hesitation, the magician is able to reveal the chosen card. This effect takes advantage of a "glimpsed" card. It should be performed briskly and, as you will see, you do not even need to pull *the chosen card out of the deck; you can simply say the name of the card out loud. For some reason it seems more impossible if you just say the name of their card, as opposed to physically finding it. Try both ways and see which method you prefer.*

1 Using one of the techniques explained, "glimpse" and remember the bottom card of the deck (in this example, the King of Hearts). This becomes your key card.

2 Spread the cards for a selection, emphasizing the fairness of choice open to the spectator.

3 Ask for the selected card to be remembered (in this example, the Five of Diamonds). Simultaneously square the deck.

4 Swing-cut the top half of the deck into your left hand.

5 Have the card replaced on to your left-hand cards, then place the right hand's cards on top, positioning your key card above the selection.

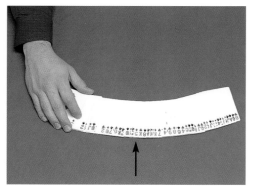

6 You can make a quick face-up Ribbon Spread along the surface of the table, or alternatively spread the cards between your hands, towards you.

7 Either way, find your key card, and the selected card will be the one directly above it. Remove it from the spread and reveal the selection.

the next card is yours

A card is chosen and returned to the deck. The magician deals the cards one at a time, face up on to the table. While dealing, he states that the next card to be turned over will be the one selected. Even though the spectators are sure the magician has failed, since they have seen that the selected card has already been dealt, much to their amusement and surprise the next card to be turned over is indeed the selected card. This trick is a "sucker" trick – your audience thinks the trick has gone wrong, but it is really part of the presentation.

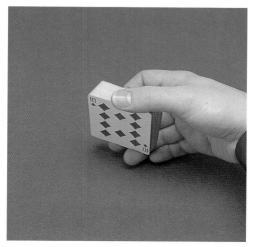

1 Secretly "glimpse" the bottom card of the deck, using one of the methods described earlier. This will be your key card. (In our example it is the Ten of Diamonds.)

2 Using the Two-Handed Spread, offer the cards to a spectator for a selection.

3 Cut half the deck to the table and have the selected card placed on top of this packet. As you place the other half on top to bury their card, you will automatically position your key card directly above their selection. Cut the deck and complete the cut a few times, but do not shuffle!

4 Deal the cards face up, one at a time. When you see your key card, the very next card dealt will be the one selected, but do not pause; carry on dealing about ten more cards. Then say, "I bet you the next card I turn over will be yours". The spectator will immediately accept the bet.

5 Wait a second or two, then watch the spectator's face as you reach for the card immediately next to your key card, which will of course be the one selected.

6 Turn it over and you will win the bet! You will definitely have fun with this one!

do as I do

Two decks of cards are used. Both the magician and the spectator choose a card from their respective decks, then put them back into the centre. The decks are swapped and each looks for their selection. Both cards are placed side by side and, despite the odds against it

happening, the cards mysteriously match each other. This is one of the cleverest cards tricks ever invented. Try it and you will amaze everyone who watches it. It simply defies explanation, and has become one of the all-time classic card tricks.

1 Give a deck of cards to the spectator and keep a second deck for yourself. Have both shuffled. As you shuffle your deck, remember the bottom card. This is your key card.

2 Swap decks so that you now know the card on the bottom of the pile in front of the spectator. Explain that they must copy every move you make as closely as possible.

3 Cut approximately half the deck to your right. The spectator will mirror your actions.

4 Pick up the card you cut to and instruct the spectator to remember theirs. Look at your card, although you do not need to remember it. Just pretend to do so.

5 Place the card back on the right-hand pile. Your spectator will copy you.

6 Place the left packet on top of the right. The spectator's card is now directly under your key card. At this stage you can cut the cards as many times as you wish, although it is not necessary to do so.

7 Swap the decks over again and comment to your spectator on the absolute fairness with which you have both chosen a card.

8 Tell the spectator to find their chosen card at the same time as you find yours. Spread through the deck until you see your key card. The card immediately above it will be the one selected.

9 Place your card face down on the table in front of you. The spectator will do likewise.

10 Explain that you both made the same moves at exactly the same time and so in theory you should have arrived at the same result. Turn over the cards to show a perfect match.

impossible card location

A deck of cards is split in two and thoroughly shuffled by two spectators. Each chooses and exchanges a card. The cards are shuffled again. Incredibly, and without hesitation, the magician is able to find both cards immediately.

The more your spectators try to figure out how you achieved this, the more impossible it will seem. The secret preparation is actually shown as part of the presentation of the trick, but it is so subtle that it remains absolutely invisible!

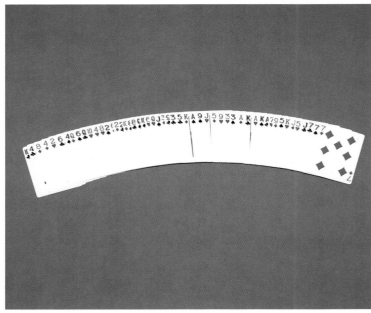

1 Set the deck by dividing all the odd cards from all the even cards. Place one set on top of the other. Spread or fan the deck towards two spectators and explain that although the cards are already mixed, you want to have them mixed some more. A casual glance at the set-up cards will not be enough to see that the deck has been split into odd and even cards.

2 Split the deck at the point where the odd cards meet the even cards. Hand half the deck to each spectator. Ask them to shuffle their cards well. Really stress to the spectators that they can mix the cards as much as they like. This apparent fairness simply increases the overall effect.

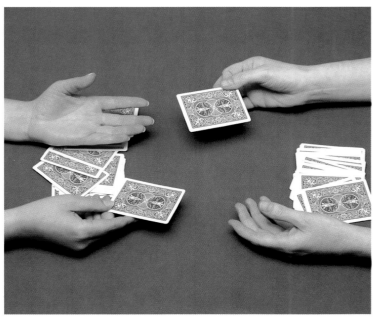

3 Request that the cards are spread out on the table face down and that one from each half be chosen, remembered and swapped with the other person's selection.

4 The selected cards are then placed back somewhere in the middle of the opposite half from where they came.

5 Have both half-decks shuffled well again and reiterate the fairness of the procedure thus far. Ask the spectators to leave the half-decks squared on the table in front of them.

6 Pick up one packet and spread through it with the faces of the cards towards you. It will be easy to find the chosen card as it will be the only even card in the odd packet. Remove it and place it in front of the spectator who chose that card.

7 Repeat the same procedure with the second packet, placing the second selection in front of the other spectator. A little acting ability will go a long way at this point. Make it look as though you are having trouble finding the chosen card, or perhaps you can just start eliminating individual cards, scattering them to the table one at a time until there is only one card remaining in your hand.

8 Ask each spectator to verify the name of their card. Turn each card over and show that you correctly divined the selections. The ease of the method used for this trick allows you to focus on the presentation. Experiment with different styles until you find one that suits you.

magic time

A prediction is made and placed in the centre of the table. A random hour in the day is thought of by a spectator. Twelve cards are laid in the formation of a clock face and a card is chosen to represent the thought-of hour. The magician reveals the thought-of hour and the prediction in the centre of the table is found to match the chosen card.

This trick works on a mathematical principle, and is very clever indeed. Try it with a deck of cards in hand and you will amaze yourself! At the end of the explanation there is a variation of the first method, using a marked card. This has the advantage of being even more deceptive.

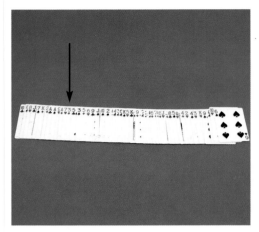

1 The only preparation is to remember which card is thirteenth from the top of the deck. In our example it is the Three of Diamonds.

2 Set the deck face down on the table and write a prediction on a piece of paper, with a question mark on the reverse. Your prediction is the card you remembered. Place it on the table, with the question mark uppermost, not letting the audience see your prediction.

3 Ask someone to think of their favourite hour in the day, and to take that many cards off the top of the deck and put them on the bottom. Turn your back while this happens so that there is no way for you to know what hour it is. Let us assume that they think of 4 o'clock and move four cards from the top to the bottom.

4 Take the deck and deal twelve cards on to the table, reversing their order.

5 Pick up this pile and set the cards out face up in a clock formation around your prediction so that the first card you deal is at 1 o'clock, the second at 2 o'clock, etc. (The 12 o'clock position should be placed so that it is the furthest card from the spectator.)

6 Your prediction card will automatically position itself at their thought-of hour. However, do not reveal it just yet. Build up the suspense by asking the spectator which wrist they wear their watch on. Ask them to hold that wrist over the centre of the circle. Hold their wrist as if trying to pick up a psychic vibe, indicating what hour they chose. Reveal the thought-of hour.

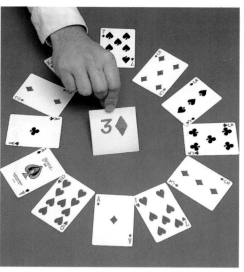

7 Ask the spectator to confirm that you are correct, then call attention to the card at their chosen hour (in this case 4 o'clock). It will be the Three of Diamonds.

8 Turn over your prediction to show a perfect match.

9 If you mark the back of the thirteenth card down (Three of Diamonds), you can lay the cards face down instead of face up. As the cards are dealt, the marked card will indicate the thought-of hour.

secret view

10 This close-up view of the card shows the normal design compared to the subtle mark which is easy to spot if you are aware of it. Part of the design on the back of the card has been filled in with a permanent marker pen which matches the colour of the card.

11 At step 7, after the thought-of hour is revealed and confirmed as being correct, reverse the appropriate card at the thought-of hour.

spectator cuts the aces

A deck of cards is placed in front of the spectator, who cuts it into approximately four equal packets. Although the magician never touches the deck and the spectator mixes the cards some more, the top card of each packet is found to be an Ace.

Four-Ace tricks are very popular with magicians. In fact, four-of-a-kind tricks make up a large percentage of card tricks. This self-working card trick is amazing; the method is simple and the impact on an audience is powerful.

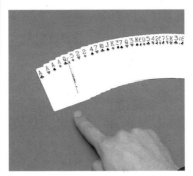

1 To prepare, secretly find the four Aces and move them to the top of the deck.

2 Place the deck on a table and invite a spectator to cut it into two approximately equal halves. Keep track of the original top of the deck at all times (that is, the packet with the four Aces at the top).

3 Ask the spectator to cut one of the packets in half again, and indicate where they are to place the cards.

4 Ask for the other half-deck to be cut in half again in the opposite direction, indicating both verbally and with your hand where the final packet should go. Make sure you still know which pile has the four aces on top.

5 You should have four approximately equal packets in front of you. The four Aces should be on the top of one of the end packets, depending on which way the cards were cut. In our example, the four Aces are on the top of the packet on the far right. Explain that four random points in the deck have been found.

6 Point to the packet at the opposite end to the Aces. Ask the spectator to pick up the deck and to move three cards from the top to the bottom. The fact that the spectator makes all the moves increases the apparent fairness of the whole procedure.

7 Now tell your spectator to deal one card from the top of the packet in their hand to each of the piles on the table, in any order they wish.

8 Having replaced the first packet, the spectator should pick up the second packet and repeat the same procedure; that is, take three cards from the top and place them at the bottom. They should deal one card to the top of each packet on the table.

9 This exact sequence should be repeated with the third packet. Each time explain which moves to make and watch to ensure that the spectator follows your instructions correctly. If any wrong moves are made, it may be because you did not explain the procedure clearly enough.

10 The fourth packet is treated in exactly the same way. This will result in four packets face down on the table, which you have not touched from the very beginning.

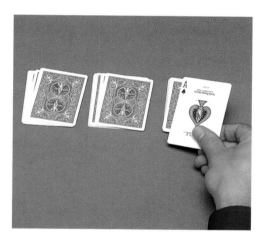

11 Explain the randomness of the cuts and that without even touching the cards you have been able to influence the actions taken. Turn over one of the cards on the top of one of the packets. It will be an Ace.

tip *During the sequence of movements what actually happens is that you add three cards on top of the Aces, then move those three added cards to the bottom and deal one Ace to each of the other three piles. All of the other moves are simply a smokescreen to help hide the method!*

12 Turn over the top cards of the remaining three packets, revealing an Ace on each.

four card poker

This is an ideal sequel to Spectator Cuts the Aces. Four groups of four cards are mixed and dealt into four "hands". The spectator chooses a "hand" of cards. Despite the fairness of the selection, the chosen pile is shown to consist of the four Aces!

Although there are several outcomes to this trick, your audience must believe that there is only one. This will only happen if you perform confidently and practise each of the possible scenarios until you are able to do this without hesitation.

1 Set the four Aces out on to the table next to each other. If you have just performed Spectator Cuts the Aces, you will already be in this position.

2 Deal three cards on top of each Ace. Place the rest of the deck to one side.

3 Collect each pile, one on top of the other, into one packet. Turn the cards face down and square them neatly.

4 Cut the cards several times, each time ensuring that it is a complete cut. Cutting will not mix the order of the cards; it will merely change the cyclical order. You can even let a spectator do the cutting, which seems to increase the impossibility of any sleight of hand.

5 Re-deal the cards into four piles, side by side. So long as the cards have only been cut and not shuffled, the four Aces will automatically be dealt together in one pile.

6 Square each pile, secretly "glimpsing" the bottom card each time. You must discover which pile the Aces are in, but do so without making your glimpse obvious.

7 There are now several possible outcomes to this trick. Ask a spectator to point to a pile with one hand. If they point to the pile of Aces, simply turn over that pile and show that, despite a completely free choice, they have found all four Aces.

8 If they point to a different pile, ask them to point to another packet with their other hand. If both piles picked do not contain the Aces, remove them, explaining that they are to be discarded. This will leave you with two piles. If, however, the second pile pointed to does contain the Aces, remove the other two piles, leaving two piles on the table.

9 Either way, one of the remaining piles will consist of the four Aces. Explain that you are going to play a very simple game of Four Card Poker and that the spectator must choose a hand for you and a hand for themselves. Ask the spectator to push one pile of cards towards you. Give them an opportunity to change their mind.

10 If the Aces are pushed towards you, turn both packets face up and display them. Explain that even though they had every chance to change their mind, they gave you the winning hand! If the Aces are kept by the spectator, simply show your cards and ask to see theirs, exclaiming that they are extremely lucky and that you would not want to play cards with them! If you are not 100 per cent confident with the three possible outcomes of this trick, your audience may be confused as to what was meant to have happened. Practise until you can perform this without thinking what to do next.

spell-a-card

A card is selected and replaced in the deck. The magician seems to be in trouble and fails to find the chosen card. It is suggested that maybe the card will answer to its name in the same way that a dog would!

The cards are dealt one at a time on to the table, one card for each letter. The final card proves to be the one selected. This is yet another example of how the use of a key card can create a different effect.

1 Secretly "glimpse" the bottom card of the deck. This will become your key card. In this case it is the Three of Hearts.

2 Using a Two-Handed Spread, offer the cards to a spectator for a selection.

3 Swing-cut the top half of the deck and have the selected card replaced on to the original top card. Place the rest of the deck on top, positioning the key card directly above the selection.

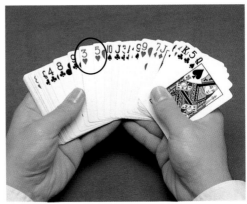

4 You can give the cards a false shuffle at this point, as long as the selected card and key card stay side by side. Spread through the deck face up and explain that you are going to find the selected card. Find your key card. The card above it will be the one selected. In this case the chosen card is the Five of Hearts.

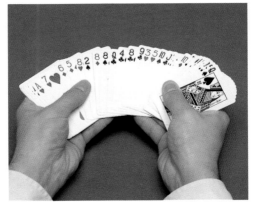

5 Starting from the selected card, begin to mentally spell its name. For every letter, move one card to the left. This is done as the cards are spread and should be practised until you can do it without concentrating too much. When you reach the final letter, ask if you have passed the selected card. The spectator will tell you that you have and will think something has gone wrong. Cut the deck and complete the cut at the card reached on the last letter. It is possible you may reach the top of the deck before you have finished spelling (*see* Tip for this eventuality).

6 Turn the deck face down and ask for the name of the selected card. When it is given to you, start dealing the cards face down to the table one at a time, one card for each letter. The card that is dealt on the final letter will be the one selected.

tip *Occasionally you may run out of cards when spelling the name of the selected card. This is because you cut too deeply when the selected card was replaced. Just continue spelling from the face of the deck, acting as if you need to go through the deck again. Cut the cards as before and continue.*

controlling a card

One of the most important sleights to learn is how to control a chosen card to the top of the deck. It will give you the ability to perform literally hundreds of different card tricks. Discussed here are several ways to control a card. It is always better to learn one really well than to learn several badly. In order to learn how to control a card, it is also important to understand a few other techniques and grips.

finger break

This break is used in a great number of tricks. It is one of the sleights most widely used by professional card magicians, predominantly for keeping control of a desired number of cards and also to aid the shift of the required cards from one position to another. It is an essential sleight that must be mastered if further study of card magic appeals to you. Because it uses the fourth finger, this particular sleight is also known as the Pinkie Break. It is not too difficult to learn, and is worth learning well.

secret view

1 Hold the deck in the left-hand Mechanics' Grip or Dealing Grip. With the right hand, approach from above in the Biddle Grip position and using the right thumb, lift approximately half of the cards about 1cm (½in). Release the cards, but allow the pad of the left fourth fingertip to stop the cards from falling flush.

2 The gap between the two packets need not be large – just enough for you to locate at a future point in the particular routine. If pressure is applied from the thumb on top of the deck, the gap will close enough to remain hidden from both the front and sides.

thumb break

The Thumb Break is similar to the Finger Break and is used for the same purposes – to maintain control, or to aid the repositioning of certain cards. It is a vital sleight to learn, but you will be pleased to know that it is not at all difficult and will take no more than one or two trials to understand. It's even easier than the Finger Break!

secret view

Hold a Finger Break as described above. With the right hand, approach the left hand from above and pick up the deck in the Biddle Grip position. However, as the thumb grips the back short edge (nearest you), the gap between the two packets is maintained by squeezing lightly between the right thumb and fingers. The cards are held entirely by the right hand, freeing the left hand.

double cut

The purpose of a Double Cut is to bring a card or block of cards from the middle of the deck to the top. It is a very useful move to master *and, as you will learn, can also be used to control a selected card to the top of the deck.*

1 Using the right hand, hold a Thumb Break about halfway down the deck. Drop approximately the bottom quarter of the deck into the left hand.

2 Grip these cards between the thumb and first finger and replace them on top of the right-hand cards.

3 Almost immediately loosen the right thumb's grip, letting the remaining cards (up to the Thumb Break) fall on to the fingers of the left hand.

4 Replace the left hand's packet on to the top of the right-hand cards in exactly the same way. The cards that were immediately below the Thumb Break are now on top of the deck. Square the deck and the Double Cut is complete.

double cut control

The Double Cut is also a neat and effective way to control a selected card to a wanted position in the deck. The same set of moves are seen here to show how the card is controlled to the top. Performed swiftly, it allows you to control the selected card in an unsuspicious and smooth manner. Your audience will assume you are merely cutting *the deck to mix the cards further. No attention should be called to the sequence of cuts. Study and practise this until it becomes second nature. The selected card is marked with a black border so that it can be easily followed throughout the explanation. This is one of the easiest, quickest ways to control a card to the top of the deck.*

1 Assume you have had a card selected. Cut off half the deck (in the Biddle Grip) and have the selected card replaced on to the bottom half.

2 As the top half is replaced, hold a Thumb Break between the two packets. You will now perform the Double Cut as explained previously, that is, drop approximately the bottom quarter of the deck into the left hand. The left hand begins to move away with the dropped cards.

3 These cards are gripped between the thumb and first finger and replaced on top of the right-hand cards. Almost immediately, the right thumb loosens its grip, letting the remaining cards (up to the Thumb Break) fall on to the fingers of the left hand. The top card of this dropped packet is the one selected.

4 Replace the left-hand packet on to the top of the right-hand cards in exactly the same way. The selected card is now on top of the deck.

in-jog dribble control

This addition to the Double Cut Control gives a very convincing touch of extra subtlety to the overall look of the sequence. The *casualness with which the cards are handled will convince your audience that the selected card is lost in the deck.*

1 Have a card selected. Cut off half the deck (in the Biddle Grip) and have the selected card replaced on to the bottom half. Dribble the cards from the right hand on to the selected card, ensuring that the initial few cards are dribbled slightly towards you.

2 This view shows how the remaining cards are dribbled as the right hand moves forward so that the last group of cards fall square with the rest of the deck. The overlap of the cards seen in the above photo is known to magicians as an "in-jog".

3 As the right hand positions itself on to the top of the deck, allow the thumb to lift up the cards above the "in-jog" and secure a Thumb Break between the two packets. From here on, the Double Cut sequence is identical to that explained previously.

4 Drop approximately the bottom quarter of the deck into the left hand.

5 Grip these cards between the thumb and first finger and replace them on top of the right-hand cards. Almost immediately, loosen the right thumb's grip, letting the remaining cards (up to the Thumb Break) fall on to the fingers of the left hand. The top card of this dropped packet is the one selected.

6 Replace the left-hand packet on to the top of the right-hand cards in exactly the same way. The result is that the selected card is now on top of the deck.

run and back control

This is yet another way to control a card, and looks like a legitimate shuffle. You simply shuffle the selected card from the top to the bottom and back to the top again. It is an easy shuffle to master, and is deceptive because it looks so like the shuffle everyone is familiar with. As with any control, do not call attention to what you are doing but simply get on with it, perhaps describing what is going to happen next or asking someone a question. The more casually you handle the cards, the less suspicious people will be. The selected card is shown with a black border so that it can be followed easily during the explanation that follows.

1 Have a card selected and replaced on top of the deck. Begin an Overhand Shuffle by running one card (the card selected) into your left hand.

2 Follow this single card with a regular Overhand Shuffle until all the cards in your right hand are used up.

3 The situation at this stage is that the selected card is now on the bottom, followed by the rest of the deck on top.

4 Start another legitimate Overhand Shuffle.

5 When you are left with a small packet in your right hand, run the cards singly on to the left-hand cards.

6 You will finish with the selected card back on top.

simple overhand control

If you can Overhand-Shuffle a deck of cards, you will not have a problem learning this simple method for keeping track of and controlling a chosen card once it has been replaced in the deck. It can be used in conjunction with other shuffles and controls learnt previously, but is most suitably used with the Run and Back Control, as the motions of the cards match each other and one shuffling sequence will simply become an extension of the other. The selected card is shown with a black border for ease of explanation.

1 Have a card selected and replaced on top of the deck. Begin an Overhand Shuffle by cutting approximately half the deck from the bottom.

2 Toss this packet on to the selected card as you pull up another group of cards. However, when the first packet is tossed it should be "in-jogged" approximately 1cm (½in) back from the top of the deck.

3 Throw the second packet on top, flush with the original packet.

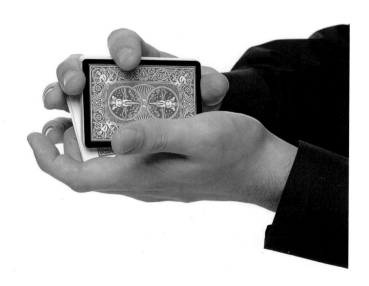

4 As your right hand returns to the deck, the right thumb is able to push all the cards above the selected card forward to grip the original top section of the deck. This is made easy thanks to the "in-jog".

5 Throw this final packet on top of everything, and the selected card is back on top.

a false cut

This sleight allows you to create the illusion of mixing the cards even though the order of the deck never changes. Used properly, it is a very useful technique to master. There are many different types of False Cut. Some are flashy and difficult to learn; others, like this one, are simple and invisible because it looks as if you cut the deck when in reality you do nothing!

Success relies on timing the moves so that the cut looks natural. See and feel what it is like to actually cut the cards, then try and match the look and pace of the real cut while executing the False Cut. Performing a real move before attempting a false move is widely practised by professional magicians. Once again, the top card is shown with a black border for ease of explanation.

1 Hold the deck face down high up at the fingertips of the left hand. Your thumb should be on one of the long edges, your second, third and fourth fingers on the other long edge and your first finger at the short edge furthest away from you.

2 With your right hand, approach the deck from above. The right first finger lies across the top card and the thumb and other fingers hold the long edges.

3 With the right thumb, split the cards about halfway down. It is the bottom half of the deck that is held by the right thumb; the top half is held entirely (and only) by the left hand.

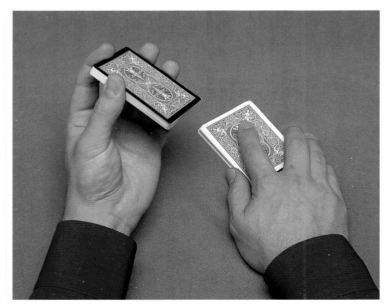

4 With the right hand, pull the bottom half of the deck away from the top half. The right first finger naturally slides over and off the top card and on to the top card of the bottom packet. This half is cut to the table.

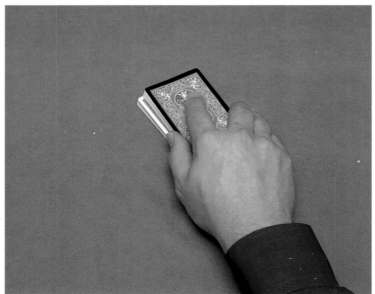

5 The right hand returns to the left and completes the cut by placing the remaining half on top of the cards on the table.

card tricks requiring skill

The following card tricks are a little more complicated than the self-working variety taught earlier. Many of the routines use the techniques previously discussed and will require a certain amount of rehearsal, practice and dedication to master. As you will notice, many sleights are interchangeable, and you should aim to experiment in order to find techniques that work well for you.

countdown

A card is selected and shuffled into the deck. A spectator is asked for a number, and that number of cards are dealt to the table. The final card dealt is turned over, but is not the chosen card. The spectator counts the cards again. This time the last card dealt is found to be the one selected. The method to this trick may seem obvious, but people will be amazed because they do not know about controlling cards.

1 Fan the cards for a selection, stressing the spectator's freedom of choice.

2 Have the card returned and prepare to control it to the top of the deck.

3 You can use any control technique. This is the Simple Overhand Control.

4 Ask for a number between 1 and 52. Deal that number of cards to the table, one on top of the other. You will notice that the first card dealt to the table is the one selected. Assume the number chosen was 14. Deal thirteen cards to the table and turn over the fourteenth card. It will not be the one selected.

5 Act surprised by this failure and re-assemble the cards by placing all the dealt cards back on from the top of the deck. As you have just reversed the top fourteen cards, the selected card will now automatically be the fourteenth card down.

6 Give the deck to the spectator and ask them to try. Watch as they deal the chosen number of cards to the table. This time the final card will be the one selected.

tip *If you are able to convince your audience that the selected card has really been shuffled and lost into the deck, the outcome will appear to be a near impossibility. Of course, the best-case scenario occurs if the spectator should happen to choose the number "1". Then you will be able to perform a miracle without having to do anything else – simply turn over the top card. Should this ever happen, stop performing immediately because it is doubtful that anything you do could follow that!*

gliding home

This wonderful trick, based on the Glide, is especially good for a large audience. It is a "sucker" trick, which means that the audience thinks the trick has gone wrong when in reality you are in total control. It never fails to amaze people, but should be performed with a tongue-in-cheek style so as to entertain rather than frustrate or annoy the spectator. Remember, it is alright to fool a spectator, but you should avoid making someone feel or look foolish.

1 Spread the cards for a selection, using either a Ribbon Spread or a Two-Handed Spread.

2 Split the deck in half, pushing off the top two cards of the bottom half and holding a Finger Break beneath them. The selected card is replaced on this pile.

secret view

3 Once the selected card has been replaced, square the deck, maintaining the Finger Break.

4 Cut all the cards above the break to the table.

5 Place all the cards remaining in your hand on top of the packet on the table. The selected card has now been controlled to the third card from the bottom of the deck.

6 Explain that you are going to eliminate some cards and that you do not want the audience to give you any clues as to whether you are right or wrong. Hold the deck in the left hand, in preparation for the Glide. Tip the deck backwards to show the bottom card, and explain that you do not think it is the chosen card.

7 Tip the deck down again and slide off the bottom card of the deck. This resembles the Glide, which you will perform soon.

8 Once again, tip up the deck so that the next card can be seen. Remind the audience not to give you any clues.

9 Deal this card to the table next to the first in a similar fashion.

10 Tip the deck up one last time. This time the selected card will be seen, but carry on regardless. Explain that you do not think this is the chosen card.

11 Start to deal this card to the table next to the first two cards. However, you actually perform the Glide so that the penultimate card is secretly removed instead.

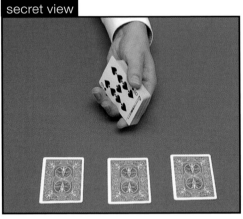

secret view

12 Keep the selected card in the Glide position and ask for a number between one and ten. Let us assume that "four" is chosen.

13 Deal three cards off the bottom of the deck, using the Glide. The fourth card you pull off is the selection. Hold it towards you and ask which card was chosen. When you hear the response, act as if there has been some mistake.

14 The spectator will rush for the last card you eliminated and will turn it over. They will be amazed to find it is no longer their card. Turn over the card in your hand and show that you had the correct card all along.

trapped

The two red Queens are placed to one side. A card is chosen and returned to the deck, which is then shuffled. The Queens are cut, face up, into the centre of the face-down deck. In an instant the cards are spread on to the table to reveal one card trapped between them. It is revealed to be the card selected.

This is an involved routine, which will encourage you to become proficient at controlling a card while using the Double Lift and Finger Break. Once you have mastered it, you will have learnt the necessary sleights to perform a whole range of different effects, several of which follow later in this book.

1 Openly remove the two red Queens from the deck and place them face up to one side. Use the Two-Handed Spread to fan the cards for a selection. Ask the spectator to look at and remember their chosen card. Whenever you get a card chosen it is always a good idea for your spectator to show it to at least one other person in case they forget it later in the trick.

2 Control the selected card to the top of the deck, using any of the methods described, or this slight variation of the Double Cut, which is easy to perform and very convincing. Lift half the deck with the right hand and have the selected card replaced on to the left-hand cards. Hold a Finger Break between the two packets as the right hand places its half back on top.

3 Cut approximately one-quarter of the deck to the table.

4 Now cut all the cards above the break on to the packet on the table.

5 Finally, place the last packet on top of everything. The selected card is now on top.

6 Hold the deck face down in the left-hand Mechanics' Grip. Obtain a Finger Break below the top card by pushing the top few cards over to the right with your left thumb. Square the cards with one hand, inserting your fourth finger into the deck one card from the top. Pick up the two Queens and display them in the right-hand Biddle Grip. The bottom Queen should be pulled to the left so that both can be seen clearly.

7 Call attention to the two Queens as you move them to a position just above the deck. Square them together by pushing the left long edge of the bottom Queen against the side of your left thumb. As this happens, secretly add the selected card to the bottom of the two Queens. This is easy because of the Finger Break.

8 The left thumb moves across the face of the top Queen and holds it in place as the right hand moves to the right with the lower two cards (perfectly squared to look like one). This displays one Queen on top of the deck.

9 Place the second Queen (with the hidden card underneath) on top of the first. Essentially what you have done is to display two cards while secretly loading one card in between them.

10 Cut the top half of the deck neatly and squarely to the table with your right hand.

11 Complete the cut by placing the remaining cards on top of those on the table. The deck should now be face down and squared in front of you.

12 Make a magical pass over the cards, then ribbon-spread them across the table to reveal that a face-down card has magically appeared between the two face-up Queens.

13 Show this card to be the one selected.

card through handkerchief

A card is chosen, then shuffled back into the deck. The deck is wrapped in a handkerchief and held aloft. Slowly but surely the selected card starts to melt through the material until it is completely free of the handkerchief. This routine is a classic of magic and visually *striking to watch. If performed well, the card really looks as though it is melting through the fabric. The best type of handkerchief to use is a medium-sized gentleman's silk handkerchief of the kind that is usually worn in the breast pocket for show.*

1 For this trick, you will need a deck of cards and a handkerchief. Have a card selected and returned to the deck.

2 Using any of the controls taught previously, bring the selected card to the top of the deck. Hold the deck in a left-hand Mechanics' Grip.

3 Cover the deck of cards with a coloured silk handkerchief.

4 Reach under the handkerchief with your right hand and remove all but the top card.

5 Place these 51 cards on top of the handkerchief and square them, with the single card beneath. The deck is still held in the Mechanics' Grip.

secret view

6 Fold the side of the handkerchief nearest you up and over the deck of cards. The bottom card should remain hidden.

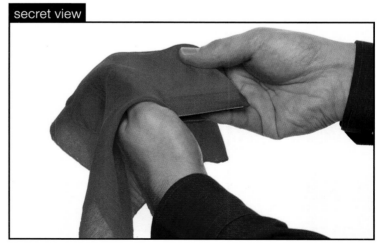

secret view

7 Now fold the material on the right side, underneath the deck. Your left hand will have to alter its grip to accommodate this.

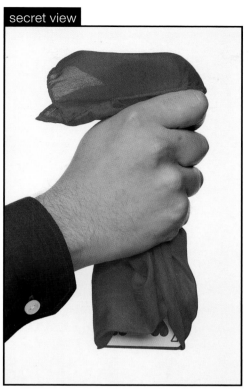

8 Finally fold the material on the left side, under the deck. Hold the loose corners together in your right hand, out to your right-hand side.

9 From behind, you can see that the selected card is trapped on the outside of the handkerchief, within the folds of the material. The folds stop the card from falling out prematurely.

10 Shake your right hand up and down and the card will start to emerge. This is the view that your spectators will see from the front.

11 Continue to shake until just before the card falls out completely. With practice, you will know when the card is about to fall free of the handkerchief.

12 Reach up with the left hand, remove the card and reveal it to be the one selected. The deck can now be unwrapped and you will be ready to perform another card trick.

cards across

Two packets of ten cards are carefully counted and two spectators each hold on to one packet tightly. Three cards are caused to fly invisibly from one packet to the other so that when the cards are counted again one person has seven and the other thirteen. This is *a classic of magic for which there are many methods, most requiring some form of sleight of hand. The techniques taught here are relatively simple yet effective. Practise the false counts until you are super-confident with them. They are the key to the success of this trick.*

secret view

1 Hold a deck of cards in your left hand and openly push off ten cards into the right hand. Secretly push off another three cards, obtaining a Finger Break beneath them. Due to the ten-card spread there is a huge amount of cover for this "get-ready".

2 Flip the top ten cards face up and square them on to the top of the deck. Lift up everything above the Finger Break. You will now be holding ten face-up cards with three face-down cards at the bottom of the packet. Place the rest of the deck off to one side. It is now necessary to count these thirteen cards as ten as follows.

3 Hold the packet in the right-hand Biddle Grip. With your left thumb, pull off the first card and, using the edge of the right-hand packet, flip it face down on to your left hand, counting out loud, "One". Pull off the second face-up card in the same manner as you place the first card back on to the bottom of the packet. Count "Two". Place this second card to the bottom, as before, and continue counting the cards out loud until you reach the end of the face-up cards. You will have counted ten face-up cards but will have secretly added three face-down cards.

4 Give this packet to the spectator on your left, asking them to hold it tightly between their hands. At this stage they will be convinced they are holding just ten cards. Now pick up the deck again and openly spread off another ten cards, counting each card as you push it off to the right.

5 Lift only seven of the ten cards and immediately square the edges of these against the cards in your left hand. Don't make a move out of it; just act casually and nonchalantly.

6 Put the deck to one side so that you can recount the seven cards as ten, as follows. Hold the packet in the right-hand Biddle Grip and use the left thumb to peel off the top card into the left hand, counting out loud, "One". The left hand approaches to take the second card on top of the first, counting "Two". Peel off one more, counting "Three".

7 As the fourth card is taken, place the previous three back on to the bottom of the packet. Do not pause here; just peel off the fourth card, counting "Four". For a second there will only be one card in your hand when there should be four, but your hands do not stop moving and continue to peel off the fifth card as you count "Five". Continue in this fashion until there are no more cards left. You will have counted seven cards as ten. This false count is not easy, but practice will eventually enable you to perform it without hesitation, which is absolutely essential.

8 Give this packet to the spectator on your right and have them hold it securely. Ask each person to confirm how many cards they hold. They should automatically say that they have ten each. Mime sneaking three cards from the spectator on your right and placing them into the hand of the spectator on your left.

9 After this comical byplay, ask the person on your right to count the cards out loud to the table one at a time. There will be only seven cards.

10 The other spectator counts their cards to the table and incredibly they will now have thirteen!

card under glass

Here is a clever little routine that makes use of the Double Lift and Turnover explained earlier. Learning this will make all the hard *work and practice worthwhile! A chosen card is caused to magically change places with an indifferent card isolated under a glass.*

1 Have a wine glass on the table, to your side. Spread a deck for a selection.

2 Hold a Finger Break above the card as it is replaced into the centre of the deck.

3 This photograph shows an exposed view of the Finger Break.

4 Double-cut the cards below the break to the top of the deck. You have controlled the selected card to the top.

5 Perform the Double Lift, showing an indifferent card.

6 Place the double card back on to the deck as your right hand lifts up the glass. Push off the top card of the deck and deal it to the table, putting the glass on top.

7 Dribble the deck on to the top of the glass, holding on to the last card.

8 Turn it over to reveal it was the card just placed under the glass!

9 With a flourish, turn the card under the glass face up to show that it has changed to the one selected.

forcing a card

In many routines it is necessary to make the spectator take a particular card. Using several techniques explained here, even though you "force" a particular card upon the spectator, the selection procedure seems quite fair and above board. A card force properly executed should arouse no suspicion. Several forces are explained here – in most cases you can use whichever you feel most comfortable with.

hindu force

This and the Slip Force, which is explained next, are the most practical ways to force a card. The Hindu Force is direct, convincing and relatively easy to execute. A small amount of practice is all that is required to learn how to do this successfully.

1 The card to be forced should be at the bottom of the deck.

2 Hold the deck high up in the fingertips of your left hand. Your left first finger should be at the outer end of the deck.

3 With the right hand, approach from above and take the bottom three-quarters of the deck away. The thumb is on one side, the second, third and fourth fingers on the other, and the first finger bent lightly on top.

4 Allow the cards in your left hand to fall down to the palm as the right hand returns and the left fingers grab a small group of cards from the top of the deck. Allow these to fall on to the cards below.

5 The bottom card in the right hand always remains the same. Ask a spectator to stop you as you Hindu-shuffle the deck. When he or she says "Stop!", show the bottom card of the packet in your right hand. It will always be the force card.

slip force

This card force is simple yet effective. If performed casually and comfortably, it will be successful every single time. The card to be *forced must be on top of the deck at the outset. It is shown with a black border for ease of explanation.*

secret view

1 Hold the deck in the left-hand Mechanics' Grip. Bend the first finger under the deck and run your thumb down the corner of the cards. Ask the spectator to say "Stop!" as you riffle through the cards.

2 The right hand approaches the deck from above and grips all the "riffled off" cards. Lift this packet straight up. Pressure is maintained on the top card of the deck (force card) so that it falls flush with and becomes the top card of the bottom half.

3 Tapping the long edge of the right-hand cards on the top of the left-hand cards to square them will add plenty of cover for the move. Extend your left hand and have the top card (supposedly the card stopped at) looked at and remembered.

cut deeper force

This is an extremely simple way to force a card. However, while this forcing procedure fits some tricks well, it is too laborious to have a *card chosen this way every time. In practice, it is highly advisable that the spectator does the cutting and turning of the cards.*

1 The card to be forced should be at the top of the deck. In our example it is the Three of Hearts.

2 Hold the deck face down in your left hand and cut about a quarter of the cards face up, replacing them on the deck.

3 Now cut about half the deck face up and replace that group of cards on the deck.

4 Explain that you will use the first face-down card you come to. Fan through the cards and cut the deck at the first face-down card. Place all the face-up cards on to the bottom of the deck, turning them face down as you do so.

5 The top face-down card will be the force card.

cross cut force and prediction

This is a very useful force, easy to accomplish and very deceptive, but only if done correctly. It is taught here as part of a simple trick, as its success relies largely on something known as "time misdirection". This is the concept of using time in between a secret move and the result of that secret move, the idea being that when the spectator tries to reconstruct what happened, they cannot recall the exact sequence of events. Even a few seconds is sufficient. As you will soon see, it would look ridiculous to mark the cut and then immediately reveal the card. The spectator would know instinctively that something illogical had happened.

The back of the force card is here marked with a black border for ease of explanation.

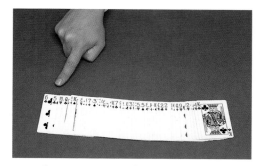

1 When you are ready to start the trick, take a moment to secretly note the top card of the deck. In this example it is the Six of Clubs. This is the card you will be forcing on the spectator.

2 Begin by giving the cards a shuffle or a False Cut that leaves the top card in position. Either way, the cards should be in front of you, face down, with the Six of Clubs on top. Explain that you are going to write a prediction. Draw a question mark on one side of a piece of paper and the Six of Clubs on the other side.

3 Place your prediction off to the side of the table but in full view.

4 Ask a spectator to cut the deck at any point into two packets, side by side. It is important that you keep note of where the original top half is placed.

5 Pick up the bottom half of the deck and place it on the top half of the deck at right angles. As you do this, explain that you are marking the exact position the spectator cut to, for reference later on.

6 Now "time misdirection" is employed by diverting the spectator away from the deck and on to the prediction. Remind your audience that you made a prediction before the cards were cut and that the cards were cut at a completely random location. Reveal your prediction to be the Six of Clubs.

7 The true orientation and order of the deck will have been forgotten by the time the audience's attention returns. Lift up the top packet and explain that you are finding the exact point in the deck marked earlier. In reality you are about to turn over the original top card of the deck.

8 Turn over the supposed cut-to card and reveal that it matches your earlier prediction.

special gimmicks

There are a variety of specially made playing cards, available from magic shops, which will enable you to perform some amazing tricks. These cards look normal but are specially faked in some way.

Explained here are several special gimmicks you can construct yourself. They are not difficult to make and they give you the ability to show people tricks that they will have never seen before.

pips away

The Two of Diamonds is picked by a spectator. The card is placed into the centre of the deck and the magician explains that it will magically appear at the top of the deck again. The top card is turned over but it is the Three of Diamonds. With a flick of the fingers one of the pips flies off the card, leaving the magician holding the Two of Diamonds!

1 Using a scalpel, carefully cut out one of the diamond pips from a spare card.

2 Attach a tiny piece of reusable adhesive to the underside of the diamond pip.

3 Stick the diamond pip in the centre of a duplicate Two of Diamonds so that at a glance it resembles the Three of Diamonds.

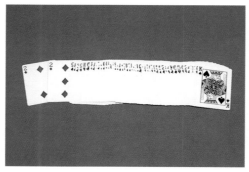

4 Set up a deck so that the real Two of Diamonds is on top and the special Two of Diamonds is second from the top.

5 You will need to force the Two of Diamonds using the Cut Deeper Force. Hold the deck face down on your left hand and ask a spectator to cut off about a quarter of the cards and to turn them face up on top of the deck.

6 Now ask them to cut about half the cards and to turn them face up on top of the deck. Explain that you will use the first face-down card you come to.

7 Spread the deck until you come to the first face-down card. That is the force card. Remove all the face-up cards and place them face down on the bottom of the deck.

8 Lift the top card and show that it is the Two of Diamonds. Do not look at the face of the card yourself.

9 Push the Two of Diamonds clearly into the centre of the deck, then slowly square the cards.

10 Riffle up the end of the deck and explain that the chosen card will pass through all the cards and return to the top again.

11 Hold the cards in the left-hand Dealing Grip and push the top card to the right with your thumb. With your right hand, grip the card at the top right-hand corner so that as the card turns face up, your fingers are automatically covering the corner pip, which should show "3" but actually shows "2".

12 Turn the card face up, hiding the far corner pip under your left thumb. Display the special "Three" of Diamonds and ask whether it is the chosen card.

13 When the spectator tells you that the chosen card was the Two of Diamonds, say "Watch!" and prepare to flick the centre pip with your right finger and thumb.

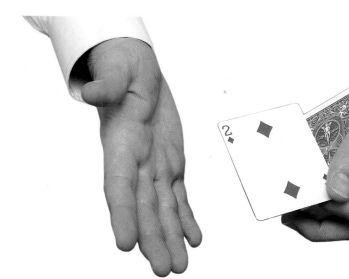

14 As you flick the pip, it will fly off so fast it seems to disappear, leaving you with the chosen card, the Two of Diamonds.

tip *Remember that there is a duplicate Two of Diamonds in the deck, so be sure to remove one of them before giving the deck out for examination.*

changing card

A card is selected and shuffled back into the deck. You remove one card from your pocket. It is seen to be incorrect. With a shake of the hand, the card changes into the correct card.

As a variation, you could force two cards, in this example the Six of Clubs followed by the Jack of Spades. Then you can show the first prediction and magically change it to the second.

1 Choose two different cards (in this example they are the Six of Clubs and the Jack of Spades), plus a spare third card. Fold both of the chosen cards inwards with a sharp crease across the centre.

2 Glue one half of the folded cards back to back, ensuring perfect alignment.

3 This will create a card that can be shown as either a Jack or a Six.

4 Apply glue to the remaining area of the back.

5 Glue it to the face of the third card. This will strengthen the gimmick.

6 Fold the flap into the "up" position, with the Six of Clubs facing outwards. Place this card face down into your breast pocket.

7 Take a deck of cards and place the Jack of Spades on the bottom in preparation for a card force.

8 Shown here is the Hindu Force, but you can use any force that you feel confident performing.

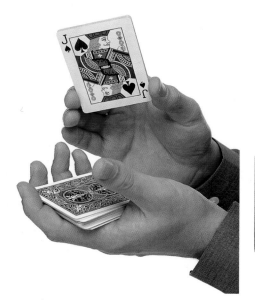

9 Ask a spectator to say "Stop!", then show the bottom card. It will be the Jack of Spades. Shuffle it into the deck and put the cards to one side.

10 Reach into your pocket and remove the fake card, displaying it in your left fingers. Hold it tightly so that the double thickness remains hidden. Ask if you have the correct card. The spectator will tell you it is wrong. Ask which card was chosen.

11 Bring your right hand in front of your left and let the top of the fake card spring forward.

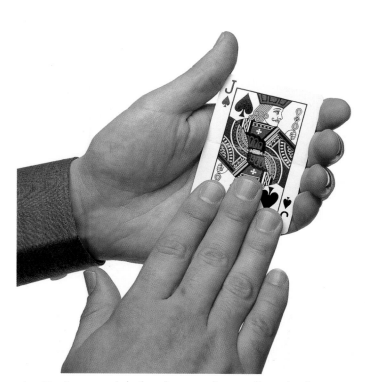

12 As your right hand moves down, allow the flap to open completely so that the card appears to change.

13 Re-grip the card so that the entire surface can be displayed. Try to keep the flap aligned.

find the lady

This trick is a famous illegal swindle, often seen played on the streets of cities worldwide, in which people lose their money by betting on the card they believe to be the odd one out. It has many other names, including Three Card Monte and Chase the Ace. Show your friends why they should never play this game.

Three cards are displayed – two Eights and a Queen. Even though your spectator is sure they know where the Queen is, when they turn over the card they find the Queen has changed into a Joker. With some thought, the Joker can be made to change into many other things, including your business card!

1 Using scissors, cut a piece off a Queen card. The exact size does not matter, but try to cut about a third of the card. It should taper towards one end, as shown here.

2 Trim about 5mm (¼in) off the tapered end. This is so that the gimmicked card will work more smoothly, as you will see.

3 Attach a piece of adhesive tape along the back of the long outer edge of the Queen, and stick it to one of the Eights in a slightly fanned position. The tape acts as a hinge. Experimentation will make this clear.

4 This is how the completed fake card should look.

5 Insert a Joker behind the flap on the fake card and align the edges.

6 Lay another Eight on top so that it looks like a fan of three cards. The Joker will be completely hidden, and it looks as if you are holding two Eights with a Queen in the middle.

7 Display this fan of cards and explain that the spectator simply has to keep their eye on the Queen and remember where it is.

8 Turn the fan of cards face down by turning your wrist, then ask them where they think the Queen is. They will tell you it is in the middle. Ask them to remove the middle card.

9 When they turn it over, they will be amazed to find it is a Joker. Close the fan of cards slightly so that you can turn the cards face up again to flash the two Eights.

card through tablecloth

This effect is simple. A chosen card vanishes from the deck and reappears under the tablecloth, or indeed anywhere you wish to make it appear – your pocket, under a plate, under a spectator's chair or in their pocket. Wherever you decide, make sure you plant it there a long time before you begin the trick. If you were to be seen setting up the trick, the ending would be spoilt.

This is the perfect example of a method that is so simple yet so very baffling. When performed well it should look like a miracle and would probably even fool knowledgeable magicians! After reading through the method, think about other ways in which the vanish of the card could be used.

1 There are two stages to this routine: the disappearance of the chosen card and its reappearance at the end. The card that vanishes is forced. Begin by taking any card from the deck (in our example, the Ace of Clubs) and, using scissors, trim off about 1mm (¹⁄₁₆in) from one short end.

2 Take any card from a spare deck (in our example, the Eight of Hearts). This will be the card that vanishes. Apply glue (here marked black) to the bottom third, and glue it to the Ace of Clubs along the untrimmed end, so that the glued edges align perfectly.

3 Leave the glue to dry. This is how the faked double card should look. Notice how the Eight of Hearts is easy to lift away because of the strip you trimmed off the Ace earlier. (This trimmed card is known as a "short card".)

4 Insert this double card into the middle of the deck, remembering the orientation so that you know which is the unglued end.

5 The second stage to this trick is the reappearance of the card. From the deck, take the card that matches your duplicate card (the Eight of Hearts) and place it secretly under the tablecloth. (This should be done before the audience arrives.)

6 The preparation is now complete. Hold the deck of cards face down in the left-hand Dealing Grip. (The open side of the short card should be facing away from you.)

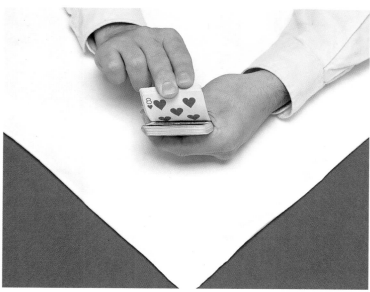

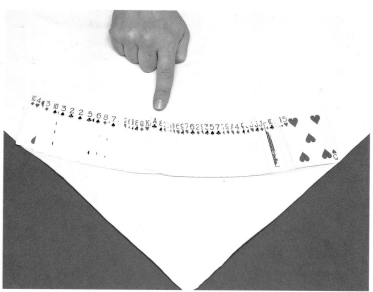

7 Using your right first and second fingers, riffle up the edge of the deck. The cards will automatically stop at the duplicate Eight of Hearts because of the short card. If you listen carefully you will hear a click. With practice, you will be able to stop at the short card every single time. In performance explain that as you riffle the deck of cards you want the spectator to say "Stop!" at any time. Begin the riffle and watch their lips. You must time the riffle so that when they say "Stop!" you are able to let all of the cards below the short card fall. This will take a little practice but is not too difficult, especially if you start the riffle slowly. If you start too fast, you may pass the short card before the spectator has a chance to say "Stop!" Ask the spectator to remember the card they stopped at, then allow the remainder of the deck to riffle off your fingers.

8 You have several options here to show that the card has vanished from the deck. You could spread the cards neatly along the table in a Ribbon Spread (as seen here). In our example, the Ace of Clubs is actually a double card with the Eight of Hearts hiding secretly behind it. Nobody will ever suspect this. Ask the spectator to find their card and they will have to admit that it is no longer there. Another way to do this is to give the deck to the spectator and ask them to deal the cards one at a time on to the table until they find their card. Nobody ever notices the difference in thickness of one card. This is perhaps the most convincing way of proving that the card has actually vanished from the deck.

9 Slowly reveal the card under the tablecloth. Do not underestimate how effective this routine is. This is one of the cleverest ways to vanish a card from a deck, and there seems to be no explanation for its disappearance. As mentioned in the introduction, with a little thought the card can be made to reappear just about anywhere. You are limited only by your imagination.

rising card from box (version 1)

A chosen card is shuffled into the deck, which is then placed inside the card box. The box is held at the fingertips and one card rises up into view. It is the card selected.

The best thing about this simple trick is that it does not require a special deck, so as long as you keep the cards in the special box you will be ready to perform it at any time. It is the perfect "end" trick to your act, as you finish with the cards back in the box, ready to put away in your pocket.

The special box is very simple to make and will only take a few minutes of your time, yet the result is a trick that will truly mystify your audience.

1 Remove a deck of cards from the box. Using a scalpel, cut a section from the flap side of the box approximately 1.5cm (⅝in) wide x 5cm (2in) long.

2 Place the box to one side so that the cut-out section remains unseen throughout the trick. Spread the cards for a selection.

3 Control the selected card to the top. Shown here is a Double Cut to the table. With the right hand, lift the top half off the deck and have the selected card replaced.

secret view

4 Replace the top half of the deck, holding a Finger Break between the two packets.

5 Cut approximately a quarter of the deck to the table.

6 Now cut all the cards above the break on top of those on the table. The cuts should be made briskly.

7 Finally, place the remaining cards on top. The selected card has now been secretly controlled to the top. You can follow this with a false shuffle and False Cut if you feel confident enough.

8 Place the deck in the box so that the faces are pointing outwards. Make sure the cut-out section at the back of the box remains hidden.

9 Hold the box in the fingertips of your right hand. Notice how the box is held in such a way that the right first finger cannot be seen.

10 Insert your first finger into the back of the box through the hole and slowly push up the top card of the deck.

11 From the front, the selected card is seen to rise mysteriously from the box.

rising card from box (version 2)

The idea of a chosen card rising from a deck is an old one, and believe it or not there are literally dozens of methods for accomplishing this effect. This is a clever version that is easy to master.

In this version a card is freely chosen and returned to the centre of the deck. The deck is placed in the card box and a small "handle" is inserted through a hole in the side of the box. The handle is "cranked" and the chosen card comically begins to rise out of the deck.

It is best to use a new deck of cards for this trick, and the preparation is a little more elaborate than most tricks require, but you will find the reaction you receive from your spectators more than worth the extra time and effort.

1 Perfectly square a new deck of cards. Using a pencil, mark a very light, straight line along the edge of the deck approximately 1.5cm (⅝in) from the top. This line should not be obvious at a casual glance, but clear enough for you to see. The line shown here is thick for clarity.

2 Using a scalpel, cut a small square hole in the side of the card box so that it matches up with the pencil line.

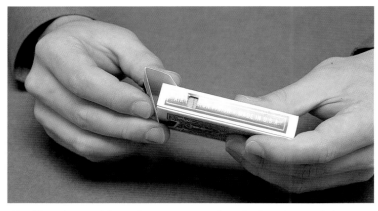

3 Test the position of your cut-out by placing the cards into the box and viewing the line through the hole.

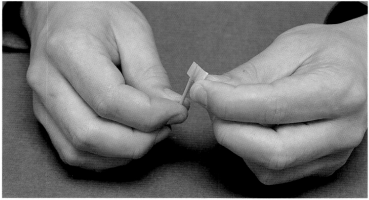

4 Attach a small piece of double-sided adhesive tape to the end of a toothpick. It may help to roll the tape between your fingers so that your natural skin oils reduce the stickiness of the tape slightly. Experimentation will make this clear.

5 Begin by having a card selected. While the spectator is looking at the card, secretly turn the deck end to end.

6 Ask the spectator to replace their selected card anywhere into the centre of the deck.

  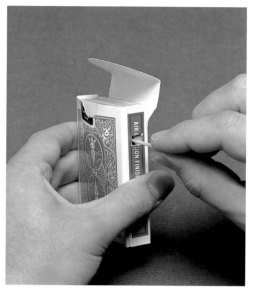

7 Replace the deck in the card box, positioning the secret pencil line on the opposite side to the cut-out.

8 Produce the toothpick. Insert the end that has the adhesive tape attached to it into the deck through the cut-out and exactly next to the chosen card. This can be found because it will have a tiny pencil dot on the edge. (That is the reason for using a new deck; the whiter the edge of the cards, the easier it is to see the pencil mark.)

9 Push the toothpick into the deck about halfway. The adhesive tape should be touching the chosen card.

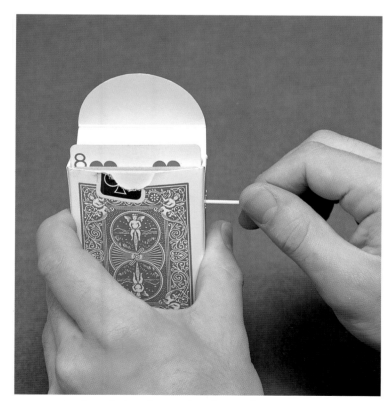 

10 Begin twisting the toothpick in a clockwise direction. The tape will adhere to the chosen card and start to "crank" it upwards from the box.

11 Continue twisting the toothpick until the card is completely exposed and has risen almost all the way out of the deck.

card to matchbox

A spectator chooses a card. You remove a card from your pocket and ask if it is correct. It is not. With a wave of your hand, the card instantly changes into a matchbox. This is opened and a folded card is discovered inside. It matches the selected card!

In order to make this gimmick, you will need a matchbox, a second matchbox cover (top and side required only), glue, a scalpel and duplicate cards. It may take some time for you to make up this particular gimmick, and you may need several trials before you make one that works perfectly. Experiment with different sized matchboxes to find one that works well.

1 Place a duplicate Queen of Hearts face down in front of you. Glue a complete matchbox on to the card at the top left-hand corner.

2 Using a scalpel, carefully score the point where the card meets the box. Fold the card inwards.

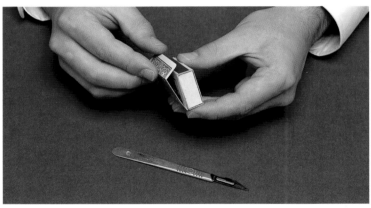

3 Score the card once again, this time where the card meets the edge of the box. Fold this side down so that it lies against the striking edge of the box.

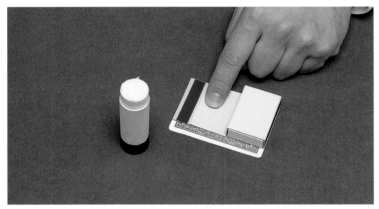

4 Unfold the card. Glue the top and side from the second matchbox cover to it as shown. The folds in the cover should match up with the scored sections in the playing card.

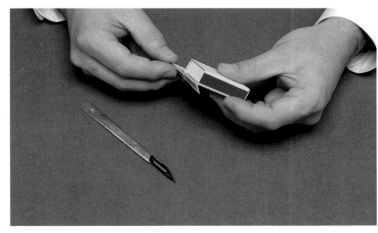

5 The card overhangs along one edge. Score along the length of the overhang so that it folds inwards.

6 When the box is now folded along the creases, the card will fold face inwards and be hidden. You may need to trim the playing card slightly in order to ensure a perfect fit.

7 Take another duplicate card (in this example, the Six of Diamonds) and fold it into quarters.

8 Place the folded Six of Diamonds in the drawer of the matchbox. Hold the matchbox with the Queen of Hearts in the open position. Place it in your left jacket pocket, in readiness for the routine.

9 Force the Six of Diamonds in the deck, using any of the force techniques described. Shown here is the Hindu Force. Start with the Six of Diamonds on the bottom of the deck.

10 Begin the Hindu Force, asking a spectator to say "Stop!" at any time.

11 Show the force card, then shuffle it legitimately into the deck again. ▶

12 Reach into your left jacket pocket and remove the card in the open position. The hidden matchbox should rest against the palm of your hand. Ask "Is this your card?" The answer will of course be "No".

13 Say "Watch!" Gently shake your left arm up and down. Simultaneously with the fourth finger of the left hand bend the overhang upwards along the crease.

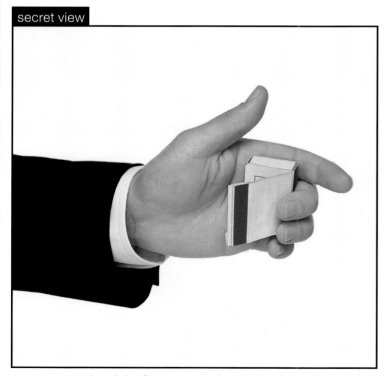

14 Now bend the fingers inwards, folding the card in half along the centre crease you made earlier.

15 Finally, with your left thumb, fold the remaining section along the edge of the box. You can now stop shaking your hand and show that the card has changed into a matchbox.

16 Explain, "Inside the box is one card." Slowly push open the drawer of the matchbox. The duplicate of the forced card that you placed inside the box will become visible.

17 Tip out the contents – a folded card. Remember to keep the gimmick held firmly so as not to expose the secret of the card stuck to the outside of the box, but try to look as though you are handling it casually.

18 Unfold the card and have the spectator confirm that it was the card they selected at the start of the trick.

advanced flourishes

The irony with sleight of hand is that one spends a great deal of time learning a "move" that usually remains secret! Of course, spectators are impressed by magic tricks when they cannot see how *they are done, but you can impress them in a different way by fancy flourishes such as the ones that follow – you are demonstrating, in a dramatic fashion, that you can make the cards do whatever you want.*

thumb fan

This is a neat fan, produced with two hands. You will need a deck of cards in good condition. Once learnt, this fan can be used whenever *you need to have a card selected. It is a prettier spread than the Two-Handed Spread taught earlier on.*

1 Hold the deck in your left hand. The base of the deck should align with the top of your third finger. The thumb grips the deck tightly along the bottom third.

2 With the right hand, approach the deck. The right thumb stretches out and reaches a position at the top left corner of the deck.

3 The right thumb moves in a small semicircle while the left thumb grips the deck tightly. The cards will automatically pivot under the ball of the left thumb. If the fan looks messy, you may need to reposition your left thumb.

4 From the front, a beautiful display of cards is seen.

pressure fan

This is perhaps the neatest fan of all. A good-quality deck of cards is essential. While similar to the Thumb Fan, this fan is even more *attractive to watch being formed because the semicircle of cards just seems to pop into shape by itself.*

1 Hold the cards in the right-hand Biddle Grip and bend them by squeezing the fingers and thumb together. Place the bowed cards into the left hand, between the thumb, second finger and third finger. The bottom edge of the deck should be level with the third finger.

2 The left hand stays perfectly still as the right hand turns, allowing the cards to riffle off one at a time, describing a semicircle. Pressure must be maintained correctly for the cards to fan smoothly.

3 This view shows how the pressure created bends the cards into a flower-like display.

4 Viewed from the front, the fan looks symmetrical, neat and very professional.

one-handed fan

In this flourish, the cards are fanned neatly and quickly with one hand. A little practice will enable you to produce a beautifully aligned fan every time. A good-quality deck of cards in perfect condition will increase your chances of success.

1 Hold the deck in your right hand. The edge of the deck sits halfway between the first and second joints of the fingers. The thumb grips the deck at the bottom corner.

2 This view shows the position of the hand without the cards.

3 Close your hand up into a fist. This view shows the finishing position of the hand without the cards.

4 As you close your fingers, the result is a fan of cards.

one-handed reverse fan

This fan results in a deck that looks blank because the indices of the cards remain hidden. As with all card work involving fans, you need a deck of cards in good condition. If you wish to create the illusion of a blank deck, you will also need to use a deck with only two indices as opposed to four, and you will require a blank card which should be positioned at the face of the deck at the start.

1 Hold the deck in a grip similar to the finishing position of the One-Handed Fan. However, the cards are not yet spread.

2 This reverse view shows how the fingers are all closed in a fist.

3 Open your fingers to spread the fan. Practise the move slowly at first, and experiment with different positions – you may find that it helps if your first and second fingers pull back slightly as they open. You should be able to make an impressive flourish.

4 The front view shows how the deck looks blank, with the indices hidden from view. If you place a blank card on the face of the deck before you begin, the illusion of a blank deck will be perfect.

giant fan

This is a nice quick flourish. A deck of cards is split in two and woven together, then the cards are fanned. The result is a fan of cards that looks like it has been made with a jumbo-sized deck! You may be able *to think of a line of patter to accompany the flourish, for example, "For those of you who can't see at the back of the room, here is a trick for you!" or "Look, a giant deck of cards…or maybe we are shrinking!"*

1 The initial sequence of moves is similar to that of the Weave Shuffle. Hold the cards high up in the fingertips of the left hand. Your thumb should be on one of the long edges and your second, third and fourth fingers on the other. Your first finger rests on the short end.

2 With your right hand, lift approximately half the deck and weave the two halves together as neatly as possible. Ensure the first and last cards of the right-hand packet become the bottom and top cards of the deck. (*See* Weave Shuffle and Waterfall for more details on weaving cards.)

3 Push the cards together until they protrude about half their length.

4 Spread the deck between both hands and you will have a magnificent Giant Fan.

comedy card force

It is always fun to make people laugh, and it shows you do not take yourself or your magic too seriously. In this flourish, you fan a deck of cards for a selection and stress how fair the choice is. As you talk, one *card sprouts out of the deck and moves backwards and forwards as if to say "Choose me!" Your spectators will laugh at the irony of this supposedly fair selection procedure!*

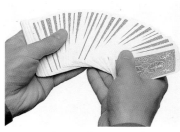

1 Fan the cards, using the Two-Handed Spread.

secret view

2 With the left fingers, manipulate the bottom card and push it to the right.

secret view

3 Take this card with the right fingertips and thrust it forwards.

4 From the top, it looks as if the card has a life of its own. You can make the card run around the perimeter of the fan by swivelling the card with the third finger, using the second finger as a pivot point. Play with this move with the cards in your hands until you develop the knack.

card spring

Picture a magician with a deck in their hand and you will visualize the cards being juggled and shuffled with dexterity and precision. In this spectacular display of skill, the hands are held wide apart yet the cards seem to take on a life of their own, springing with perfect direction out of one hand through the air and into the other hand.

Be prepared to spend most of your practice time picking cards up off the floor! The best place to practise is over a bed so that when (not if) you drop the cards, you won't have to reach so far to pick them up.

You may find it easier to start with your hands very close together until the cards start springing, then move your hands further apart, and as the spring finishes, bring both hands back together again. Trial and error is the only real way to learn how to spring cards properly. With practice, you should be able to get your hands as far as 30cm (12in) from each other – maybe even further. This is a fun flourish that you will enjoy performing. Use a good-quality deck of cards, otherwise they may become ruined when the cards are bowed.

1 Hold the deck in the right-hand Biddle Grip, at about chest level. It is important that the deck is held firmly.

2 Push the middle of the cards up with your left hand, squeezing them with your right hand to bend them.

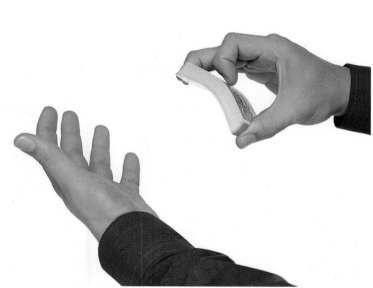

3 Hold your left hand about 10cm (4in) under the deck. (With practice, you will be able to increase this distance dramatically.) Your fingers should be outstretched, ready to catch the cards as they hit your hand.

4 Continue to bend the cards until they start to slip off the fingers. The key to success is ensuring that the cards slip off the fingers and not the thumb. (If you experience this problem, try holding the cards further up the thumb. The ideal position is usually in the middle of the first joint.) As the cards hit the left hand, begin to tighten your fingers to hold the cards in place.

back palm

If you have ever seen a magician pluck cards from the air, you will know how wonderful this illusion is. It is not easy to perform well and requires plenty of practice but, like riding a bicycle, once you have learnt the basics you will never forget how to do it. This type of magic is best suited to stage acts and performances where there is some distance between you and the audience.

If you go on to learn more about magic, you will discover moves and sleights that enable you to produce a constant fan of cards at your fingertips, and even moves that allow you to show that the back and front of the hand is empty before producing a card. Some magicians make a very successful living from acts that contain nothing but card manipulations such as this.

1 Hold a card in the fingertips of the right hand, with the fingers on the back and the thumb on the front.

2 Bend your middle two fingers inwards and push with your thumb while straightening your first and fourth fingers. The view seen here is from above.

3 Bring your first and fourth fingers around to grip the card from the front at either side. Curl the fingers until they are level with your middle two fingers, making sure that the top of the card is below the ends of your fingers.

secret view

4 Close the gaps between your fingers (these gaps are known to magicians as "windows") and straighten them out so that the card is carried around to the back of the hand. The cards are gripped by the first and fourth fingers only. From the front, the hand should look completely empty.

5 This back view shows the true situation – the card is pinned to the back of your hand. The moves should happen one after the other, very quickly. Added "misdirection" can be created by gently waving the hand up and down.

6 To make the card reappear, reverse the sequence above, but with some subtle differences. Close your hand into a fist, bringing the card to the front of the hand. The thumb is positioned on the front and pinches the card against the middle two fingers as before.

7 With the thumb, drag the card between and through the first and second fingers. As the card is pulled, open the fingers.

8 The card pivots until it is completely straight. The first finger moves behind the card, so that you finish with the card held between the tips of the thumb and fingers.

9 Try experimenting with other similar-sized objects. For example, hand out your business card with a magical flourish! Magic always works best when it occurs unexpectedly.

dinner table magic

The dinner table is an ideal place to perform magic for your friends and family. If you take the time to learn a few clever routines, you will be able to entertain and astound people at any time. Most of these tricks can be performed without any set-up, and the items you require can be found at the restaurant or dinner table.

introduction

Glasses, napkins, cutlery, straws, cups and sugar cubes are just some of the objects often found on tables at meal times. It is a good idea to learn some magic tricks with these items so that whenever you dine with other people you are in a position to entertain. An ordinary dinner party can become a very memorable occasion with an impromptu performance, and if your guests do not know each other magic is an ideal icebreaker. You can be sure that your performance will lead to conversation and no doubt speculation as to how you achieved your miracles.

One magician known for his love of intimate performances was Max Malini. Born Max Breit in 1873 on the borders of Poland and Austria, he was taken at an early age to live in New York. Between then and his death in 1942, Malini made a name for himself in many countries around the world. While other magicians were busy performing in theatres and music halls, Malini would work for small intimate groups, often at top hotels, and for the most distinguished dignitaries of the time – including royalty and numerous world leaders. One feat of magic that will always be associated with his name is the production of a huge block of coal or

ice from under his hat. His table guests, who had been in his company for several hours, were understandably astounded by the sudden production of the block, and in the case of the ice were most curious as to how such an item could be stored and hidden without melting! However, if he deemed the time and mood to be wrong, he would sometimes decide not to perform at all, despite having prepared for the trick hours in advance.

Another great story is that of Malini bending, ripping and soiling an old playing card that he would then throw face down in the gutter. Later that day, while walking with a friend, Malini would boast about his ability to name any playing card just from looking at its back. His friend might then spot the dirty card in the gutter and challenge Malini to name it. Such elaborate preparation may seem like a lot of work considering the friend might not have spotted the card in the gutter, but this kind of magic and the response it

Below: *L'Escamoteur, sur le Boulevard, Près le Chateau d'Eau* is a late nineteenth-century engraving which shows a street magician in mid-performance of one of the greatest tricks of all time – the legendary Cups and Balls.

receives is what reputations were, and still are, made on. Using Malini's philosophy, why not practise and prepare the Torn and Restored Napkin trick for your next dinner party? Wait for the right time in the evening to perform it, and cause a sensation. After dinner is usually a good time to perform because people are generally relaxed by the time they have finished their meal. If you are hosting the dinner yourself, there is no reason why you could not ensure the correct items were conveniently nearby for when you needed them.

Explained in the following pages are several effects which can be strung together (for example, Sugar Rush and Sugar Rush Uncovered). This allows you to make your performance short or long depending on how responsive your audience is. Bouncing Bread Roll and

Above left: Max Malini, the early twentieth-century conjuror, caused a sensation whenever and wherever he performed.

Top: This fork seems to be defying gravity. Or is it? Find out in Clinging Cutlery.

Above: A typical dinner table setting. Most of the items seen here – a glass, knives and forks, a napkin, a salt shaker and a pepper grinder – can be used to perform magic.

both versions of Bending Knife are quick, off-the-cuff stunts, while Vanishing Glass, All Sugared Up and The Cups and Balls are longer routines which can form part of a small, impromptu after-dinner show.

rolling straw

A straw is set on the table in front of you, and you then rub a fingertip against your sleeve. As you hold your finger above the straw, it rolls forward as if repelled by a magnetic force. The best kind of straw to use is one of the type that are supplied free in fast food restaurants. As will become apparent when you read through the method to this trick, it may be a good idea to fail a few times before finally succeeding. Your audience will become accustomed to watching you rub your finger on your sleeve and this will provide you with perfect misdirection. If a drinking straw is not available, this quick stunt will work just as well with a cigarette.

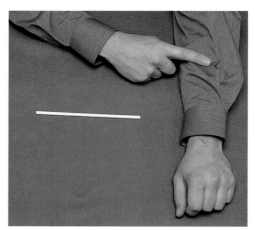

1 Place a straw in front of you on the table and rub your first finger on your sleeve. Explain that you are generating static electricity.

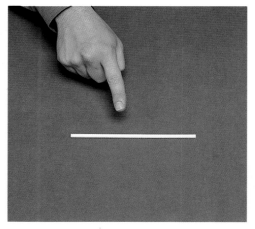

2 Hold your finger directly above the straw.

3 Move your finger forward and, as you do so, secretly blow at the table in front of the straw. The breeze will cause the straw to roll forward. Try not to change the shape of your face as you blow; all eyes should be on your finger.

clinging cutlery

This is a perfect dinner table stunt. It is easy to perform, yet completely mystifying. A fork is made to cling to the outstretched palm of your hand. The secret is explained, but moments later it transpires that you were not being entirely honest, as the fork is once again made to cling to your hand in an even more amazing fashion! The set-up takes just a few seconds.

secret view

1 Hold a fork in your closed left fist. Grip your left wrist with your right hand and open the left fingers wide. The right first finger secretly stretches out to hold the fork in place.

2 From the front, it looks as if the fork is stuck to your hand. You can stop the illusion here, but you can also go a step further. Turn your hands around, exposing the method to the trick. Return to the same position.

3 The right hand is now removed completely, yet the fork still stays suspended from the left hand. How?

secret view

4 This exposed view shows how a knife is held under your watchstrap from the outset. When you pretend to reveal your secret, the knife is covered by your first finger (see step 1).

bending knife (version 1)

A knife is held between the fingertips and gently shaken up and down. The metal seems to turn to rubber and the illusion is created of the knife bending. This illusion also works with rulers, nails, pens and many other objects. It is the perfect effect to show just before the even more impressive Bending Knife (Version 2), described next.

This optical illusion dates back a long way and is a good example of "retention of vision", which is the term used to describe the effect whereby an image remains in view a few milliseconds after it has been moved away.

At about chest level, hold a knife loosely by one end, between the thumb and first finger of the right hand. Quickly and continuously move your right hand up and down about 10cm (4in). As the knife begins to shake, it appears to become wobbly, as if made of rubber.

bending knife (version 2)

This is a great follow-up to Version 1. A knife is bent in half at right angles, then straightened out again. The optical illusion is perfect.

It is not necessary to use a coin, as seen below, because the trick works almost as well without it, but the coin does give conviction to the illusion.

secret view

1 Hold a knife in the right hand with the tip against the table. The fourth finger should rest behind the handle and the other fingers in front. Hold a coin at the top of the knife between the finger and thumb. Only the tip of the coin is seen, and it is mistaken by the observer for the top of the knife.

2 The left hand closes around the right hand as shown. The knife is supported entirely by the right hand. The left hand simply helps to hide the method.

3 The knife is pushed against the table and although the hands stay straight, the knife is allowed to fall flat pivoting between the right third and fourth fingers, as seen in this exposed view.

4 From the front, with both hands covering the method, this is how the illusion looks. Finish by raising the hands, therefore straightening the knife and showing that it has unbent itself.

bouncing bread roll

A bread roll is picked up off the table and apparently bounced on the floor, like a tennis ball. It shoots up into the air and you catch it as if it was the most natural thing in the world. This trick would work equally well with a piece of fruit such as an apple or orange, and even a pool ball at a pool table! As long as you use an object that would not ordinarily bounce, the effect will register well.

1 This trick is easiest to do sitting at a table, although once you understand the principle you can also do it standing. Hold a bread roll in your right hand, at about shoulder height.

2 Bring your hand down below the table's edge, exactly as if you were about to bounce the roll on to the floor.

3 As soon as your hand passes the edge of the table it will be out of sight. This is where you have to work with split-second timing if the illusion is to be a success. Notice how the foot is ready to tap against the floor, simulating the sound of the roll hitting the ground.

4 The moment the hand is below the table's edge, it turns at the wrist and flicks the roll up into the air as straight as possible. There should be no movement from the arm itself; only the wrist should move. A split second before you toss the roll, tap your foot on the ground.

5 Follow the movement of the roll with your head. The combination of sounds and visuals will provide the perfect illusion of the bread roll bouncing.

vanishing glass

In this amazing impromptu trick a coin is covered with a glass, which in turn is covered with a paper napkin. While the audience's attention is focused on the coin, the glass is somehow caused to disappear. You can also make it pass straight through the top of the table.

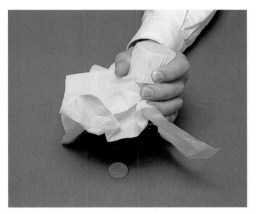

1 Perform this sitting at a table. Place a coin on the table in front of you, then place a glass, mouth down, on top of it. Cover the glass with a paper napkin from the top downwards so that the paper is stretched around the top and sides and would hold its shape even if the glass were removed; the bottom should remain open. Ask a spectator if the coin on the table is heads up or tails up.

2 Lift the covered glass up and back towards the edge of the table with one hand, exposing the coin. Bring attention to the coin by pointing to it with the other hand. This is simply misdirection to divert the attention of the spectators away from what happens next.

3 The glass should be resting on the edge of the table in front of you. Allow it to slip out of the napkin and safely on to your lap. There is no "move" as such – simply lift the glass away from the coin and allow it to fall silently. The napkin will hold its shape so a casual glance should not arouse any suspicion.

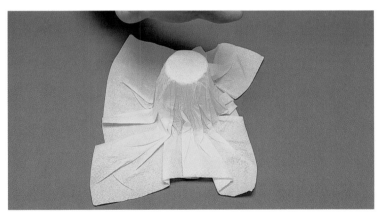

4 Carefully place the napkin shell back over the coin and remove your hand.

5 Tell the audience to watch as you proceed to smash the "glass" flat to the table under your hand. This sudden noise will create the moment of impact you should strive for. One moment the glass is there, the next it has completely disappeared!

tip *As a variation, ask the spectator to hold their hand out just above the "glass". Place your hand above theirs and bring your hand down on to theirs as the paper is flattened. This directly involves the spectator, who is expecting to feel the glass. Instead of creating the illusion of the glass disappearing, you can also finish by telling the audience that the glass went straight through the table. Simply produce the glass from beneath. If a glass is not to hand, you can do the same trick with a salt shaker or pepper grinder.*

torn and restored napkin

A paper napkin is torn into small pieces and squeezed between the hands. The pieces magically weld themselves together again. The napkins in the photographs are shown in different colours for ease of explanation.

A little experimentation with napkins will reveal that the paper is easy to tear in one direction because of the direction of the grain. Try to orientate the napkins correctly when you set up this trick so that the tearing is made easier for you.

1 To prepare, apply a small amount of glue to the top right corner of a paper napkin (at the point here marked "X").

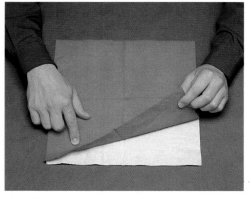

2 Glue a second napkin to the first at this point. Wait for the glue to dry.

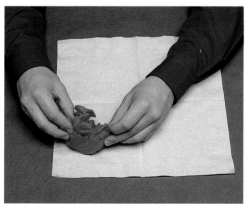

3 Scrunch up the top napkin into a ball. Neatness is not important.

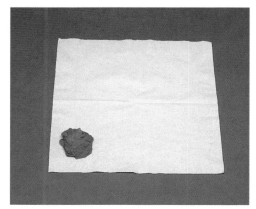

4 Continue to squeeze the ball, making it as small as possible. You are now ready to start performing the trick.

secret view

5 Hold the flat napkin in both hands so that the duplicate ball is at the top right corner on your side of the paper. Begin to tear the napkin in half down the centre.

6 From the front, the duplicate ball is hidden completely and must remain so. The napkin provides lots of cover.

secret view

7 Place the left half of the napkin in front of the right half. Tear the paper down the centre as before.

secret view

8 Place the left pieces in front of the right, then turn the strip sideways so that you can tear the strip down the centre.

9 Place the left pieces in front of the right again, then make one final tear down the centre.

10 Place the final pieces of paper in front of the right-hand pieces as before and squeeze the edges together.

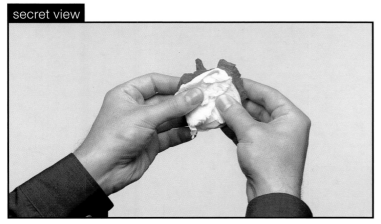

11 While you are squeezing the napkins, secretly turn them over so that the duplicate napkin is facing the front. As the real napkins are the same colour, this move will be invisible.

12 Start to open out the napkin along the top edge, smoothing out the wrinkles as you go.

13 Continue to straighten it out until the entire napkin is revealed to be restored.

14 The torn pieces are safely hidden behind the duplicate napkin at the top right corner. To finish, crumple all the paper into a ball and discard it.

sugar rush

This is a very popular effect in magic which is also known as "Matrix". Four sugar cubes are set out in a square formation. Two playing cards are shown and used to cover the cubes briefly. The sugar cubes jump about, seemingly of their own free will, until they all meet in one corner. This is similar to the next routine, Sugar Rush

Uncovered, but it does not require difficult sleight of hand because of the extra cover created by the two cards. If no playing cards are available, you could also perform the trick using coasters or even menus – whatever is to hand. If you learn both routines, you will have a nice set piece to perform at a dinner table.

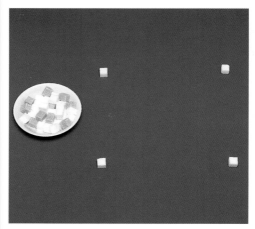

1 Set out four sugar cubes in a square formation. The cubes should be about 30cm (12in) away from each other.

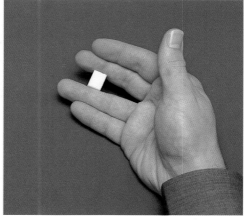

2 Grip an extra sugar cube between your second and third fingers, as shown. In performance, there will always be a card on top of your fingers so this cube will remain hidden.

3 Hold a playing card in each hand, so that they both look the same and the extra sugar cube cannot be seen. Cover both the upper right and left cubes.

secret view

4 This exposed view shows how the right hand is about to let go of the hidden sugar cube while the left hand is getting ready to take a cube away under the card.

secret view

5 Move both cards to show that one cube has supposedly jumped. (Be careful not to expose the hidden sugar cube.)

6 Cover the upper right and the lower right cubes, repeating the same move as before. Both hands should move together and at a constant pace.

7 Move the hands back to show that a second cube has moved across to join the others. Do not pause for long, but continue to move your hands to the next position.

8 Cover the upper right and lower left corners, in preparation for the final sugar cube to travel.

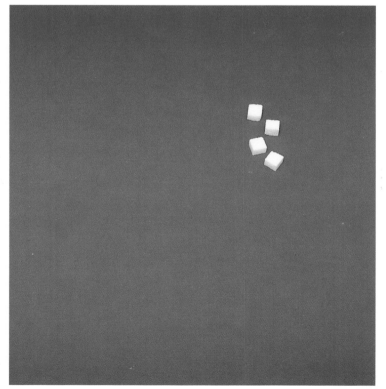

9 Repeat the move one last time and show that all the sugar cubes are together at the top right corner.

sugar rush uncovered

Four sugar cubes are placed in a square formation on the table. The hands cover the cubes for the briefest of moments and they start to jump from corner to corner until all four cubes join together in one corner. This routine is a perfect follow-up to Sugar Rush. The order of moves is basically the same, but instead of using cards as cover, this version *relies entirely on a convincing Classic Palm. Palming a sugar cube is as easy as palming gets, which is why they are ideal for this trick. You could also use upturned bottle tops, which are equally easy to palm because of their shape and easy-to-grip edges. In order to achieve success with this effect, some dedicated practice is required.*

secret view

1 For this trick you will need a bowl of sugar cubes. Take five cubes from the bowl, secretly palming one in the right hand (*see* Money Magic chapter for a description of the Classic Palm technique). Set the bowl off to your left-hand side and set out the remaining four cubes in a square formation in front of you.

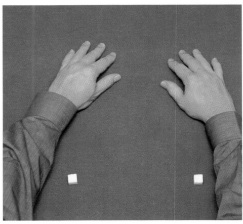

2 Cover the furthest two cubes with your hands. As you will notice, the sequence of moves is similar to that of Sugar Rush, so once you are familiar with that trick this one will be easier to learn.

secret view

3 Drop the palmed cube in your right hand and palm the one under your left hand. This should take no more than a second, and both moves must happen simultaneously. With practice, you will be able to palm and drop the cubes without any noticeable movement from the back of your hand.

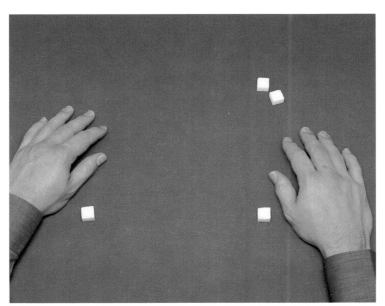

4 Move both hands away to reveal that one of the cubes appears to have jumped.

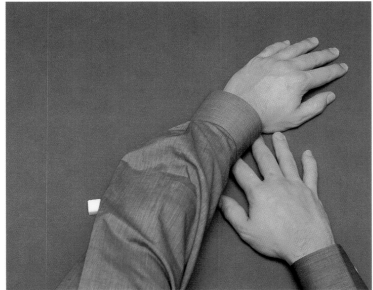

5 Without hesitation, cover the top right corner with your left hand and the bottom right corner with your right hand. Do the same move again, dropping the left-hand cube and picking up the cube at the lower right in a right-hand Classic Palm.

 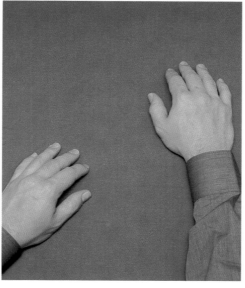 

6 Move your hands to show that the second cube has moved.

7 Finally, cover the top right corner with your right hand and the bottom left corner with your left hand.

8 Perform the move one more time to show that all cubes are now at the top right corner.

secret view

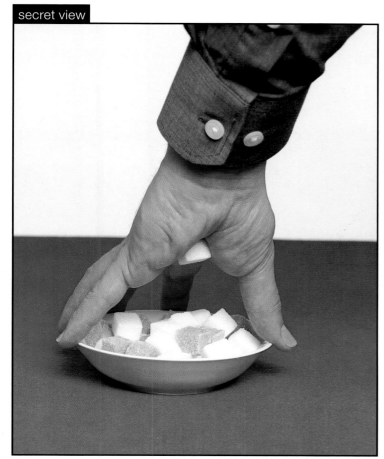

9 You will finish with a sugar cube palmed in the left hand. This is easy to get rid of. Simply pick up the sugar bowl to your left-hand side and, as you lift the bowl up, allow the cube to fall in, along with the other cubes.

10 Pick up the remaining cubes on the table and openly drop them back into the sugar bowl. The great thing about this routine is that you finish completely "clean"; that is, you destroy the evidence of the extra cube when you drop it back into the bowl.

all sugared up

A number is chosen at random and written on the side of a sugar cube. The cube is then dissolved in a glass of water and the written image is made to appear on the palm of the person who chose the *number. You will need to use a very soft pencil and a sugar cube that is smooth on all sides. This routine will cause massive reactions because the effect actually happens in the spectator's hands.*

1 Before you begin the trick, secretly dip your right second finger into a glass of water to moisten it. If the liquid is cold, you may be able to moisten your finger by touching the condensation on the outside of the glass. Either way, you must ensure there is some moisture on your fingertip.

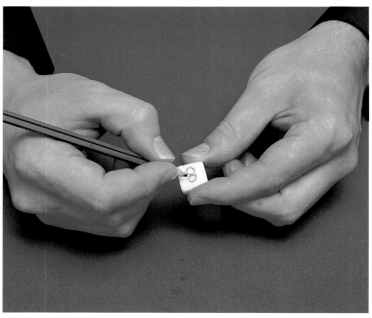

2 Ask a spectator to choose a number. Using a pencil, clearly print the number on one side of a sugar cube.

3 Squeeze the cube between your right thumb and second finger as your left hand moves the glass into view. The written number should be pressed against the moist second finger. Drop the cube into the water.

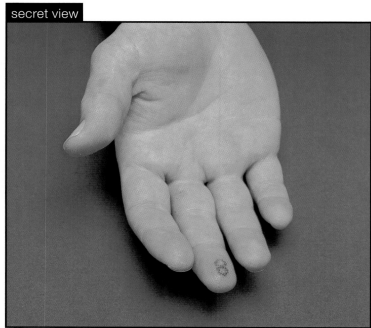

4 You have secretly transferred the graphite in the pencil to your fingertip. Now you must secretly transfer this to the palm of the person who chose the number.

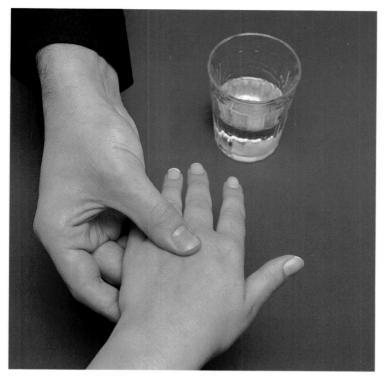

5 Ask them to hold out their hand, then take hold of it and move it to a position above the glass. As you do so, lightly press your second finger against their palm.

6 This will transfer the image without their knowledge. The spectator should not notice because you are touching them for a reason, that is, under the pretence of repositioning their hand.

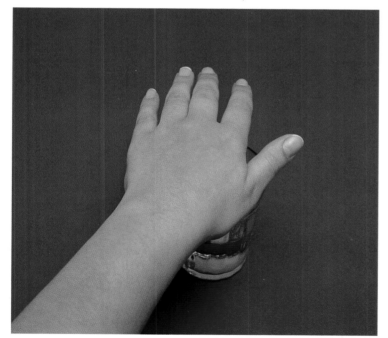

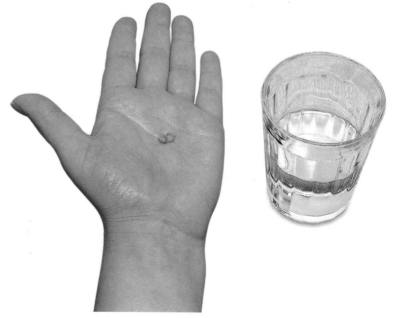

7 Ask the spectator to move their hand up and down above the glass. Explain what is going to happen: "As the sugar cube dissolves, the graphite will float to the surface of the water and the heat of your hand will cause the particles of graphite to turn into a vapour which will rise from the glass and attach itself to the palm of your hand."

8 Ask the spectator to turn their hand palm up and they will see the duplication of their number, drawn on the sugar cube moments before.

two in the hand

Three sugar cubes are displayed. Two are put into the left hand and one is placed in the magician's pocket, yet there are still three cubes in the left hand. This little mystery is repeated several times, culminating in the disappearance of all three!

If you enjoy this type of magic, then it may be worth investing in some magicians' sponge balls from a magic shop. They are quite inexpensive and come in a variety of different sizes and colours. They are the ideal prop to use for sleight of hand such as this, although you will find that it is also possible to use other small objects for an impromptu performance.

secret view

1 Place three sugar cubes in a row on the table and have an extra cube secretly hidden in your right-hand Finger Palm. This cube must remain hidden throughout.

2 Pick up the cube at the far right and display it in the right fingertips. Hold out your left hand flat and count "One", placing the cube in your left palm.

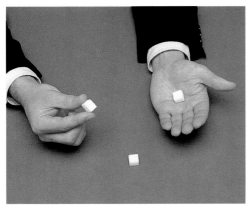

3 Display the second sugar cube in the right fingertips and count "Two".

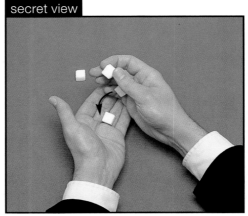
secret view

4 As the second cube is placed into the hand, drop the extra cube along with it.

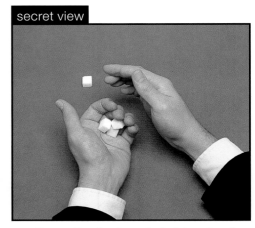
secret view

5 Immediately close the left hand and say, "Two sugar cubes in my left hand."

6 Say "One in the pocket." Suiting your action to these words, pick up the remaining cube from the table. Display it and pretend to put it in your right jacket pocket, but secretly retain it using the right Finger Palm.

7 Ask how many cubes are in your left hand and the response should be "Two". Say "Close!" as your left hand sets out the three cubes in a row on the table. Repeat steps 1 to 7, however at step 6 really place the cube in your pocket and leave it there.

8 The third time, change the routine ever so slightly. Pick up the cube at the far right and place it on to your left palm. Count "One".

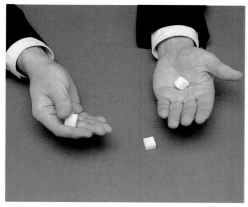

9 Pick up the second cube and display it in your fingers as before.

10 Count "Two" as you supposedly place this in your left hand along with the first cube. Continue your patter by saying, "Two cubes go into my left hand."

secret view

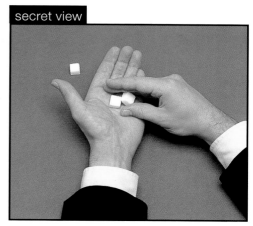

11 What you actually do is secretly pick up both cubes by pinching them against your fingers with your thumb. There must be no hesitation.

secret view

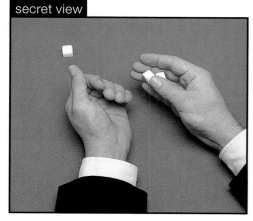

12 As the right hand comes away with the two hidden cubes, the left hand closes as if it still contains them.

13 Pick up and display the third cube. Say "One in the pocket", but in fact place all three cubes in your pocket.

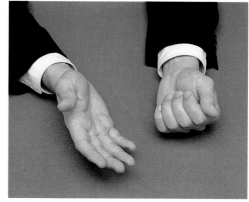

14 Ask how many cubes are in your hand. The audience may assume two, or even three.

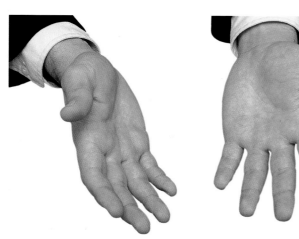

15 Open your left hand, showing that both your hands are completely empty and all of the sugar cubes have mysteriously disappeared!

16 This trick will work with a variety of small objects. You could, for example, tear up a paper napkin and roll the pieces into small balls. As mentioned in the introduction, magicians' sponge balls are also perfect for this trick.

knife and paper trick

Paper spots are stuck to the blade of a knife on both sides. The spots are removed, but reappear at the magician's command. The sleight taught here has been used by magicians for decades and is still popular today. It includes the Paddle Move, which involves showing the same surface of an object twice while the spectator thinks they are seeing two different sides. This move has many applications.

1 Tear off six tiny pieces of paper from the corner of a paper napkin.

2 Dip the tip of your finger into a glass of water, then touch the blade of the knife to transfer the spot of liquid.

3 Repeat this at two more points on the knife, then place a paper spot on each wet point – the water makes them stick.

4 To practise the sleight you will use throughout this trick, hold the knife between your fingers and thumb with the blade pointing downwards. The paper should be on the top side of the blade.

5 Twist your wrist towards you so that the knife turns over and the blank side can be shown to the spectator.

6 Twist your wrist back again, reversing the action of step 5.

7 Repeat this wrist action once more but, as your wrist turns over, push the handle of the knife with your thumb so that the knife turns over at the same time as your hand. This time the spots will appear to be on the back of the knife as well. This is the Paddle Move. Turn your wrist back again, using the Paddle Move to flip the knife over at the same time.

8 To proceed with the trick, after step 3 add three more pieces of paper to the blank side of the knife. This completes the preparation.

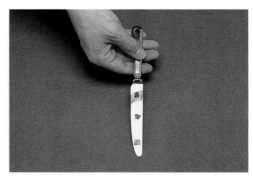

9 Now that you are familiar with the Paddle Move, you are ready to learn the sequence of moves for the routine. Display the knife in the right fingertips as shown.

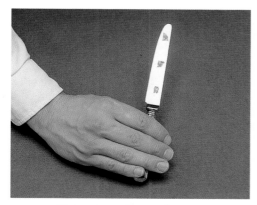

10 Twist the wrist (without performing the Paddle Move) and show three spots of paper on the other side of the knife blade.

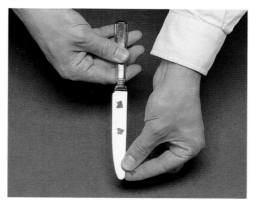

11 Bring the knife back to the start position and pull off the lowest spot. Pretend to slide off the spot on the underside of the knife at the same time.

12 Perform the Paddle Move, which allows you to show that the spot on the underside has also apparently been taken.

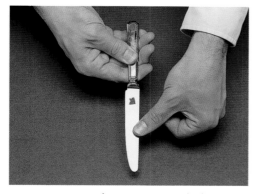

13 Repeat these moves with the second spot, in fact only taking the spot off the top of the knife.

14 Execute the Paddle Move again to show that both spots have supposedly been taken.

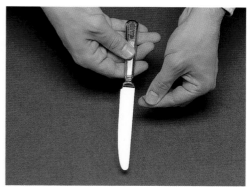

15 Repeat once more for the last spot remaining on the knife.

16 Using the Paddle Move, show that both sides of the knife are now blank.

17 With a shake of the wrist, quickly twist the knife between your fingers and thumb to make all three spots reappear. These can be shown to be apparently on both sides, using the Paddle Move one last time. Finish by removing the three spots, thus destroying the evidence.

the cups and balls

It has been said that a magician's abilities can be measured by the performance of this great trick, of which there are many versions. Some use just one cup, others two or three, but the effect is always similar. A number of small balls are caused to vanish, penetrate and

reappear under the cup or cups, often changing into fruit and even live mice and chicks along the way! This basic version uses three balls and three cups. It is easy to perform and amazing to watch. Professional sets of the cups and balls are available from magic shops.

1 You will require four small ball-like objects. You can use sugar cubes for an impromptu performance, or you can fashion balls from a paper napkin torn into four strips.

2 Roll each strip into a ball. Although you will be using four balls, the audience will only ever be aware of three of them.

3 Stack three cups together, secreting a ball in the centre cup. Set the other three balls in a row in front of you. You are now ready to perform the incredible Cups and Balls.

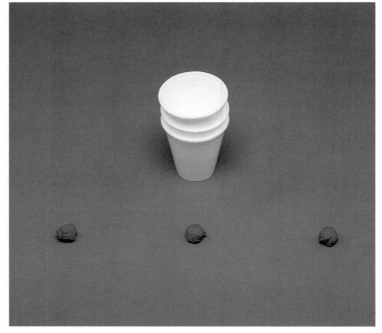

4 This shows the preparation completed and is how the cups should be set before you begin the routine.

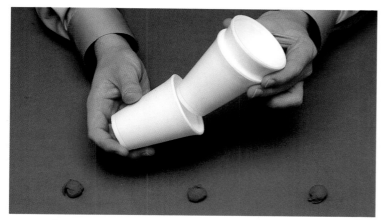

5 Pick up all three cups in a stack with your left hand. The right hand takes the bottom cup from underneath and pulls it off the stack. Keep the mouth of the cup away from the spectator.

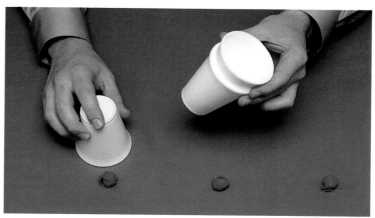

6 Turn this cup upside down next to the ball on your far right, as shown above.

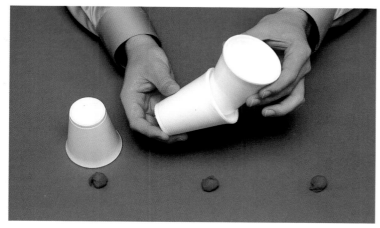

7 Repeat step 6 with the second cup. Although there is a ball hidden inside this second cup, it will remain unseen and will not fall out if the cup is turned at a constant speed.

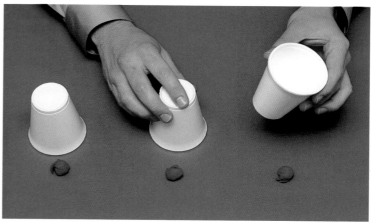

8 Place the second cup next to the centre ball, with the secret ball hidden beneath it. You must practise this until you can position the cup without fear of the extra ball falling out.

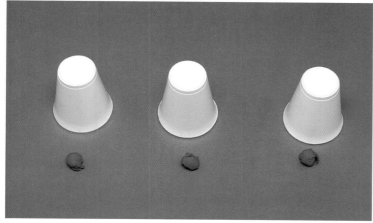

9 Finally, turn over the third cup and place it next to the ball at the far left. The extra ball is hidden under the middle cup.

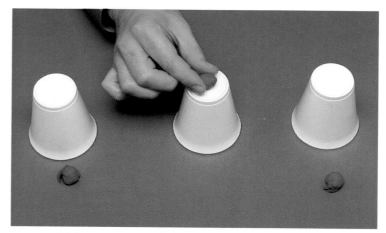

10 Pick up the centre ball and place it on the base of the middle cup. ▶

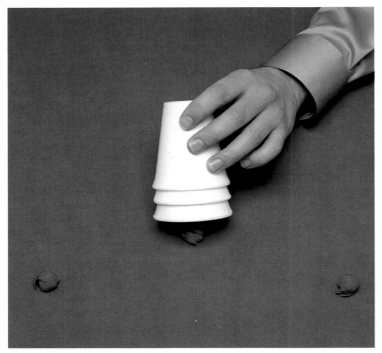

11 Stack the outer two cups on top of the centre one. Make a magcial gesture, then tilt back the stack of cups to show that the ball has apparently penetrated the centre cup and is now on the table. Pause to let this effect register with your audience.

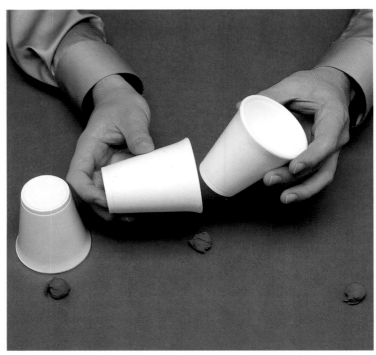

12 Pick up the stack of cups and turn them mouth upwards again. Now repeat the set of moves and turn each cup over again. Place the first cup at the right, next to the ball. Place the second cup (containing the extra ball) over the centre ball.

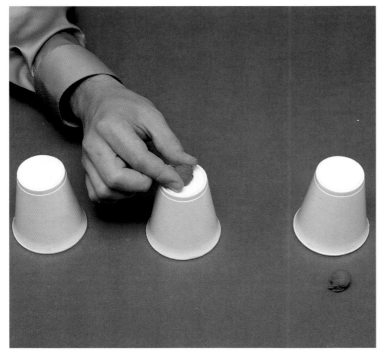

13 The third cup goes next to the ball on the left. Pick up the right ball and place it on top of the middle cup. This sequence of moves is almost identical to the sequence at the start of the routine.

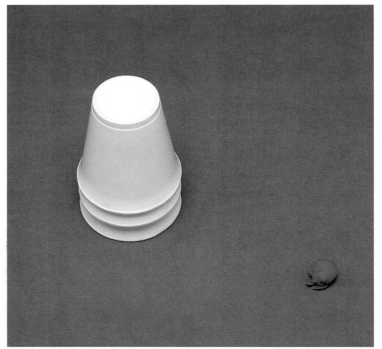

14 Stack the other two cups on top as before. Make a magical gesture above the cups.

15 Tilt the cups back to show that the second ball has arrived to join the first.

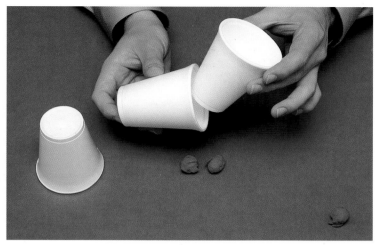

16 Repeat the moves one final time. Place the first cup to the right, the second cup over the balls already on the table, and the third cup to the left.

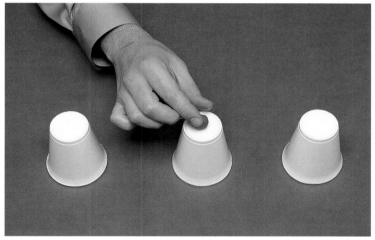

17 Pick up the last remaining ball and place it on the underside of the centre cup (*see* Tip for an alternative move).

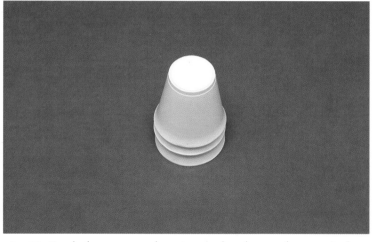

18 Stack the cups one last time and make another magical gesture over them.

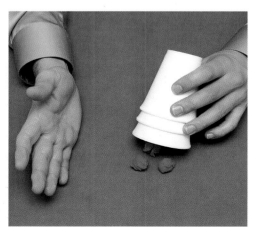

19 Tilt the cups back to reveal all three balls together.

20 That is the mystery of The Cups and Balls!

tip *When you reach step 17, instead of placing the final ball on the cup you can "vanish" it using a Fake Take (see Money Magic chapter) or any other technique that you are familiar with. The final ball will then be shown to have magically reappeared under the final cup.*

match magic

Matches are a common household item and can be found almost anywhere. Their very existence is a reminder of our ability to perform real magic and create fire at will. The shape and size of ordinary matches, together with the matchbox or matchbook they are housed in, create ideal opportunities for optical illusions and simple magic tricks. With a box of matches in your pocket, you can be ready to perform an entire magic show!

introduction

One of humanity's greatest achievements was discovering how to create fire. Perhaps this was the first magic trick ever performed – it certainly must have felt like magic at the time. Our desire for "instant" fire was not satisfied until approximately 1.5 million years later, in about 1680, when a match similar to our modern ones was invented. The phosphorus used was deadly, and despite several attempts to create non-toxic alternatives, it wasn't until around 1910 that matches were made with harmless chemicals. They were then sold throughout the world. Well over 500 billion matches are now used each year – that's a lot of matches!

As a result, matches can be found everywhere. Most people have a box or two at home, and restaurants, bars and clubs will certainly have them.

> **WARNING: Safety of yourself and others around you is the most important thing to remember when using matches. It is strongly advised that children should not play with matches, and they must be supervised by an adult if attempting any of the following tricks.**

There are magicians who use fire as a major theme in their act, and build a reputation on effects of this nature. Most of the following tricks do not require you to actually light a match, so they can also be performed with cocktail sticks. As has been mentioned throughout the book, always try to be adaptable to whatever props are around you. It is advisable to learn several stunts and tricks that you can perform "impromptu" –

Above: British magician Colin Rose is well known for his fire-themed acts. One of these acts – "Fantasy in Flame" – thrilled audiences on television and in casinos and nightclubs the world over. In the 1970s his superb and dramatic manipulations of fire were enjoyed by hundreds of thousands when he toured with the legendary Richiardi Jnr.

Left: An artist's impression of the discovery of fire. Such an event would have been incredibly magical and wondrous to watch, but would probably have been met with severe apprehension.

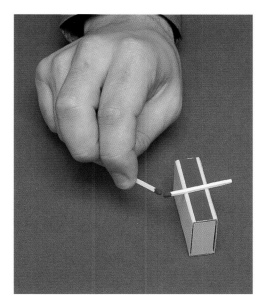

Above: Can matches really conduct static electricity? Your friends will believe so when you show them the Static Match!

Above: The next time you need to light a candle, cigarette or cigar, magically produce a lit match from behind your lapel – Lit Match Production.

Above: A match is torn from a matchbook and lit. Seconds later it disappears, only to be found reattached inside the book – Burnt Match in Matchbook.

such tricks can often be more impressive than a fully prepared show. Performing impromptu magic should not mean that your tricks are unrehearsed; it simply means that you are able to do an off-the-cuff routine.

If you learn some of the simple stunts in the following pages, you will be able to amaze your friends by making a lit match appear before using it to light a cigarette or candle (Lit Match Production). Then you will learn how to "vanish" it using a relatively unknown method (Vanishing Match). To demonstrate

the idea that wood can channel static electricity, you can make matches move and jump (Static Match and Jumping Match).

You will also learn how to make two solid matches pass through each other several times under impossible conditions (Match through Match), and how to rip a match from a matchbook, light and "vanish" it only to show the burnt match re-attached back inside the matchbook (Burnt Match in Matchbook). These are two of the best impromptu tricks in magic.

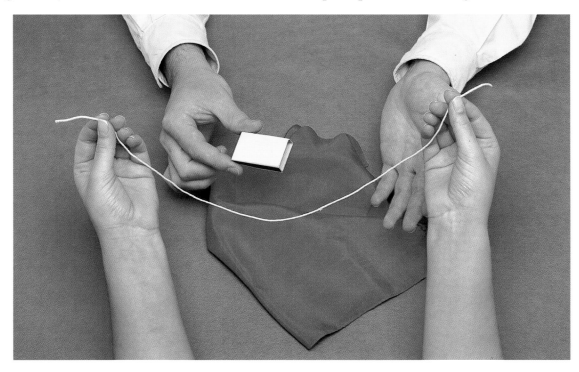

Right: Matchbox off String is the impossible penetration of one solid object through the other. The concept of penetration forms the basis for many "effects" in magic.

match through safety pin

The illusion created by this little stunt is that of a match passing through the bar of a safety pin. Although not a particularly difficult magic trick, it is a good example of how speed can deceive the eye.

It is a small party trick which can be made up quickly and cheaply with objects that most people would be able to find in their houses or place of work.

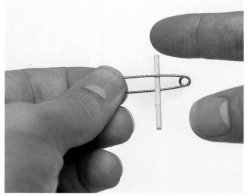

1 Using a scalpel, carefully cut the head off a match and push the sharp point of a safety pin through the centre. Close the safety pin and the set-up is completed. You may find that the match splits when you insert the pin. If this is the case, try first soaking a match for a few minutes in water in order to soften the wood.

2 Hold the safety pin with the left hand and position the match so that the top half is against the top bar of the pin. Flick the match, striking the point marked "X".

3 If you strike the match correctly, it appears as if the match passes straight through the top bar of the pin and on to the other side. In reality, what happens is that the match bounces off the top bar and rotates backwards in a complete revolution so quickly that it is virtually impossible for the human eye to see.

self-extinguishing match

You light a match and hold it in your right fingertips. You then extinguish the flame by blowing up your left sleeve! Often the best time to perform magic is when nobody is expecting anything to happen – if you catch people off guard, you can really amaze them.

Try this trick the next time you light a match. Don't call attention to your actions; just do it as if it is the most natural thing in the world. The match extinguishing itself looks very magical. Sometimes these little magic tricks can be as enjoyable as the more involved routines.

secret view

secret view

1 Strike a match and hold it up in the air away from your body.

2 Hold the match in between your right first and second fingers, so that your thumbnail is in a position to flick the match as you blow up your left sleeve.

3 Blow up your left sleeve and at the same time allow the end of the match to flick off your thumbnail.

4 The sudden movement of the match causes the flame to extinguish itself.

broken and restored match

A match is wrapped in the centre of a handkerchief. A spectator breaks the match into two pieces through the fabric, but when the match is unwrapped, it has magically restored itself. This trick is very old, but rarely seen. It is easily prepared and simple to execute, so is ideal for those times when you are asked to perform "at the drop of a hat". It also works with cocktail sticks.

1 Push a match into the seam of a handkerchief. The material of the handkerchief should hide the secret match perfectly – if it does not, then try using a thicker handkerchief.

2 When you are ready to perform, set the handkerchief on the table with a corner at the top and the hidden match in the corner nearest you. Openly place another match in the centre. With your right hand, bring the corner with the hidden match up into the centre.

3 Immediately fold the left corner into the middle, then the right corner, and finally the top.

4 Lift the secretly hidden match through the cloth. Hand it to a spectator and ask them to break it in half. The spectator will assume this is the same match they saw just a few moments ago.

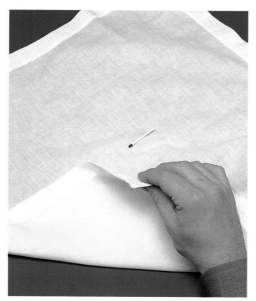

5 Unfold the handkerchief one corner at a time. With the right hand, grip the last corner to cover the hidden match.

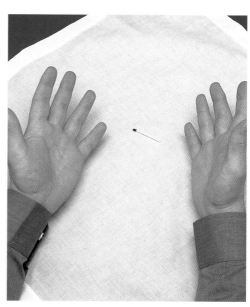

6 Show that the match has completely restored itself. Finish by folding up the handkerchief and pocketing the evidence of the hidden, broken match in the corner!

vanishing match

A match is held at the extreme fingertips and magically dissolved into thin air. In order to perform this amazing trick, you need to be wearing a ring on your right third finger.

This is another simple trick which is ideal for a spur-of-the-moment performance. You could also vanish a cocktail stick, but you must be careful not to stab yourself with it!

1 Hold a match between the tips of your thumb and first finger.

2 Curl your third and fourth fingers in, so that your second finger can angle the match towards the ring.

3 Use your thumb to push the match behind the back of your third finger and underneath the back of the ring.

secret view

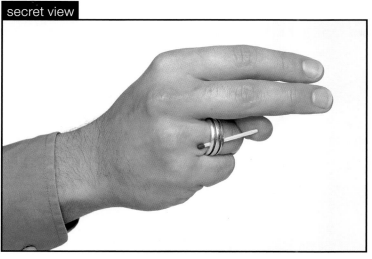

4 This is what the move looks like from the other side. You must make sure that nobody is watching you from behind.

5 Straighten out your fingers and rub your thumb as if dissolving the match.

6 Hold your hand out flat, but with your fingers closed together.

7 Finally spread your fingers wide to show that the match has completely gone.

vanishing box of matches

A box of matches is shaken and a spectator is asked to guess from the sound alone how many matches are inside. Whatever their answer, they are proven to be wrong when the box is opened and the matches have vanished! The effect of sound is strong and can be used in many different ways. For instance, once you are familiar with the workings of the principle described below, it is possible to

demonstrate a similar game to the old street swindle Three Card Monte. Three empty matchboxes are placed next to each other; one supposedly contains matches. The spectator has to keep their eye on the "full" box of matches as you move them and mix them around. You can prove that any of the boxes are empty or full at any time, depending on which hand you shake the box with.

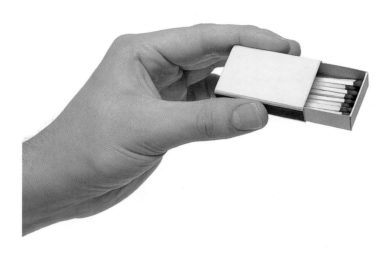

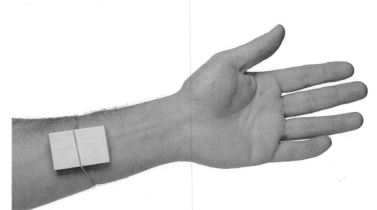

1 To prepare, half fill a matchbox with matches and close the box. Do not overfill the box, otherwise the sound the matches make when shaken will become muffled.

2 Put a rubber band on your left forearm, under your shirt sleeve. Place the box under the rubber band. You are now ready to perform the trick.

3 Shake an empty matchbox with your left hand. The rattling sound that is emitted comes from the hidden box up your sleeve. Ask the spectator to guess how many matches are inside the box. It doesn't really matter what their answer is.

4 Open the box and show that it is completely empty. You can hand it out for examination and allow your spectator to dismantle it if you wish.

static match

This is similar to the Jumping Match which follows, but is slightly easier to perform. One match is balanced on the edge of a matchbox and the other match rubbed against your arm to create "static

electricity". As the two match heads touch, the "static" is transferred and the match on the box shoots off like a rocket. In fact static has nothing to do with the method but it makes an interesting presentation.

secret view

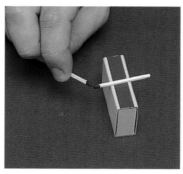

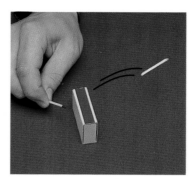

1 Remove one match from a matchbox. Stand the matchbox on its side and carefully balance the match on top at right angles, as shown here.

2 Rub the second match on your sleeve, supposedly to generate static electricity. Rub your foot on the floor at the same time, as if trying to harness as much electricity as possible. Hold the match between your thumb, first and second fingers. Its tip should sit under the second finger's nail.

3 Slowly approach the balanced match until the heads touch each other. You should act as if you might be about to receive an electric shock so that your actions interest the spectator.

4 As soon as the heads touch, allow the match to snap out from behind your fingernail. The force of the resulting jerk will be transferred through the first match and into the second. The second match will fly away at speed.

jumping match

Two matches are held at the extreme fingertips. One is rubbed on the sleeve and is held underneath the other. A few seconds later one of the matches flies away as if charged with electricity. The secret to the trick is the vibrations that are caused by rubbing a match against your fingernail. These vibrations make the match jump. They travel

along one match and through the other, making it move without any apparent cause. If you practise enough, you can make the match jump completely off your finger and on to the table.

This effect will also work with toothpicks and even chopsticks. Try linking this trick with the Static Match explained above.

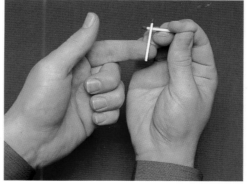

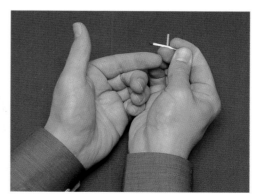

1 Rub a match against your sleeve, saying that you are charging it with static electricity. Then hold its edge between your right thumb and first finger. Position your second finger so that the match is pulled against the base of the fingernail.

2 Balance the second match on the first match, using your left first finger.

3 Pull the right hand's match back against your fingernail and scrape it against the nail. This is a tiny movement, which is completely unseen. The balanced match will begin to jump as the vibrations travel along.

lit match production

The next time you need to light a cigarette or a candle, simply reach behind your lapel and produce a lit match! As with all effects using matches and fire, you must be extremely cautious.

This is not really a trick in itself, but it does provide a small, visual magical moment. It is nice to be able to make things happen magically; after all, if you are a magician it is only right that you can produce fire at will – why would a magician need a lighter or a box of matches?

1 To prepare, fold the striking panel from a matchbox in half.

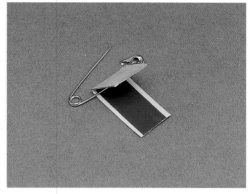

2 Thread the striking panel through the bars of a safety pin, as shown above.

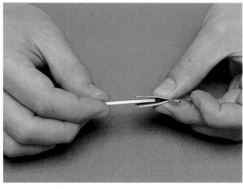

3 Carefully position a match with its head between the two surfaces of the striking panel.

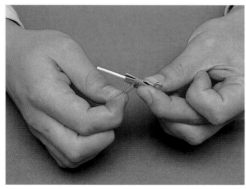

4 Wrap a rubber band tightly around the match and panel to keep everything locked in place.

5 Attach this "gimmick" under your right lapel. You can leave it in position for as long as you like.

6 When you are ready to perform, reach behind your lapel and grip the match tightly with your right hand.

7 Quickly pull the match downwards and outwards. The match will strike against the panel and ignite as it leaves the gimmick.

match through match

The idea of one solid object passing through another is a wonderful concept. It is simple to understand and everyone knows that it is impossible. This superb effect can be performed at any time as long as you can find two matches (or toothpicks). Two solid objects are caused to pass through each other not once but twice!

Most magic tricks should never be repeated, but if you perform this one well you can repeat it many times without fear of the method being detected. You will need to practise this effect until you can perform the secret moves without thinking. Just a little practice is all it will take to become confident.

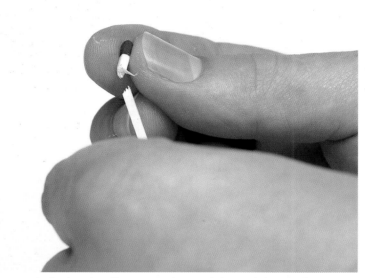

1 Break the heads off two matches and discard them. They are no longer needed.

2 Hold one match in each hand between the tips of your thumb and first finger. Your right first finger should be holding a rough, broken-off end. Squeeze it tightly so that the rough end sticks into the skin of your finger.

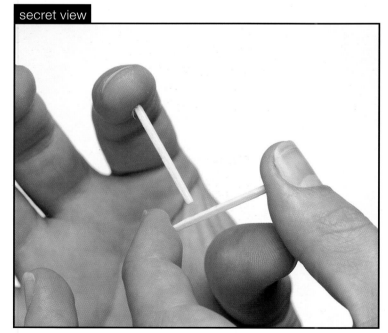

secret view

3 Tap the matches together three times. On the third tap, lower the right thumb. Because the match is wedged into your skin, it will remain suspended in the air for a fraction of a second as your thumb passes under the other match.

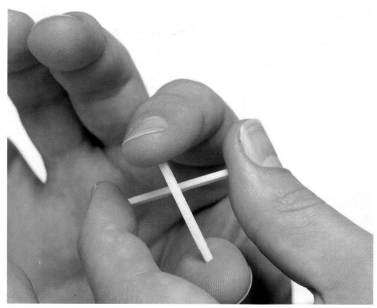

4 As soon as your right thumb is on the other side, re-grip the match again. The action takes place in under a second and the illusion created is of one match passing though the other. You can now reverse the above actions and remove the matches from each other. This is a great close-up magic trick.

matchbox off string

The cover of a matchbox is threaded on to a length of string. Both ends are held by a spectator and a handkerchief is placed over the centre. The magician reaches under the handkerchief and without any tearing or cutting is able to remove the box from the string.

To make the trick self-contained, find an opaque silk handkerchief that is thin enough to fold up and place inside the box together with the string. This way you can carry the whole trick around in one box.

1 Carefully prise open the glued joint of a matchbox cover, using a scalpel. Try to keep the card as flat as possible. It may take several attempts with different covers to split the box open without damaging the card.

2 Apply some reusable adhesive to a couple of points along the joint so that you can open and close the box repeatedly. When closed, the matchbox cover should look normal and arouse no suspicion. You are now ready to perform the trick.

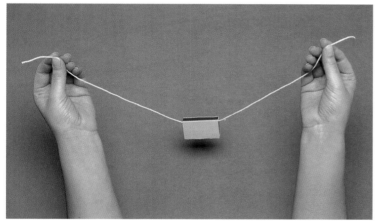

3 Thread the matchbox cover on to a piece of string. Ask a spectator to hold one end of the string in each hand.

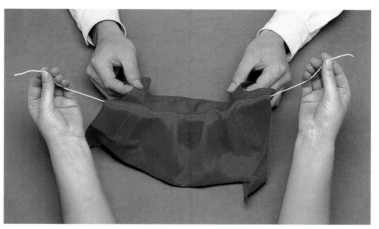

4 Cover the box with a handkerchief, explaining that the magic has to happen under the cover of darkness.

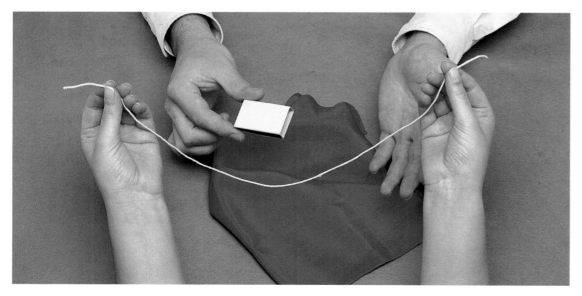

5 Reach under the handkerchief and unstick the prepared cover. Remove it from the string, then re-stick the join, making sure that you line up the sides of the box as evenly as possible. Display the box and remove the handkerchief. Try linking this trick with another that utilizes a piece of string, silk or a matchbox. There are many suitable effects in this book.

burnt match in matchbook

A match is torn out of a matchbook and lit. The burnt match vanishes and is found re-attached back inside the book. If you *learn this trick well, you will have a very strong piece of magic at your disposal wherever there is a book of matches around.*

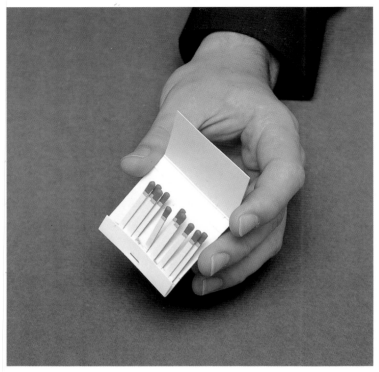

1 Before you begin the performance, open a matchbook and tear out a match.

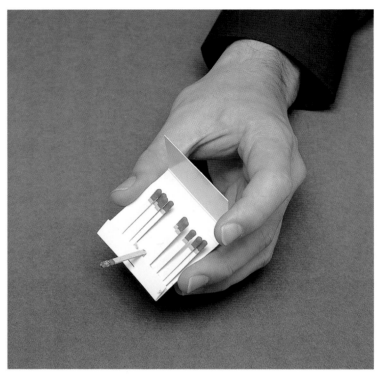

2 Bend another match forward and set it alight using the first match. Be very careful not to set alight the other matches. Blow out the flame and wait a few seconds for the match to cool.

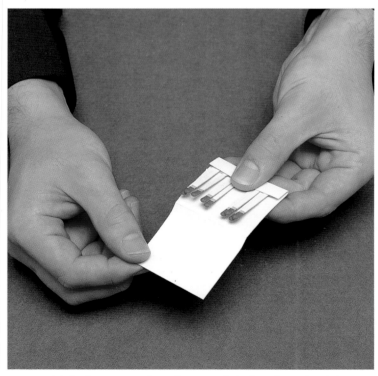

3 Hold the burnt match under your left thumb so that it is hidden from view. The preparation is now complete.

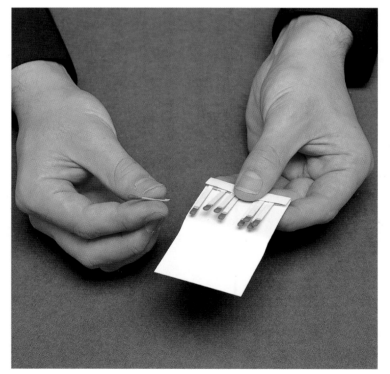

4 Show the matchbook and openly tear out one match, making sure the bent match remains hidden underneath your thumb.

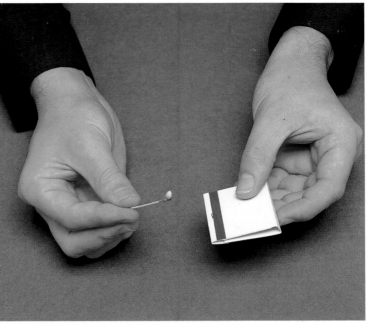

5 Close the matchbook by folding it backwards in order to keep the burnt match hidden. As the cover is closed, the burnt match is unbent and goes back into position next to the others.

6 Light the torn match and place the matchbook on the table, in view. Extinguish the flame.

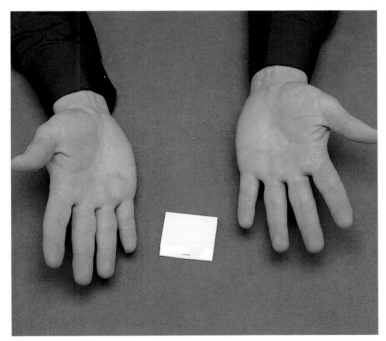

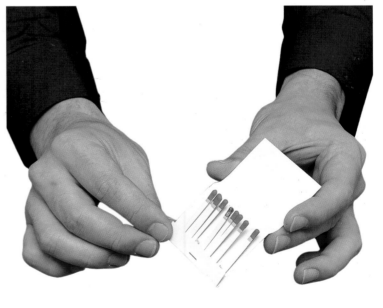

7 You must now "vanish" the match using any method you feel comfortable with, such as Vanishing Match or Fake Take (*see* Money Magic chapter). Another simple vanish can be accomplished while shaking the lit match to extinguish the flame. In a continuing motion, throw it over your shoulder and across the room. (Make sure the match is extinguished before you let go!) Continue to shake your hand up and down as if the match were still there. Give a few more shakes, then slow down to a halt and show that the match is gone.

8 Open the matchbook and show that the burnt match has miraculously re-attached itself inside!

string, cord and rope magic

There is a well-known saying, "Give a man enough rope and he will hang himself." There is another, less well-known saying, "Give a magician enough rope and he will show you a trick!" The following pages explain a variety of tricks using string, cord and rope. You will soon be able to cut and restore them, make them pass through human flesh and make knots mysteriously disappear at will.

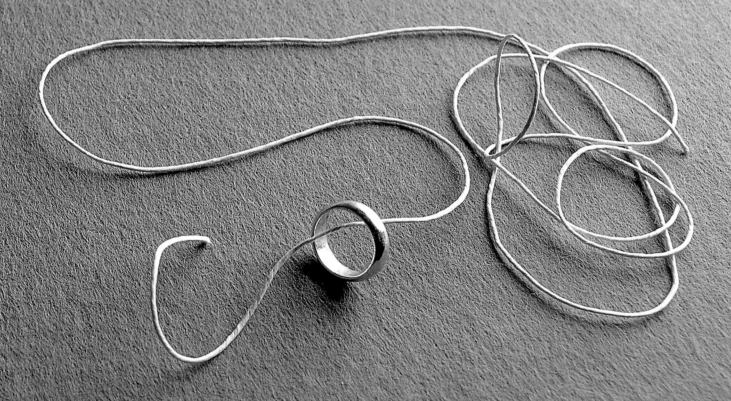

introduction

One of the most famous stories in magic is that of the legendary Indian Rope Trick. There are many versions of this trick. In one version a fakir caused one end of a long piece of rope to rise slowly into the air, where it would disappear through the clouds and remain perfectly rigid. A small boy would then climb the rope until he too vanished into the mist. In a rather gruesome moment the boy would fall from the sky limb by limb. His limbs were placed inside a basket and the rope would fall to the ground. From the basket would then rise the boy, who was found to be in perfect condition. In some stories the boy was chased up the rope by the fakir, and in others the boy simply vanished when he reached the top. The variations seem to be endless.

It is hard to pinpoint exactly when this illusion first came into existence because accounts vary and most, if not all, of those who wrote these accounts did not experience the illusion first-hand. It is believed that the first reported sightings were around 1350. Centuries later, in the early 1900s, many well-known illusionists, such as Thurston, Goldin, Hertz, Kellar and Kalanag,

Above: A typical nineteenth-century depiction of a suspension/levitation which would have been performed by fakirs trying to convince the public of their special powers. Such illusions were easily duplicated by magicians of the time.
Left: This drawing of a magic trick was published in *The Discoverie of Witchcraft* (1584) and suggests that string, cord and rope have been used by conjurors for centuries.

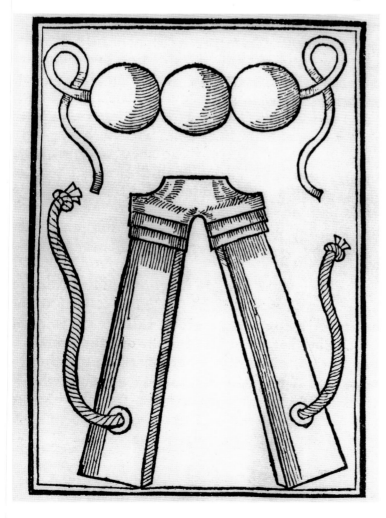

began performing elaborate versions of the trick in theatres across the world, much to the delight of their audiences. The addition of the famous Indian Rope Trick to their repertoire and the legend that surrounded it guaranteed valuable publicity.

Even though many of the principles of rope magic are old, there are still many new techniques being developed and invented. The French magician Tabary is currently one of the freshest innovators in rope magic. His performances have astonished magicians and non-magicians across the world and won him a coveted first place at the FISM international magic convention in 1991, making him a close-up world champion.

Magic shops sell "magicians' rope" in hanks. This is relatively inexpensive and available in a wide range of colours. You can use any type of rope, but try to find one with a high cotton content which is soft and flexible. You may find the rope needs to be cored – some ropes are made up of an outer layer and an inner core. The core can often be removed by pulling it from one end. You will be left with the sleeve of soft cotton, which makes perfect rope for manipulating and cutting.

The ends of the rope may begin to fray, and there are several ways to avoid this happening. The easiest is to stitch the ends with a thread of similar colour. Alternatively you can paint clear glue on to each end to seal the ends completely.

A staple of many magicians' repertoire is the Cut and Restored Rope effect. A length of rope is cut into two – sometimes three – pieces and caused to restore itself. There are dozens of methods in existence, and several are explained in this book. With a little thought, you can link several of these routines together to create a small performance that can be used as an act on its own or as part of a larger programme.

Above right: Seen here is a demonstration of a version of the Indian Rope Trick being performed in England, 1935.

Right: A publicity poster for nineteenth- and twentieth-century magician Carl Hertz, who regularly featured a version of the Indian Rope Trick in his illusion show.

Below: A popular rope trick wherein several silk handkerchiefs magically pass through a length of rope to which they are securely tied.

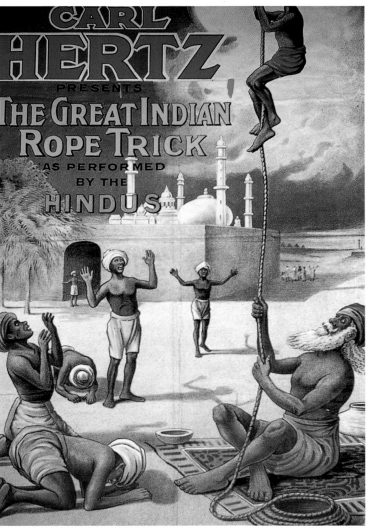

cut and re-strawed

A long piece of cord is threaded through a straw, which is then bent in half. The straw and cord are cut through the middle and displayed in two pieces, but when the cord is removed from the straw, it has *magically restored itself! The best straws to use are those found in fast food restaurants. The only preparation required is a slit which must be cut and which will remain hidden by the stripes on the straw.*

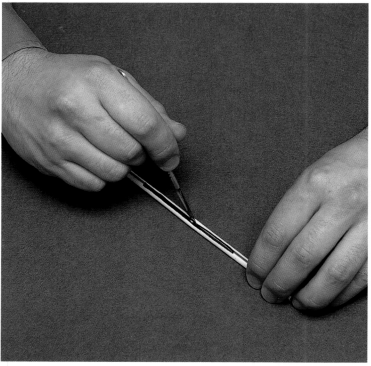

1 To prepare, carefully cut a slit in a drinking straw, using a scalpel. The slit should not go all the way to the ends. It is seen as a black line here for ease of explanation.

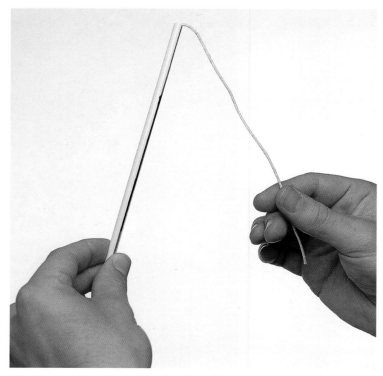

2 Hold the straw so that the slit is facing towards you and therefore hidden from anyone viewing from the front. Thread a cord through the straw so that a piece hangs from each end.

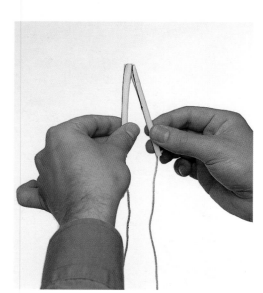

3 Hold one end of the straw in each hand and bend it in half so that the slit is on the inside.

secret view

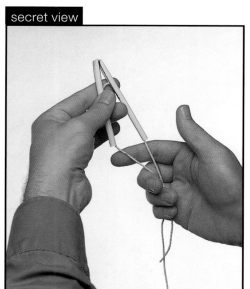

4 Hold the straw in the left fingertips and pull the ends so that the middle of the cord slips out of the slit and behind the left first finger. Pinch the cord together with the straw between the left first finger and the thumb.

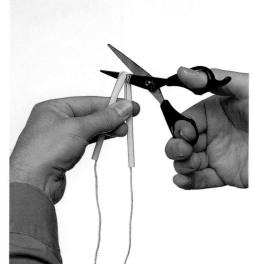

5 Cut the straw neatly in two. The middle of the cord remains hidden but the illusion created is that both the cord and the straw have been cut.

6 From the front, it can be seen that the cord is hidden behind the left forefinger, which looks very natural holding the straw in two pieces.

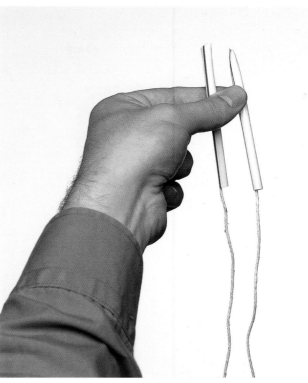

7 The view from your side is almost as convincing! Begin to pull one end of the cord downwards.

8 Continue pulling until the cord is removed completely. Pause to let the effect register with your audience.

9 Show that the cord is completely restored. If you wish, you can immediately hand the cord out for examination, but be sure to discard the straw in case the slit is discovered.

jumping rubber band

A rubber band is placed over the first and second fingers, then magically caused to jump to the third and fourth fingers. This is a very simple trick which you will have no trouble in mastering. You could perform this before another trick such as Linking Paper Clips.

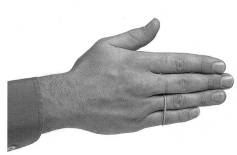

secret view
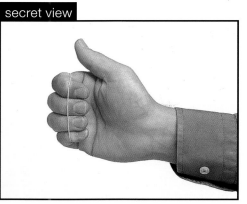

1 Place a rubber band over the first and second fingers. The back of your hand should be towards the audience. Pull the band away from your hand.

2 Close your hand, inserting all the fingers into the rubber band. Let the band snap over the fingertips. From the front, it will simply look as though the band is on the first and second fingers.

3 Quickly open your hand. The band will automatically jump over to the third and fourth fingers.

secret view
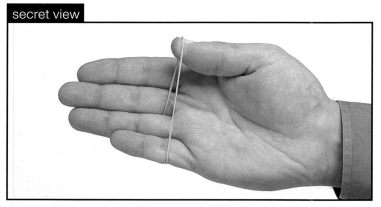

secret view
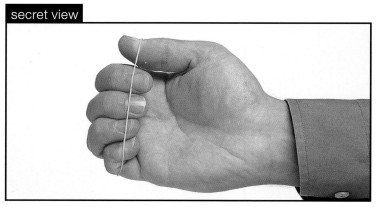

4 It is possible to make the band jump back again. The move can also be accomplished with one hand. Hook your thumb under the band and stretch it up so that you create a gap, as before.

5 Close the fingers again, inserting them into the gap created. Release your thumb from the band.

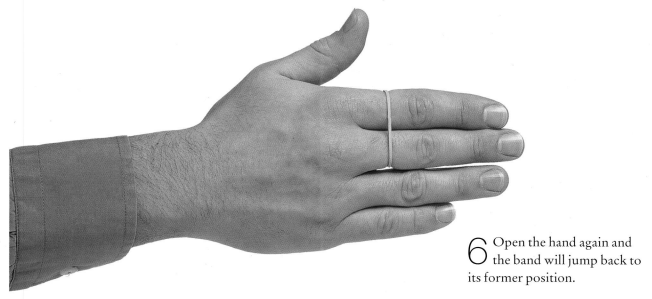

6 Open the hand again and the band will jump back to its former position.

string through arm (version 1)

A piece of string is tied into a continuous loop. It is wrapped around a spectator's arm and magically penetrates the flesh and bone without any damage whatsoever! The principle relies on your moves being quick and smooth. The secret move is covered by the speed of the hand which, in this case, really does deceive the eye. A piece of string is a simple, compact prop to carry around.

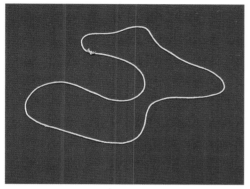

1 Tie a piece of string, approximately 90cm (3ft) long, into a loop with a strong knot.

2 Hold the loop under a spectator's arm and ask them to create an impenetrable barrier by gripping their hands firmly together, as seen here.

3 Bring both ends of the string up to meet each other, then pass one loop through the other. Grip the string and tug it gently to show that it is unquestionably trapped on the arm.

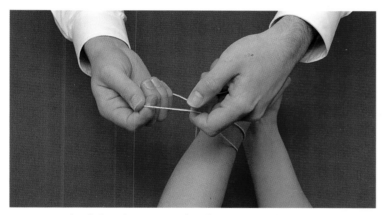

4 Move both hands up to each other again, then hook the left first finger around the top strand of the right hand's string.

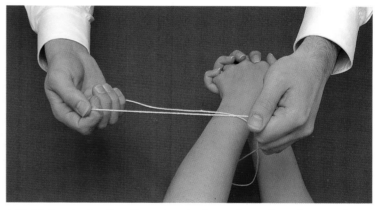

5 Maintain the first finger's grip, but release the other portion of string from the left hand.

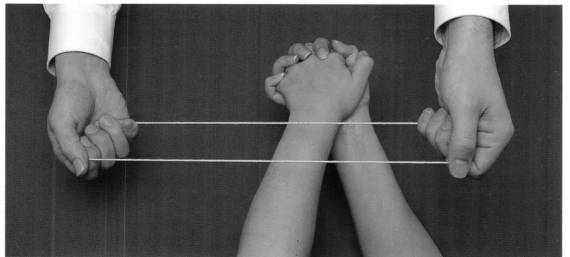

6 Pull both hands apart until the string is held taut. It will now be above the spectator's arm. It is important that steps 4, 5 and 6 happen together in one smooth motion in order for the illusion to look its best.

string through arm (version 2)

A spectator holds out their arm and a piece of string is held underneath. A few tugs and the string passes straight through their arm to the other side! Or does it?

To prepare for this trick you need to thread two small beads on a piece of string, approximately 45cm (18in) long, tying a knot at each end. The beads should be loose and free to slide from one end to the other. These beads are not meant to be a secret but neither should you call attention to them. When you pinch your finger and thumb around them, you should hardly be able to see them. Try to ensure that the knots at the ends of the string are tied as tightly as possible so that they do not come undone while performing.

1 Starting with both beads at the left end of the string, place the string under the outstretched arm of a spectator. The string should be held taut and at the fingertips.

2 Bring both ends of the string together. Grip one of the beads tightly with your right fingers, keeping the end bead gripped in your left hand.

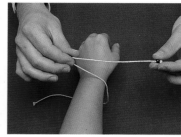

3 Allow the end of the string held by the right hand to drop, then quickly pull both beads taut. What really happens is that the string passes under the arm.

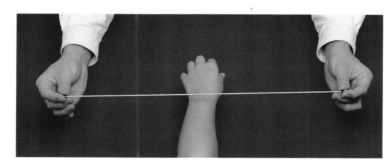

4 At full speed the eye cannot detect the route the string takes. The illusion of the string passing through the arm to get to the other side is very convincing!

string through ring

You can make a piece of string pass through many other solid objects. Here the same trick is performed using a spectator's finger ring.

As before, you need to attach two small beads to a piece of string. Then ask a spectator to lend you a ring. The best type of ring to use is a plain wedding band. In any event, you should avoid borrowing rings that have precious stones, in case one of them should fall out.

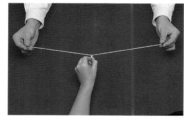

1 Ask a spectator to pinch a ring tightly between their finger and thumb. Thread the string through the ring. Both beads must be to the left.

2 Bring both hands together, pinching a bead between finger and thumb of each hand.

3 Drop the end held in your right hand and pull the beads apart.

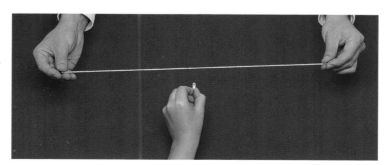

4 The string appears to have melted through the band of metal. A little thought will reveal many other objects which could be used instead of a spectator's arm or a finger ring – the handle of a mug, for example.

rope through neck

The two ends of a piece of rope are seen hanging over both shoulders. Despite the fact that the rope clearly passes around the back of the head, with a sharp tug it visibly penetrates the neck. This trick also works very well with a tie, which is perhaps a more appropriate item to have hanging around your neck! Please note that care should be taken when wrapping any sort of cord around your neck.

1 To prepare, run the rope across the front of your neck, and tuck it just under the edge of your shirt collar.

2 Once this secret preparation has been accomplished, you are ready to perform. Viewed from the front, it looks as if you have a piece of rope hanging around your neck and over your shoulders.

3 Hold both ends of the rope and pull gently until the line becomes taut.

4 With one quick action, pull the rope hard with both hands. As the rope stretches out, it is pulled from under your collar so quickly that the eye will be unable to detect the secret.

rope through neck again!

The general rule is "Never repeat a trick" but there are exceptions, for example when you have several methods for achieving the same effect. This is the ideal follow-up to Rope through Neck because the *method is completely different, even though the two tricks look very similar. Once again, a tie will work just as well, and as mentioned before you should take care whenever looping cord around your neck.*

1 Hang a piece of rope, approximately 1.8m (6ft) long, around your neck so that the left side hangs lower than the right. Experimentation will make it clear exactly how much rope should be hanging from either side.

2 With the right hand, grasp the left side of the rope between your thumb and first finger about a quarter of the way down. Now reach over with the left hand and pinch the right side of the rope about a quarter of the way up from the bottom.

3 Lift the right hand, with the rope, across the front of your neck and around to the middle of the back of your neck.

4 A split second after the right hand has started moving, the left hand begins its journey. It takes its piece of rope and wraps it around the back of your neck from right to left (the same way as the first piece). Your left arm moves over your head to achieve this.

secret view

5 The result is a bight or loop of rope, which is trapped by the loop made by the shorter piece.

6 From the front, it looks as if you have wrapped the rope around your neck. Hold one end in each hand and pull the rope taut.

7 Pull sharply with both hands. The bight of rope will slip out of the other loop and the rope will fall away from your neck. Make sure the rope is pulled completely taut.

hunter bow knot

In this trick, a slip knot is tied into a length of rope with a pretty flourish. This method of tying a slip knot is quite tricky to learn, but once you understand the moves you will never forget them.

The beauty of this particular tie is that the knots created look completely tangled until they all dissolve into thin air! You can incorporate the Hunter Bow Knot into other rope tricks and routines.

1 Extend the first and second fingers of your left hand and hang the centre of a piece of rope over them. Position your right first and second fingers about 2.5–5cm (1–2in) down the rope, below the left second finger.

2 Move the right hand back, under and up, curling your fingers enough to pull the rope back, and loop it around the tips of your left fingers.

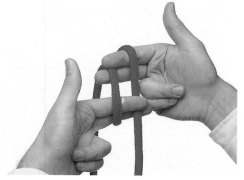

3 With both hands, grip a portion of the rope between your first and second fingers, as shown here.

4 Gripping tightly, pull the right hand to the right and the left hand to the left. The result will be a bow.

5 Reach into the tops of both loops and pull the ends through.

6 Slowly pull both ends of the rope, tightening the knot.

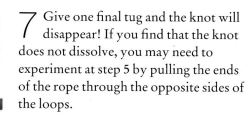

7 Give one final tug and the knot will disappear! If you find that the knot does not dissolve, you may need to experiment at step 5 by pulling the ends of the rope through the opposite sides of the loops.

impossible knot

Challenge a spectator to tie a knot in the centre of a piece of rope without letting go of the ends. Although you may find this difficult to learn initially, once you understand which hand goes where you will be able to make the Impossible Knot in an instant, without thinking.

1 Hold one end of a piece of rope tightly in each hand.

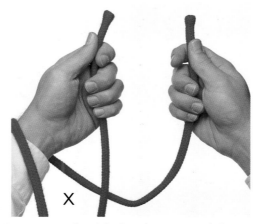

2 Loop the right hand over your left arm and behind the rope held in your left hand. Bring it back to a position similar to that at the start. Now move your right hand through the loop marked "X".

3 Once your hand has passed through the loop, pass it through the second loop marked "X".

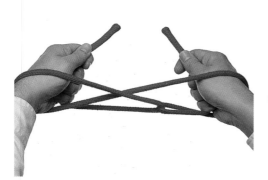

4 Stretch both hands out. You should now be in this position.

5 Allow the rope to slip off your left wrist, then pull the rope taut.

6 Repeat this with the right loop. You will be left with a knot in the centre of the rope.

7 Tug both ends and the knot will disappear before your eyes!

slip knot

A knot is tied without letting go of the ends of the rope. The knot is then plucked off the rope and thrown into the audience! This is a great *"bit of business" to add to a longer rope routine because it always receives a laugh from the audience.*

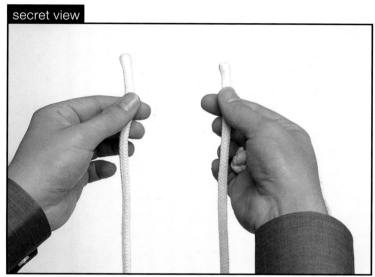

secret view

1 You will need a length of rope and a knot cut from a spare piece of rope. To prepare, hide the extra knot in your right-hand Finger Palm position (*see* Money Magic chapter). Hold one end of the main piece of rope in each hand.

2 Tie a knot without letting go of the ends of the rope, as described in Impossible Knot. Hold one end of the rope in the left hand.

secret view

3 With the right hand, approach the knot in the rope, and with the little finger, grip the rope just under the knot. The fourth finger tugs the rope, undoing the knot as you simultaneously pluck the knot off the rope, bringing the hidden knot into view in the fingertips.

4 Viewed from the front, the illusion looks very convincing. Finish by tossing the knot high into the air and into the audience.

cut and restored rope (version 1)

A length of rope is unmistakably cut in half, yet is magically restored to its former condition. This is an absolute classic of magic and is still performed today by many magicians. You can follow this version with the next. They work perfectly together.

1 To prepare, place a pair of scissors in your right pocket. Bend an offcut of rope, approximately 10cm (4in) long, in half and hold it secretly in the left hand between the thumb and first finger. This piece must remain hidden at all times.

2 To begin your performance, hold a longer piece of rope, approximately 1.8m (6ft) long, next to the short piece, as shown. From the front, it looks as though you have only one piece of rope.

3 With the right hand, grab the centre of the rope and bring it up to the hidden short piece. It will look as though you are simply repositioning the middle of the rope so that it can be displayed. In reality you are going to switch the ropes.

4 Clip the "real" centre between your left thumb and first finger while extending the short piece up into view. The move should take seconds and should arouse no suspicion.

5 Remove the scissors from your pocket. From the front, the image is very clear. You have simply found the centre of a piece of rope and are holding it before cutting it in half.

6 Cleanly cut the rope in half. Of course you are actually cutting through the centre of the short piece.

7 Trim the ends of the rope, allowing the pieces to drop on to the floor. Continue trimming until all of the short piece of rope has been cut and dropped so that you destroy the evidence in front of the audience! Make a magical gesture, then stretch out the rope between both hands to show that it is completely restored.

cut and restored rope (version 2)

This version of this famous trick follows very well after the first. Try it out and you will fool yourself! As you will see, with the extra knot in your right hand, you can follow this with the Slip Knot trick. This *illusion works because it becomes difficult to follow exactly which section of the rope is being cut and, while it looks like the centre, it is actually a piece just a very short distance from one of the ends.*

1 Hold the centre of a piece of rope, approximately 1.5–1.8m (5–6ft) long, with your left hand and bring the right end of the rope up to meet it. With your left thumb and fingers, grip the rope about 7.5cm (3in) from the end.

2 Loop the short end of the rope away from you and over the top of the centre. Bring it back underneath, as shown. Thread the end through the gap marked "X".

3 Pull the short end of the rope and the part that emerges below the knot, to tighten the knot.

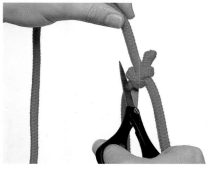

4 Cut the left-hand side of the loop just under the knot.

5 Clearly display what looks like a piece of rope cut in two and held together with a knot. Actually the rope is in one piece and the knot is simply a tiny section of rope tied around the centre.

secret view

6 Begin to wind the rope around the fingers of your left hand. As you reach the knot, allow it to slip along, hidden in the fingers of your right hand.

secret view

7 Continue to wind the rope until the knot falls off the end. Keep the knot hidden in the Finger Palm position.

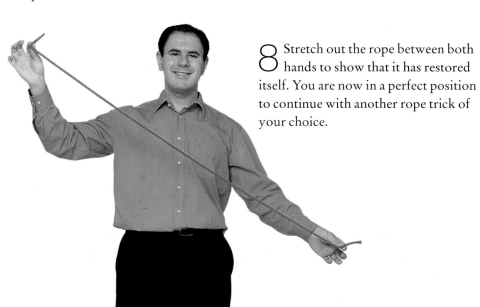

8 Stretch out the rope between both hands to show that it has restored itself. You are now in a perfect position to continue with another rope trick of your choice.

rope through apple

An apple is cored and two long pieces of rope are threaded through. To further secure the apple to the ropes, a knot is made. Despite the impossibility of the situation, the apple is pulled free of the ropes without any harm to either.

This routine is ideal for a large crowd as well as a more intimate gathering. Although only small props are used, they can be made to fill a large stage with a spectator either side of you. It is an effect that, as magic advertisements would say, "Packs Flat, Plays Big".

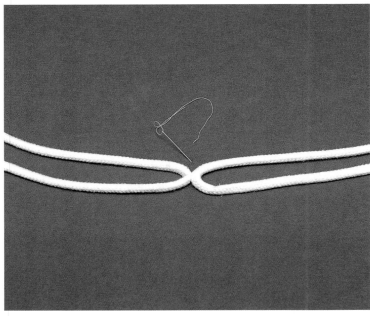

1 Prepare two pieces of rope, each about 1.8m (6ft) long, by folding them in half. Loosely stitch the centres together. The stitches should not be too tight because they must be snapped at a later stage.

2 In performance, unfold the ropes so that they run parallel to each other. Invite two people to help you, and give them two ends each. Ask them to tug on the ropes to prove that they are exactly what they appear to be.

secret view

3 Hold on to the centre of the ropes and ask your helpers to let go. As the ends drop, grip the centre of the ropes with both hands and switch one of the ropes around, arranging them so that they are held together by the stitches. The thread is hidden from the front by your fingers, and the repositioning happens as you raise the ropes to temporarily place them over your shoulders.

4 With the ropes now safely resting around your shoulders, your hands are free to pick up an apple corer and remove the core from the apple.

5 Remove the rope from around your neck, hiding the centre in your left hand. Thread the ends of the ropes through the apple. (The two ends that go into the apple belong to the same piece of rope.)

secret view

6 The left hand provides enough cover to prevent the centre section of the rope being seen. Continue to pull the ropes through the apple until the join is hidden inside it.

7 Ask the spectators to hold the ends of the ropes. To secure the apple further, suggest tying a knot in the ropes. Take one end from each side (it doesn't matter which) and tie a simple overhand knot. Give the ends back to the spectators.

8 Cover the apple with a handkerchief, explaining that the magic has to happen under the cover of darkness!

9 Reach underneath and ask the spectators to pull the ropes taut. The thread will snap and the ropes will automatically fall away from the apple. You may find it helpful to slide the apple back and forth along the ropes as they are pulled taut.

10 Display the apple and remove the handkerchief. Give the apple to one spectator and the ropes to the other to be examined. The secret to the trick was destroyed by the spectators themselves!

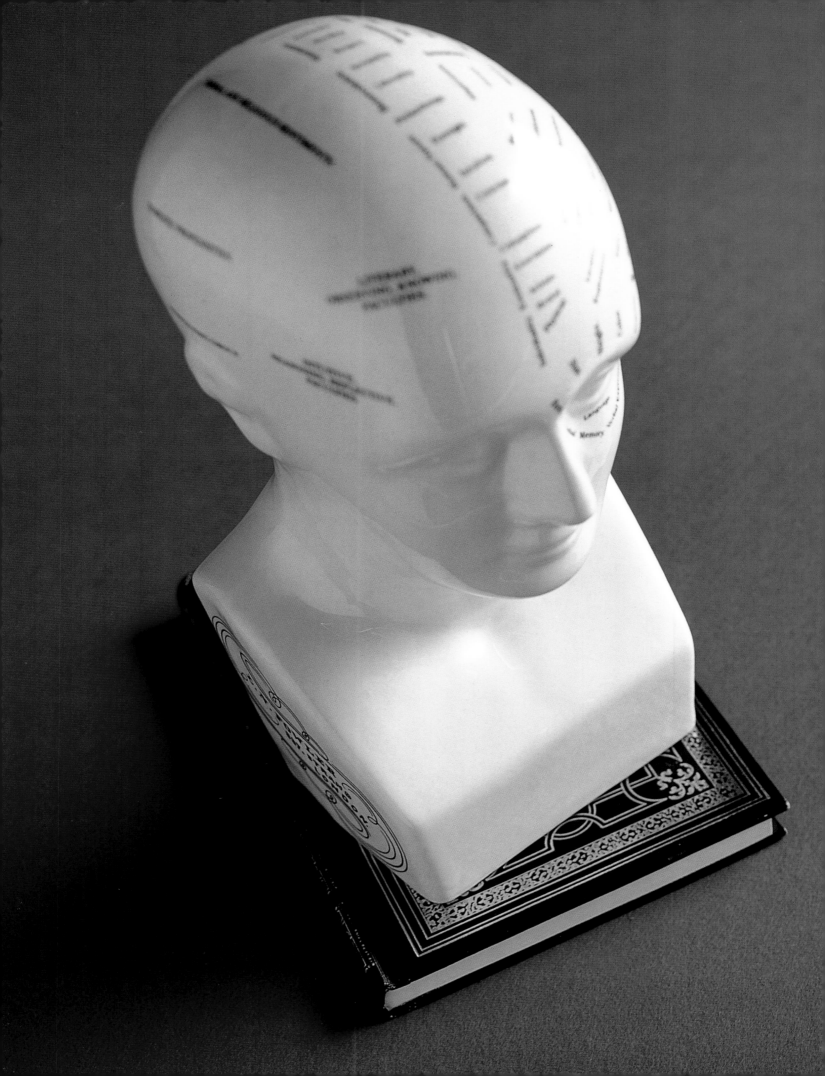

mind magic

Scientists have long subscribed to the belief that humans only use a fraction of their potential brainpower. Many people believe we have, and some even claim to have, a sixth sense with which to read people's minds and make predictions about forthcoming events. Do paranormal powers really exist? People will believe they do when you show them some of the routines in this chapter.

introduction

Inspired by the performance of a fortune-telling act at the turn of the twentieth century, American-born Joseph Dunninger became one of the greatest performers of mind magic. He originally toured with a large illusion show, but soon realized the impact his mental effects were having on his audiences. Sections of his evening show became dedicated to mind magic until he decided he wanted to be known solely as a mentalist. He subsequently worked for some of the richest and most important people in America. In the early 1940s Dunninger presented a regular radio programme and continued to do so until the late 1940s, when the world of television became an attractive opportunity to spread his reputation even further. In the 1960s Kreskin, a fresh, young American mentalist, stole the limelight from Dunninger and continues to amaze both television and live audiences with his seemingly supernatural powers.

In the 1940s, on the other side of the Atlantic, British radio audiences were being mesmerized by The Piddingtons, a husband-and-wife team many people believed were truly psychic, although they themselves

Above: A publicity poster used by the successful early twentieth-century mind-reader and magician Joseph Dunninger. Take a look at the clever design of the face and you will find the eyes and nose take on a shape of their own.

Above: David Berglas became known as television's "International Man of Mystery" following the broadcast of his series throughout the UK and Europe. Performing astounding memory feats, unusual psychological experiments, manipulation and pick-pocketing, he is one of the world's most versatile magical entertainers. He is also a past president of The Magic Circle.

never claimed this to be the case. Other prominent British mentalists between the 1940s and 70s were Maurice Fogel, Chan Canasta, Al Koran and David Berglas. Berglas has only recently retired after an incredibly successful career performing magic.

In the late twentieth century American Max Maven became one of the foremost creators and performers of mental magic. Graham P. Jolley, although not so well known, is without doubt one of Britain's finest mentalists, mixing superb mental magic with rapid-fire humour and leaving audiences enthralled, entertained and utterly astounded.

None of these performers ever claimed any real psychic ability, but there is one person who does – and as a result has become a household name. Uri Geller, known predominantly for bending spoons with nothing more than his mind, also tries to convince the public of his paranormal powers by stopping watches and duplicating drawings made by volunteers – all effects which can be replicated by known magical methods. American James Randi is one of the world's leading debunkers of phoney psychics and is well known for his numerous exposures of what he believes to be Geller's methods. The famous Harry Houdini was also known for his anger against those who claimed real psychic ability. In the early 1900s he publicly challenged anyone to show him an act of

Above: Graham P. Jolley is one of Britain's funniest and most baffling mind-readers. He is billed as "The Man You Can't Keep out of your Mind" and, among other things, will make a glass shatter with mental energy, make a table levitate, and reveal the telephone numbers of names freely selected from a huge directory.

Above: Uri Geller, the world-famous Israeli who can apparently bend cutlery and other metal objects with the power of his mind. Even scientists have marvelled at his abilities, which have been studied under test conditions on a number of occasions.

Below: One of the most popular effects for a mind-reader to perform is called a Book Test. It involves a word or selection of words being chosen from a book, which are then revealed by the performer either in the form of a prediction or as a demonstration of mind-reading.

psychic power or telekinesis that he was not able to explain. Such a challenge was bold, but only helped to increase the publicity of perhaps the greatest showman and publicist the world has ever seen.

In the following pages you will learn how to create the impression of mind-reading and even of being able to predict future events. Correctly divine a number chosen at random from the roll of a pair of dice (Dice Divination) or predict a word chosen at random from a book (Double Book Test). Transfer your psychic powers to a third party (Black Magic and Temple of Wisdom) and cause the name of a chosen card to spookily reveal itself on your arm (Ash on Arm).

Whether you choose to perform in a serious or a more relaxed style depends on your personality, but do not be put off by the simplicity of some of the methods. Remember, the simplest tricks to perform are often the most astounding.

coin under bottle tops

A coin is placed under one of three bottle tops. The caps are rearranged while your back is turned, yet you find the coin immediately. The method to this trick relies on a short length *of thread or hair which remains unseen by the spectators. Experiment with different surfaces to work on. A tablecloth with a "busy" design would be perfect.*

1 Haberdashery shops sell a thread that is almost invisible to the human eye. You will need to find some of this "invisible thread" or use a substitute such as a hair. Attach a small piece of this thread or hair to the underside of a coin with a piece of adhesive tape. (White thread is used here for ease of explanation.)

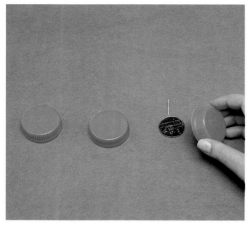

2 It is a good idea to have this coin among others in your pocket and to casually bring it out, putting the others away. Make sure that the taped side of the coin is against the table. Place three bottle tops on the table, and ask a spectator to choose any one of them to cover the coin.

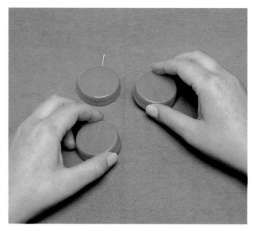

3 Ask the spectator to slide the bottle tops around while your back is turned. Explain that when you turn back you will try to divine which bottle top the coin is under.

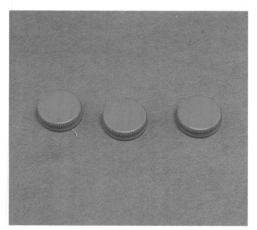

4 When they have finished mixing the bottle tops, turn around and casually glance down in order to spot the thread. Try not to make this glance too obvious.

5 Act as though you are receiving psychic vibes, perhaps hovering your hands just above each bottle top in order to feel the heat rising from the coin. After suitable byplay, lift the appropriate bottle top to reveal the coin.

whispering jack

Any five cards are removed from the deck and placed face down on the table. A spectator looks at and remembers one. The five cards are then mixed and once again placed face down on the table. Despite the fact that even the spectator is now unsure where their card is, the magician is able to find the one selected. Whispering Jack is a great

trick to perform with a borrowed deck because the owner will know that the cards could not be marked in any way and therefore will be even more baffled. You can use any number of cards for this trick, but five seems about right. Once you read the method you will realize that the older the deck of cards, the easier this trick is to perform.

1 Remove a Jack from a deck of old cards. Explain that this card represents Sherlock Holmes, the world-famous detective. Ask a spectator to remove any other five cards from the deck and to lay them face down in a row on the table.

2 Ask the spectator to pick up any of the five cards, to remember it and then replace it. This card represents the villain. Although you do not see the face of the chosen card, you must see which position the card is taken from.

3 Explain that the detective must interview each of the suspects. As you say this, tap each card with the corner of the Jack.

secret view

4 Your real reason for doing this is to create "misdirection" while you carefully look at the back of the chosen card in order to find a mark, blemish or piece of dirt which you will be able to recognize later. Study the cards secretively and quickly, otherwise someone may see you staring at them.

5 Ask the spectator to mix the cards until even they cannot know where their card is. Ask them to lay out the cards on the table as before.

6 Explain that Sherlock Holmes will now interview each suspect again and find the villain. Tap the corner of the Jack on to the back of every card as before while you secretly look for the mark you spotted earlier.

7 Turn over the card – the great detective has found his man!

"X" marks the spot

A deck of cards is placed on the table in full view. It is explained that one of the cards has been marked and the spectator has to guess which one. A card is named – it can be any card at all. This card is *removed from the deck and is shown to be the only one marked with a large "X". This is a superb card trick. It will only take a few minutes to prepare, and a little practice to learn.*

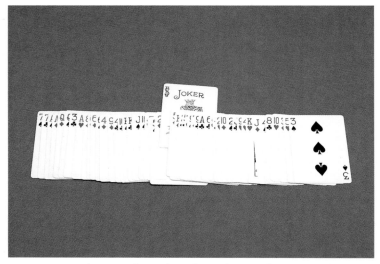

1 Prepare the cards by dividing the deck into two packets of 26 cards. Mark one packet with an "X" on the front of every card and the other packet with an "X" on the back of every card. While the "X" should be bold and clear, it should not fill the entire card, and must be positioned in the centre.

2 Arrange these cards so that (from the top down) you have the front-marked cards followed by the back-marked cards, with a Joker dividing the two packets. Square up the deck and place it back inside the card box.

3 In performance, say "Before the show I marked one of these cards with an "X". I am going to try to influence your decision and make you think of the card of my choice. The only clue I will give you is that it is not the Joker! Name any card in the deck." There are two possibilities. The first is that the chosen card will have an "X" on the back. Let us deal with this situation first.

Remove the deck from the box and spread the cards face up to find the chosen card. Do not spread the cards too wide because after the centre point of the deck you will risk exposing the "X"s. Find the chosen card (in our example, the Four of Hearts). Remove the card, keeping it face up. Spread through the first half of the deck face up, explaining that any card could have been named.

4 Turn the deck face down and display the top half of the deck in a spread or fan, subtly showing the backs of these cards. Again, do not spread too far down the deck.

5 Keep the top few cards spread wide as you reveal that the back of the chosen card has an "X" printed on it.

6 The second possibility is that the chosen card has an "X" on the front. Again, carefully spread through the cards until you find the one selected. The spread must be tight. Begin to pull out the card.

7 Before the "X" is revealed, turn the fan face down. Deal the chosen card face down on to the table.

8 Casually spread the top quarter or so of the cards, displaying the backs, and turn the deck face up. Spread them widely, explaining that any card could have been chosen.

9 Turn the selected card face up to display the "X". The great thing about this trick is that the audience are convinced that they saw the backs and fronts of all the cards.

dice divination

While the magician's back is turned, two dice are rolled a number of times and the numbers totalled. When the magician turns around they are instantly able to reveal the total.

It is a little-known fact that the two numbers on the opposite side of any die always add up to 7. Using this principle, you can gain the knowledge you need to discern the total.

 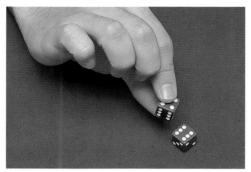 

1 Turn your back to a spectator and ask them to follow your instructions carefully. Ask them to roll a pair of dice, adding both numbers on view together. In our example it is 6 + 1 = 7.

2 Ask them to pick up one of the dice and to add its bottom number to the total (7 + 6 = 13).

3 Tell them to roll the first die again and to add the number that lands uppermost (4 + 13 = 17). Turn back and glance at both dice. Simply add 7 to whatever numbers you see facing upwards. In our example, 6 + 4 + 7 = 17.

human calculator

Six-digit numbers are selected by the spectator and the magician. Impossible as it may sound, the final total is found to have been predicted well in advance. This is a very clever mathematical trick.

As you will see, the simple formula of subtracting and adding 2 does all the work for you. The great thing about the Human Calculator is that you finish with a different number every time.

1 Give a piece of paper and a pen to a spectator and ask them to openly write down any six-figure number. Let us assume it is 2 1 7 3 4 9. You base your prediction on this number. Simply deduct 2 from the last digit and add 2 in front of the first digit. In our example, you would write down 2 2 1 7 3 4 7. Place this prediction to one side, out of view. This is written while you ask the spectator to write another six figure-number underneath the first. As soon as they start writing, jot down your prediction.

2 Let us assume their two numbers are:
   2 1 7 3 4 9
   6 1 3 9 4 8
Now you write a six-digit number underneath. Each number you write must total 9 when added to the number above. So you would write:
   2 1 7 3 4 9
   6 1 3 9 4 8
   3 8 6 0 5 1
Ask the spectator to write another number below yours:
   2 1 7 3 4 9
   6 1 3 9 4 8
   3 8 6 0 5 1
   1 2 9 3 0 6
Finally, you write one last number in exactly the same way as before:
   2 1 7 3 4 9
   6 1 3 9 4 8
   3 8 6 0 5 1
   1 2 9 3 0 6
   8 7 0 6 9 3

3 Give the spectator a calculator and ask them to work out the total:
   2 2 1 7 3 4 7
You can now reveal that your prediction matches the total. If the last digit in the first number is either 0 or 1, subtract 2 from the last two digits, that is, 3 5 7 8 3 0 would give you a prediction of 2 3 5 7 8 2 8.

impossible prediction

Three cards are displayed and a spectator is asked to choose one of them. It is a completely free choice and the spectator can change their mind as many times as they wish. The magician reveals a prediction that has been in view throughout, which matches their choice. The method to this trick relies on a principle known as a "multiple out". All three possible outcomes can be displayed as three separate predictions, but the audience is only ever aware of one of them so the prediction seems impossible. You cannot repeat this particular trick to the same audience twice, but it is one of the most baffling tricks you will ever perform.

1 To prepare the three predictions, draw a large "X" on the back of a picture card. Photocopy two other cards, reducing the size, and cut them out. Glue one of the mini photocopies on the flap side of an envelope. Keep the other photocopy loose.

2 Place all three cards, face up, inside the envelope together with the loose photocopy. With this envelope in your pocket, you will always be ready to show a miracle.

3 Casually introduce the envelope and explain you have three cards inside. The photocopy glued to the back must remain hidden. Remove the cards, taking care that the loose photocopy does not fall out, and lay them out, face up, keeping the "X" hidden. Place the envelope to one side, but in the spectator's field of vision. Ask them to choose one of the cards.

4 Give the spectator the opportunity to change their mind. There are three possible outcomes. First, let us assume the picture card is chosen. Explain that before the performance you marked the back of just one of the cards with an "X". Slowly turn over the cards one by one to reveal the "X" on the back of the selected card.

5 In this example, the second scenario would be the Five of Spades. Explain that you gave the spectator every opportunity to change their mind and that this is the card you were sure they would choose. Slowly turn the envelope over to show your prediction pasted to the back.

6 The final scenario is that the Three of Clubs is chosen. Once again explain you had a prediction, which has been in full view the entire time. Slowly tip up the envelope so that the loose photocopy falls from within the envelope. It matches the selection.

ash on arm

A card is selected and replaced into the deck. The name of the card is written on a piece of paper and the paper is burnt. The charred ashes are rubbed on the magician's bare forearm and the name of the card appears in the ashes. There are few more effective ways to reveal the name of a chosen card. With a little imagination, you can reveal lots of other information in this manner also.

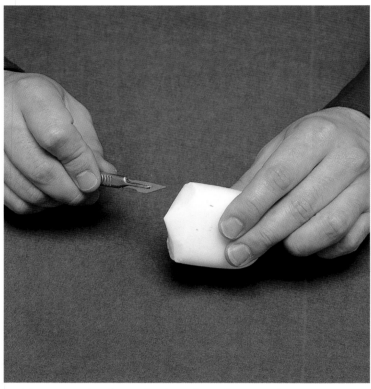

1 To prepare for the trick, slice a bar of soap with a scalpel to create a point at one end, in a similar fashion to sharpening a pencil with a knife.

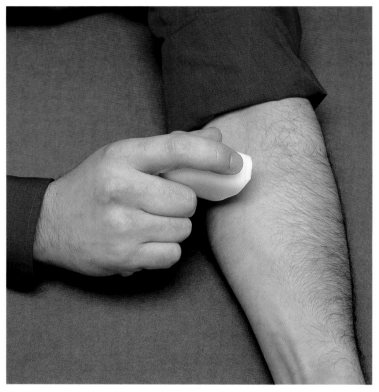

2 With the point of the soap, write the name of a card on your left forearm. In our example, it is the Four of Diamonds. This writing will remain invisible until the moment of the revelation.

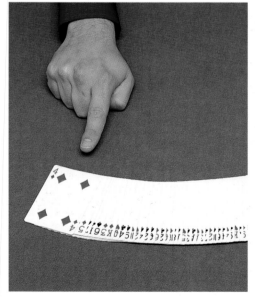

3 You will need to force the Four of Diamonds, so position that card at the bottom of the deck in preparation for the Hindu Force.

4 To begin performing the trick, start the Hindu Force (*see* Card Magic chapter) and continue cutting until the spectator stops you.

5 Show the bottom card (the force card) to the spectator.

6 Give the spectator a pencil and paper and ask them to write down the name of the selected card, then to fold the paper into quarters with the writing on the inside.

7 Light a match and burn the paper in an ashtray. As with all tricks involving matches and fire, you should be extremely careful.

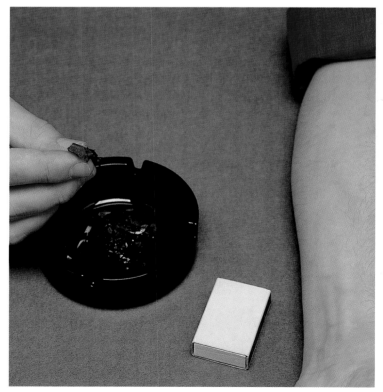

8 Roll up your sleeve (the soap will still be invisible at this point) and pick up some of the ashes in your right hand.

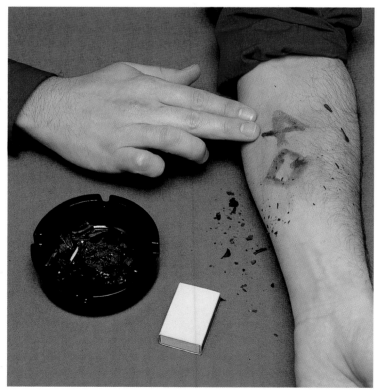

9 Rub the ashes on your forearm. The ash will adhere to the area you coated with soap earlier, and the name of the forced card will clearly be seen on your arm.

tri-thought

Three spectators are asked to make a choice. One chooses a number between 1 and 100, the second chooses a shape, and the third chooses a card. The magician has predicted all three choices. Tri-Thought uses the "one-ahead" principle. As its name suggests, you are always one *step ahead of your audience, which is how you are able to predict their choices. This routine will baffle people completely if performed with confidence and boldness. It does require you to perform well, and is not a trick for someone of a nervous disposition!*

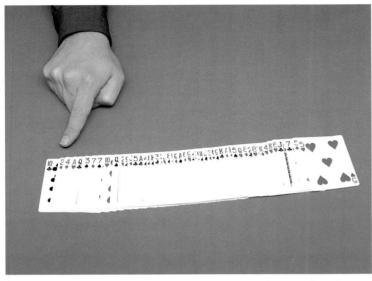

1 The "one-ahead" principle requires you to know what the final choice will be. This is why you use a deck of cards. You must know what card is on top of the deck before you begin. In our example, it is the Ten of Clubs.

2 Ask a spectator to think of a number between 1 and 100. Pretend you are reading their mind and explain that you are writing down a prediction. What you actually write on the paper is the card that was at the top of the deck (the Ten of Clubs). Fold up the paper into quarters and explain that it represents prediction number "1". However, instead of writing "1" on the folded paper, secretly write "3".

3 Drop this piece of paper into a mug so that it is temporarily out of sight. It is vital that the spectators do not see that you have incorrectly numbered the paper. The mug also prevents anyone from being able to keep track of which paper is which.

4 Ask the spectator to confirm the number they were thinking of. Let us assume they say "43". Act as though you knew all along "43" was their number and say "That's uncanny, let's try to get two out of two." Ask another spectator to think of a shape and once again pretend to read their mind as you write a second prediction. What you actually write is the number you just heard: "43". Fold this paper into quarters and write "1" on it, but say that it is your second prediction.

5 Drop the second paper into the mug. Ask the spectator to confirm their chosen shape. Let us assume they say "Square". Once again, act smug and say you will try one more prediction.

6 Now force the card, using any force method you are comfortable with. Shown here is the Slip Force (*see* Card Magic chapter). Begin by riffling down the edge of the deck until a spectator stops you, then cut the deck at this point, slipping the top card to the chosen position.

7 Offer the forced card to the spectator, but ask them not to look at it for the moment and to place it face down, off to one side.

8 Write your final prediction, but instead of writing the name of a card, write or draw the shape mentioned in step 5 – in this case, a square. Fold the paper into quarters and write "2" on it as you explain to your audience that this is the third and final prediction.

9 Drop the paper into the mug with the other predictions. Using the one-ahead principle, you have made three predictions which now match the three choices of the spectators.

10 Ask the spectator to reveal the chosen card. It will be the card you wrote at the start. Act pleased with yourself once again and tip the papers out on to the table, arranging them in numerical order.

11 Open your predictions one by one, showing your perfect mind-reading capabilities!

just chance

This is similar to the next trick, Money Miracle, but is more suitable for a large audience or a formal show. Three envelopes are displayed on a plate and two members of the audience are given absolute freedom to choose one envelope each. The remaining envelope is left for the magician. After the choices have been made, the magician explains that before the performance a banknote was placed inside

one of the envelopes. The envelopes are opened one at a time. Each of the spectators finds a blank piece of paper inside theirs, yet when the magician's is opened a banknote is revealed.

Practise this trick in a mirror to be sure that the banknote remains hidden throughout the trick. You can also replace the plate with a newspaper or magazine.

1 To prepare for this trick, you will need three pieces of blank paper the same size as a banknote. Fold the pieces of paper into eighths. Put one in each of three envelopes, sealing the flaps. Display the envelopes on a plate, flap side down.

2 Fold a banknote into eighths just as you folded the paper. Hold it in your right hand, thumb on top, fingers below.

secret view

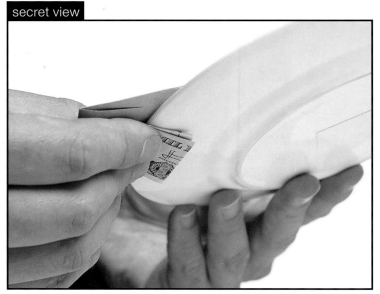

3 Place a plate on top of the note, secretly hiding it. Before the performance, put the plate on a table with the banknote just overlapping the edge. This will enable you to lift everything at once, without suspicion.

4 Explain to the audience that each of the three envelopes contains something. Offer the plate to two spectators and invite them to choose an envelope. Stress their freedom of choice. Also mention that the remaining envelope will be yours. Wait until they have removed their two envelopes. As your left hand steadies the plate, your right hand drags the remaining envelope off the plate, along with the banknote which is hidden underneath.

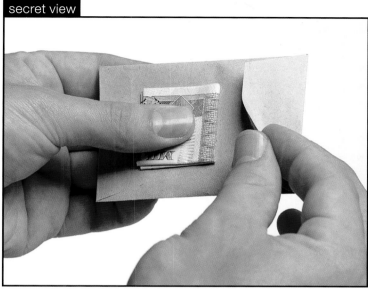

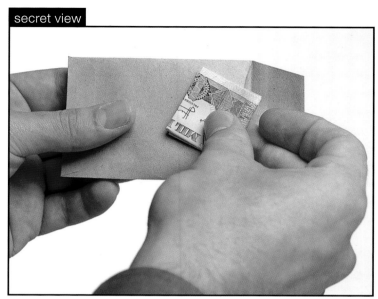

5 Orientate the remaining envelope so that the flap is towards you and the note is still hidden. Explain that before the performance you put some money into one of the envelopes and that, even though you said you would not influence the spectators, you used non-verbal communication to subconsciously direct their actions! Build up this moment so that people really do wonder if you somehow managed to make the spectators choose a particular envelope. Ask them to open their envelopes; they will find nothing but blank paper inside.

6 Open the flap of the remaining envelope and pretend to reach inside. In reality you insert your first and second fingers in the envelope while your thumb pinches the banknote on the back of the envelope. Slowly pull out the note.

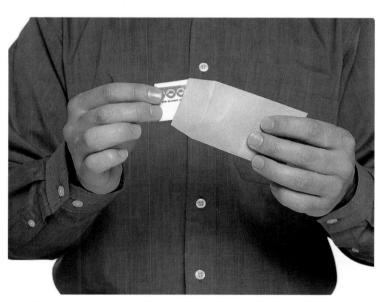

7 From the front, the illusion is perfect. It looks as if the banknote was inside the envelope the whole time.

8 Finally, unfold the note and display it at your fingertips.

money miracle

Three envelopes and two pieces of blank paper are introduced. A banknote of high value is borrowed from a trusting member of the audience. The paper and the banknote are folded in an identical manner and inserted into the envelopes. While the magician's back is turned, the spectator mixes the envelopes until even they are unsure which envelope contains the note. The three envelopes are set on the table. Immediately the magician picks up two envelopes and, without

any hesitation, tears them up into shreds and tosses the pieces aside. The final envelope is opened carefully by the spectator and inside is the unharmed banknote, much to the relief of the lender!

You could use your own banknote, but one of the most important aims in magic is to make the audience care about what you are doing. If you borrow a large sum of money, there is a lot of fun to be had from this situation.

1 To prepare, secretly mark an envelope on both sides, using a pencil. The marks should be small and very light, but clear enough for you to see. (Manila envelopes often have a natural grain with an identifying feature so you may not need to make a mark at all.)

2 Fold a banknote and two pieces of blank paper in quarters. Try to make sure that all three look identical.

3 Hand the two pieces of folded paper and the banknote to a spectator and ask them to insert each one into an envelope. Be sure to hand over the secretly marked envelope and the banknote last and watch as the note is sealed inside.

4 Turn your back and have all three envelopes mixed by the spectator so that even they are not sure which one contains the banknote.

5 Ask for all three envelopes to be laid in a row on the table. The reason you marked the envelope on both sides is because you are not sure how the spectator will set the envelopes on the table, and it is better if you do not rearrange them.

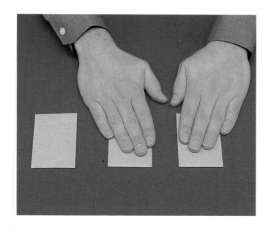

6 Turn around and, without a moment's hesitation, spot the marked envelope. Slam your hands down on to the other two envelopes. Pick them up off the table and rip them to shreds. The success of this trick relies on the speed with which you make your decision. The faster you tear up the envelopes, the more amazing the finale and the more amazed your spectators will be.

7 Ask the lender of the note to carefully open the remaining envelope and remove the contents.

1089

A number is chosen at random and is shown to match an earlier prediction. This is an interesting mathematical principle with many uses. The number will always be 1089.

1 Ask somebody to write down any three-figure number, for example:

8 3 2

Ask them to reverse the number and to subtract the smaller number from the larger:

```
  8 3 2
- 2 3 8
  5 9 4
```

Now ask them to reverse the total and to add both numbers together:

```
    8 3 2
  - 2 3 8
    5 9 4
  + 4 9 5
  1 0 8 9
```

2 Try this with various numbers. It is possible that when you reach the final stage the spectator only has a three-digit number. If so, the number will always be 198. Ask how many digits are in their final number. If they say "Three", simply add another stage. Ask them to reverse their total once again and to add them together again. This will ensure the total is 1089.

Because the number is always the same, you cannot repeat this trick to the same audience. However, you can take advantage of this knowledge, as follows.

1089 – book test

Here the distraction of the book is a smokescreen, a layer of "misdirection" designed to take the audience's attention away from the true method, which is clearly mathematical.

1 To prepare, take a book and look up page 10. Go down eight lines and look at the ninth word. Write this word on a piece of paper and seal it in an envelope.

2 At the beginning of your performance, introduce the sealed envelope containing your prediction, and ask a spectator to look after it.

3 Perform 1089 as detailed above, but do not ask the spectator to reveal the total out loud. Show your book and ask that the first two digits be used to find a page. Ask the spectator to turn to that page (page 10). The next digit, you explain, is to represent a line on that page and the final digit is to represent a word on that line. Once the word has been found, ask the spectator to read it out loud. Take back the book and have the envelope opened to show that your prediction matches the chosen word.

> tip *For an extra subtlety, choose a book in which the eighth line down on page 10 does not exist. When your spectator tells you there isn't a word there, ask them to turn to the next page instead. This little hiccup makes it seem unlikely that you knew which page was going to be chosen.*

double book test

A book is chosen from a stack of books and a page and line are chosen completely at random. The magician leaves the room so it is impossible to cheat. From the chosen line, one word is decided on. The book is closed. The magician comes back into the room and, using the hidden powers of the human mind, is able to write down the word being thought of.

1 You can use as many books as you wish, but for every book you must have a duplicate copy hidden in another room. Ask a spectator to choose one of the books and note the title. Ask for a random page number to be called out, and also a line number. Then ask for a small number between 1 and 10, to indicate the word on

the line. Explain that to avoid any cheating, you will leave the room until the book has been looked at. Once the door is closed, simply look up the corresponding page, line and word in the duplicate book.

2 When you re-enter the room, act like a mind-reader and theatrically reveal the chosen word – you could write it down on a large sheet of card and ask the spectator to shout out the word first before you show your prediction.

> tip *It is also possible to do this trick while remaining in the same room. You will need a friend at the back of the room. They look up the word for you and write it down on a large sheet and hold it up so that you can see it. Everyone else is looking at you, so they will not look behind them.*

the big prediction

A large prediction is shown to the audience and displayed in full view. Then a card is chosen from a shuffled deck. The prediction is shown and, after some comical byplay, is proved to be correct. This effect is most suitable for a large audience. It shows how a simple idea can be *made to work for a big crowd using few props – a classic example of "Packs Flat, Plays Big". If you begin in a very serious manner, the moment of comedy – when the cards are seen stuck to the back of the board – can be very funny indeed.*

1 To prepare, make a prediction by folding a board (A1 size) in half. On one of the outer sides draw a large question mark. On the other, glue one set of cards in four rows. The cards should be in suit and numerical order, and each index should be visible.

2 The inside of the board should be made to resemble a giant playing card (in this example the Ace of Clubs). Use a computer to generate the image, then cut and paste it on to the board.

3 Take another deck of cards and place a duplicate of the prediction on the bottom of the deck, in preparation to force this card on a spectator.

4 Force this card, using any force method you are confident with. (Seen here is the Hindu Force; *see* Card Magic chapter for more details.)

5 In performance, show the prediction (with the question mark towards the audience) and place it to one side. Take the deck of cards and give them a quick shuffle, making sure the force card remains in the appropriate position. Force the Ace of Clubs, then give the spectator the cards to shuffle and mix. You no longer need the cards anyway.

6 Once again show the prediction and ask the audience if they would be impressed if the chosen card was on the other side of the board. Turn over the board and show the complete deck. Appear to search for a few seconds, then point out the selected card.

7 After the laughter subsides, open the board completely to show that your prediction really does match the chosen card. Try this out the next time you get a chance to perform for a large group of people. It is a good example of how the presentation is sometimes more important than the trick itself, which in this case is fairly basic.

black magic

This is one of the few tricks for which you need a "stooge" or assistant, someone you can trust to keep the secret. The stooge is asked to leave the room (out of earshot) while a member of the audience names any object in sight. The stooge returns and the magician explains that, using the power of the human mind, he will send his thoughts across the room so that this person will be able to reveal which object was chosen. The magician points at various objects in the room – maybe ten in total – and the stooge is indeed able to choose the correct object single time.

You can repeat this trick without fear of the secret being found out if each time you change the objects and the number of things you point to.

method
The secret to Black Magic is in the title! As with many tricks, the method is very simple. Simply tell your assistant beforehand that you will point to a number of items. One of them will be black. The next object will be the chosen object. This is a very adaptable trick because you can use absolutely anything, anywhere. The stooge should act as if trying to read your mind.

Left: A number of objects, which can easily be found on a desk in an office, could be used for this trick – for example, a stapler, scissors, envelope, pen, cup and adhesive tape.

temple of wisdom

The magician explains that mind-reading requires someone to act as the sender and another to act as the receiver. A spectator is chosen to act as the receiver and leaves the room. While they are out of the room, the rest of the audience decide on a small number. Let us assume it is 12. The participant comes back into the room and places their fingertips on the temples of the magician (the sender), who pretends to send the number psychically. The receiver concentrates hard, then correctly reveals the chosen number. This can be repeated as many times as you wish.

The method relies on a "stooge" whom you have briefed before the performance and whom you can trust to keep the secret. This trick can be repeated as many times as you wish.

method
When the stooge touches your temples, pass on the chosen number by the subtle action of clenching your jaw. Your temples will pulse each time you squeeze, without anybody else noticing. Try thinking of other ways to signal the number such as the position of your feet or the number of fingers you are holding open in your lap. These subtle codes can be very baffling and are great party tricks.

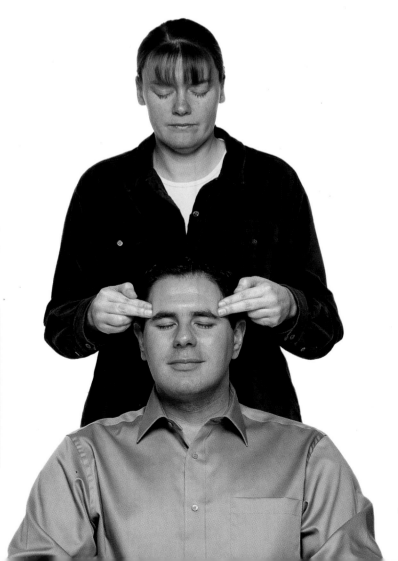

silk, thimble and paper magic

Magic tricks using simple, low-cost, everyday objects such as silk handkerchiefs and paper have always been popular. Thimble manipulation is a small but very well-explored area of magic, and a thimble is an easy object to carry around. With props that are so readily available, you are able to perform at a moment's notice. The following pages introduce you to many sleights using these conveniently sized objects.

- silk magic
- thimble magic
- paper magic

introduction

Many areas within the art of magic are relatively small when compared to, for example, card tricks. However it is important to offer your audience a variety of magical effects, and so in this chapter we have grouped together three smaller areas of conjuring: magic with handkerchiefs or "silks", magic with thimbles, and magic with paper.

Handkerchiefs are frequently used in magic. Some of them are ordinary, the kind you might find in a department store, but most are extremely thin and made of silk. These can be purchased from magic shops and are ideal – they can be displayed as a large piece of fabric, but it is also possible to squash them down into a very small bundle which can be handled and hidden easily. Magicians call these handkerchiefs "silks". Silks can be purchased in a number of different sizes, the most common being 23, 30, 45, 60 and 90cm (9, 12, 18, 24 and 36in) square. They are also available in almost every colour imaginable.

The size and shape of a thimble make it a perfect object for performing sleight of hand. One of the earliest known references to thimble magic is in *The Art Of Modern Conjuring* by Professor Henry Garenne, published in 1879. The trick was entitled "The Travelling Thimble". Since then magicians have invented many ways to make thimbles multiply, change colour, penetrate handkerchiefs, appear and disappear. Many beautiful routines can be performed with thimbles, and several of the more basic sleights and tricks can be learnt in this chapter. Magicians who perform a traditional stage act often feature thimbles as part of their programme. Although small, they are visible from a distance and provide a great example of digital dexterity.

Paper comes in every shape and size and is, therefore, often an ideal medium with which to work. One of the most popular paper tricks is Torn and Restored Newspaper. A description of the effect is unnecessary as the title says it all! This chapter will reveal a simple version which allows

Above: Thimbles can be used for close-up magic or as part of a larger stage act because they can be seen for quite a distance.

Below: This wood engraving shows the early nineteenth-century French master magician Robert-Houdin producing plumes of flowers and showers of candy from a silk handkerchief.

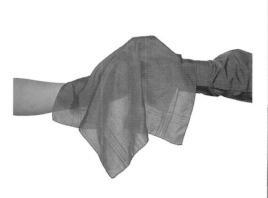

Above: Learn The Trick Which Fooled Houdini and make a spectator's watch vanish under a silk handkerchief in impossible circumstances.

Above: Baffle your audience by magically producing a thimble from a banknote. Thimbles are wonderfully versatile objects for using in tricks.

Above: Is it really possible to move an object with the power of the human mind? Your audience will believe so when you show them the Telekinetic Paper.

you to cut a strip of newspaper into two pieces and magically join them back together again. You will also learn how to perform the classic effect, Snowstorm in China. Versions of this are still being used by many professional magicians around the world, and will finish any act in a truly spectacular fashion. Many of the tricks you will learn here can be strung together to produce a very effective act, and when you have had a little experience, you will also find that you can adapt a number of the techniques to create tricks of your own.

Below left: Snowstorm in China is a spectacular trick that makes use of – among other things – an ornamental Chinese fan and coloured tissue paper torn up to form confetti. The air is filled with a snowstorm of confetti at the end of the trick.
Below: Turn a jug of milk into a large silk handkerchief in Milk to Silk.

silk magic

There are literally thousands of tricks you can do with handkerchiefs, and some of these are described here. You should not aim to put together a whole show of handkerchief magic, as this may be a little tiresome for your audience. However, handkerchief tricks can be very spectacular, and if you use them as part of your act you can make a big impression on your audience.

simple silk production

There are dozens of ways to produce a silk from thin air. This version and the Mid-Air Silk Production which follows are two of the easiest and most magical. For extra effect, sprinkle confetti or glitter into the folds as you prepare the silk.

1 To prepare, place a silk handkerchief in front of you, completely flat and with one corner towards you.

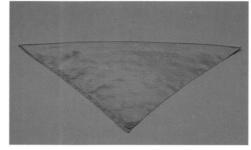

2 Fold the silk away from you, in half and along the diagonal.

3 Begin rolling the silk from the fold. Try to make the roll as tight and neat as possible.

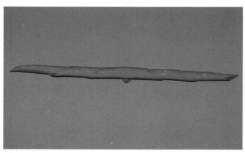

4 Continue rolling the silk until you reach the far corner.

5 Roll the silk from one end to the other, again trying to ensure a tight, neat roll.

6 Leave a tiny "ear" of silk at the end, as shown here.

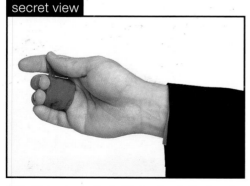

`secret view`

7 Grip the rolled silk in the right-hand Finger Palm position (*see* Money Magic chapter) so that the "ear" of the silk is clipped tightly between your right thumb and first finger.

8 Viewed from the front, if the hand is held naturally, the silk is completely hidden. With your right hand, point to an imaginary spot in the air to your left, at about chest level.

9 Reach up to that point and simultaneously, with a gentle jerk of the right hand, let the silk unroll, ready for use in another trick.

mid-air silk production

The magician's hand is shown unmistakably empty but as they reach into the air a beautiful silk appears! Practice is required to make this *always look good, but the result is so spectacular it is well worth the effort. It makes an ideal opening trick.*

1 For this trick you must be wearing a jacket or long-sleeved shirt. To prepare, bunch up a silk handkerchief in your left hand. The bundle should be very small.

2 Extend your right arm and push the silk into the crook of your elbow, covering the silk with a fold of cloth from the sleeve.

3 Keeping the right elbow slightly bent will ensure the silk remains hidden. You are now ready to begin performing the trick.

4 Show that both hands are completely empty. Keep the arms bent just enough to prevent the silk from being exposed. (This restriction of movement is the reason why the mid-air silk production is a good trick to open with.)

5 This side view shows what happens next. The right hand quickly and sharply reaches up into the air, snapping open the fabric at the right elbow. The silk is catapulted up into the air and is caught by the right hand.

6 From the front, the silk seems to appear from nowhere!

rose to silk

A red rose worn on the magician's lapel is dramatically changed into silk. It would also be possible to add the prepared silk to a *bunch of real roses. The magician could then pluck the top of a rose off a specially prepared stem as an alternative to his lapel.*

1 You will need to wear a jacket with a buttonhole on the lapel. To prepare, lay a silk handkerchief flat, with one of the corners pointing towards you.

2 Begin rolling the silk towards the top corner. Try to make the roll as tight as possible. The neater you roll the silk, the better the rose will look.

3 Continue rolling until you reach the opposite corner.

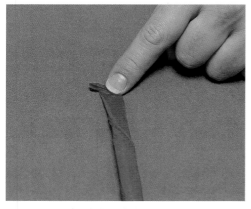

4 At one end, bend the corner at right angles to create an "ear".

5 Starting at this end, tightly roll the silk to the opposite end. You will start to form a small bundle.

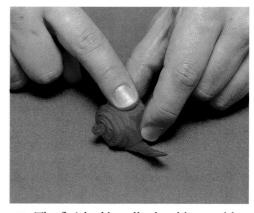

6 The finished bundle should resemble a rose. Leave a small amount of silk at the end of the roll.

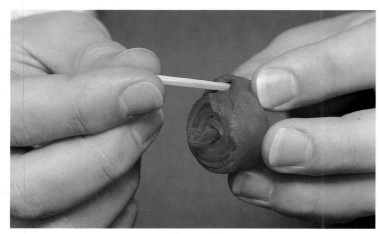

7 With a match or similar object, tuck the loose end into the fold to hold the bundle in position.

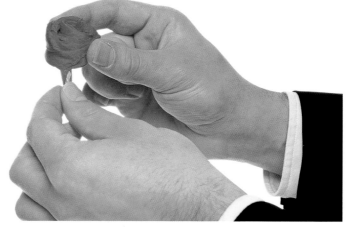

8 Push the loose end all the way through to the back of the silk, being careful not to ruin the folds that make up the rose.

9 Take this loose end and push it through the buttonhole in your lapel. You are now ready to perform. At a glance, it will look just as though you are wearing a rose in your buttonhole.

10 With your left hand, hold the rose in place by gently squeezing the sides. With your right fingers, grip the centre of the rose (the "ear").

11 Gently pull the "ear" outwards, and the rose will visibly start to transform into a large silk.

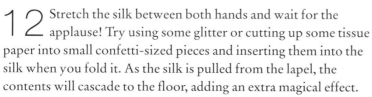

12 Stretch the silk between both hands and wait for the applause! Try using some glitter or cutting up some tissue paper into small confetti-sized pieces and inserting them into the silk when you fold it. As the silk is pulled from the lapel, the contents will cascade to the floor, adding an extra magical effect.

pencil through silk

A silk handkerchief is draped over a pencil, which is pushed straight through the centre of the silk. The handkerchief is displayed to show *that it is completely unharmed. This kind of impromptu magic gives you the ability to perform a miracle with objects that can be borrowed.*

1 Hold a corner of a silk handkerchief in your left hand and display a pencil in your right fingertips.

2 Drape the silk over the top of the pencil so that the centre lies on the point of the pencil.

3 Close your left hand around the pencil so that the shape can clearly be seen through the fabric.

secret view

secret view

4 At the same moment, secretly bend your right hand at the wrist to bring the pencil back to a position outside the silk. From the front, this move is unseen and the silk continues to hold the shape of the pencil.

5 Immediately manoeuvre the pencil back up to a position behind the silk and under the left thumb. The moves in steps 3 and 4 are achieved in one swift motion, and should only take about one second.

6 Give the pencil a push upwards and the tip will appear to penetrate the silk. In reality the pencil simply slides up against the silk and into view.

7 From the front, the illusion is perfect and your audience will believe the pencil has really been pushed through the middle of the silk handkerchief.

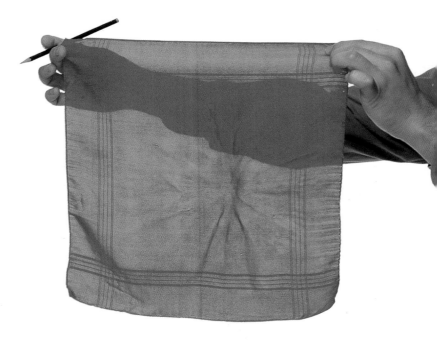

8 Pull the pencil completely free of the silk and once again display the pencil in your right fingertips.

9 Open the silk between both hands to show that it is undamaged. You can hand both the silk and the pencil to your spectators for examination, and then perhaps use the same items for your next trick.

silk vanish

A silk handkerchief is pushed into the left hand. After a suitable flourish, the hand is shown completely empty! There are many ways to "vanish" a silk. This trick uses what magicians call a "pull" – a secret holder worn out of sight, usually under a jacket. The item to *be vanished is placed inside. The holder is then pulled back into the jacket by a piece of elastic. Pulls are available from magic shops in a variety of shapes and sizes, but you can easily make your own. Pulls can also be worn within the sleeves of a jacket.*

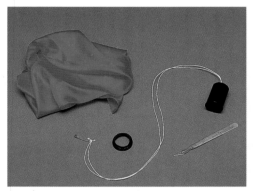

1 To make the "pull", remove the lid from a 35mm film canister and cut a hole about 2cm (¾in) in diameter. Pierce a small hole in the bottom of the canister and, with a simple knot inside, attach a piece of elastic approximately 60cm (24in) long. (The length depends on your waist size. For greater strength, cut double the length and fold the elastic in half.) Attach a safety pin to the free end of the elastic. Put the lid back on the canister.

2 Thread the elastic through your belt loops from your left side around to your right side. Attach the safety pin to a loop on the right of your body. It may take several attempts to find the correct position for the "pull" and the elastic may need to be cut down or adjusted.

3 The canister should rest at a position approximately in line with your trouser pocket, and the tension of the elastic should hold it loosely but firmly against the belt loop. Test the operation of the "pull" by pulling the canister away from the belt loop to a position in front of your chest. Let the canister go, and it should return to the position it started in. If not, readjust the gimmick.

secret view

4 In performance, hold the "pull" in your left hand. Stretch out the elastic so that your left hand can maintain a position just in front of your body. Be careful not to pull open your jacket and reveal your secret – this is an exposed view of the position you should be in.

5 Show the silk handkerchief in your right hand. Pretend to insert it into your left hand. In reality, you are pushing it into the canister through the hole in the lid.

6 Continue pushing the silk into your hand until it is completely contained within the canister.

7 This exposed view shows the position after the silk is inside the gimmick. At this stage, allow the elastic to pull the canister through your fingers and back into your jacket. Keep your hand in a position that still looks as though it holds the silk. Your spectator's view remains as in step 6.

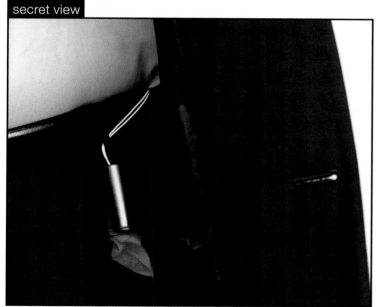

8 The canister rests back where it started, in a position under the jacket by your left pocket.

9 Move both hands to a position in front of your chest and slowly show that they are completely empty. The silk has vanished!

milk to silk

Milk is poured from a jug into a large cup. The cup is turned upside down but the milk mysteriously fails to fall out! The magician reaches into the upturned cup to reveal that the milk has changed into a white silk handkerchief. This trick creates a beautiful effect and is ideal for larger audiences. For added effect, cut white paper into confetti-size pieces and place them in the folds of the silk before placing the handkerchief in the cup. While performing this effect, it is important that you are aware at all times of the position of the cup in relation to your audience. If you hold the cup too low, the secret will be revealed. A cocktail shaker is the ideal size cup to use.

1 To prepare, carefully measure and cut a piece of board that will divide a cup internally in two. The height of the partition should be about three-quarters the height of the cup.

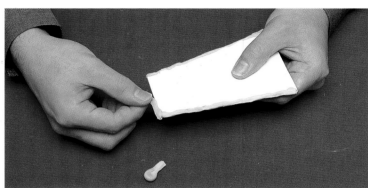

2 Mould some reusable adhesive around the bottom and side edges of the partition.

3 Push the partition into the cup and secure it to the sides with the adhesive. The idea is to create a watertight compartment. If you perform this trick on a regular basis, make the partition longer-lasting by using a sheet of plastic and a silicone sealant.

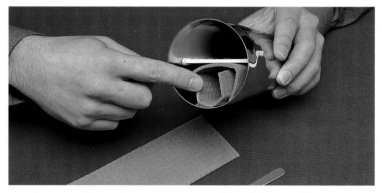

4 Insert a piece of sponge into one side of the cup. You may need to cut the sponge to shape and experiment to determine how much to use. The best sponge to use is the "super-absorbent" type which holds many times its own weight in liquid.

5 To complete the preparation, push a white silk handkerchief into the other compartment. One corner should be near the top, but make sure it is pushed down out of sight.

6 Place the prepared cup on to a table, along with a jug full of milk.

7 Begin your performance by carefully pouring some milk into the sponge side of the cup. Once again, experimentation will determine exactly how much milk to use. The milk is absorbed by the sponge.

8 It is wise to wait for a few seconds to ensure that the sponge soaks up all of the milk. Place one hand over the mouth of the cup and get ready to turn it upside down.

9 The slickest way to turn the cup is to allow it to swivel between your left fingers and thumb. When it is upside down, freeze for a few seconds as if something might have gone wrong. This creates a moment of tension and humour if acted well.

11 Slowly pull the silk out completely, allowing it to cascade from the cup.

10 Take away your hand from under the mouth of the cup and show that the milk has mysteriously defied gravity. Sometimes a small piece of silk will begin to fall from the cup but this helps to create the illusion that the milk is turning into silk.

the trick which fooled houdini

A borrowed watch is placed under a handkerchief and several spectators confirm its presence. In an instant the watch disappears without a trace. Just as mysteriously, the watch can be made to reappear. Rumour has it that one of the world's most famous magicians, Harry Houdini, was fooled by this trick back in the 1920s!

This is one of the few tricks you will learn which requires an assistant, or "stooge". Choose someone who can act well and whom you can trust to keep the secret.

1 Borrow a watch from a spectator. Place it under the centre of a handkerchief. Ask several people to reach underneath to verify that the watch is indeed still there.

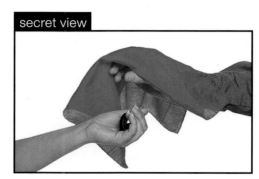

secret view

2 The last person to reach under the handkerchief is your stooge, who secretly takes away the watch. To add a simple piece of "misdirection", move the handkerchief away from your assistant's hand as the secret steal takes place. All eyes will follow the handkerchief.

3 Make a magical gesture and whip the handkerchief away to show that the watch has well and truly gone!

thimble magic

A thimble is compact enough to be carried wherever you go and will generate interest as soon as it is made to appear. By linking several of the effects together, a nice routine can be developed. For instance, after performing the Linking Paper Clips, you could produce the thimble from the banknote (see opposite) and continue your routine with the Jumping Thimble, finishing with the Vanishing Thimble.

jumping thimble

A thimble magically jumps back and forth between two fingers. Although this is a simple stunt, it is amazing how well the illusion works. The trick can also be performed with a finger ring, and is a good impromptu stunt to remember.

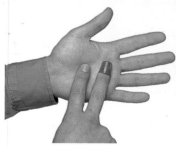   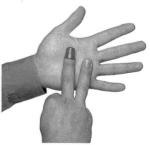

1 Place a thimble on the tip of the right second finger. Hold the first and second fingers against the palm of your left hand.

2 Tap your fingers against your palm three times. After the second tap, the fingers come approximately 10cm (4in) away from the palm.

3 The first finger quickly curls in and the third finger uncurls.

4 As the fingers reach the palm of the hand, it seems the thimble has jumped. The thimble can be made to jump back by reversing the procedure.

thimble from banknote

A banknote is shown on both sides and rolled into a cone. From within the cone, a thimble is produced. This makes a very startling and highly unusual production. As mentioned previously, stringing various effects together is a nice way to present a small impromptu show, and this is an ideal opening effect. It introduces the thimble unexpectedly and will command interest from your audience.

secret view

1 Place a thimble on your right second finger. Hold a banknote with both hands, between your first fingers and thumbs. Curl in your other fingers.

2 From the front, your spectators can see the whole surface of the banknote and the thimble is completely hidden.

secret view

3 Turn the note so that you show both sides completely. Be careful not to prematurely expose the thimble.

secret view

4 Open your second finger so that the thimble rests on the top right of the banknote. The note is clipped against the thimble, between the first and second fingers, and starts to curl in a cone shape.

5 The left hand lifts its end up and over the thimble. It continues to roll the note over and around the second finger, the first finger lifting out of the way.

6 The result is a cone, formed around the second finger of the right hand.

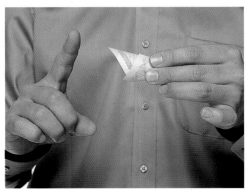

7 Pull out your finger, leaving the thimble within the cone.

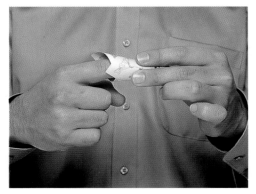

8 Dip your finger back into the cone and push it securely into the thimble.

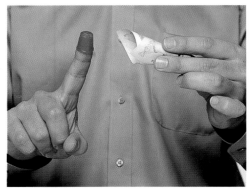

9 Remove your finger from the cone and display the thimble.

thimble thumb clip

A thimble is caused to disappear and then reappear from the tip of the fingers. Anything that fits on the end of your first finger will work perfectly well. For a really impromptu performance, try using *a candy wrapper fashioned into a thimble or a hoop-shaped potato chip. The Thimble Thumb Clip is one of the main sleights necessary to master in order to perform many thimble tricks.*

secret view

1 Place a thimble on the tip of your right first finger. Curl your first finger inwards so that the thimble rests in the crotch of your thumb.

secret view

2 Squeeze your thumb against the thimble and uncurl your finger, leaving the thimble clipped between the base of your thumb and first finger.

3 From the front, the thimble is hidden from view and the hand looks perfectly empty. In performance you will need to be aware of angle restrictions.

vanishing thimble

Once you have learnt the Thimble Thumb Clip, you can try the following routine. When executed correctly, the illusion is superb. When you have mastered the trick of making the thimble reappear *from behind your hand, you can easily use the same sleight to make it reappear from anywhere you choose, for example from behind the ear of a child or from inside someone else's pocket.*

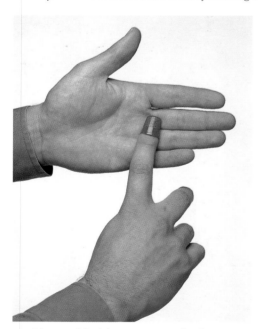

1 Place a thimble on your right first finger, and hold it against the base of the left fingers. Your left palm should face the audience.

2 Curl in your left second, third and fourth fingers. Open the fingers again to show that the thimble is still there, then start to close the fingers as before.

3 Just as the fingers cover the thimble, begin to remove the right first finger, simultaneously raising the hand and placing the thimble into a Thumb Clip.

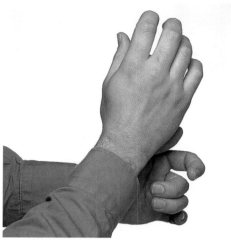

4 This view shows the right hand as it moves upwards.

secret view

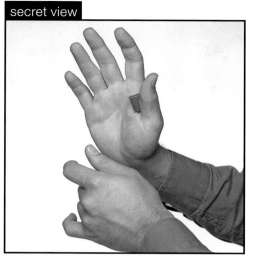

5 The view from the back shows the thimble in the Thumb Clip.

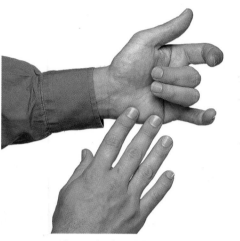

6 Bring the right hand back down to the position shown.

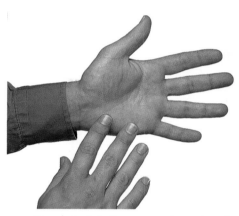

7 Open the left fingers to show that the thimble has vanished. These actions should happen smoothly and briskly. The spectators should not be aware that the thimble has gone from the left fingers until they are opened.

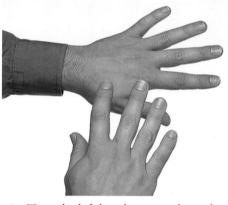

8 Turn the left hand over to show the back of the hand, then show the palm once again.

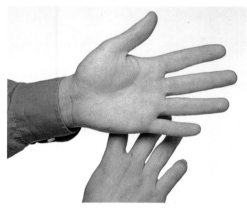

9 The right hand reaches behind the left and secretly replaces the thumb-clipped thimble on the first finger.

secret view

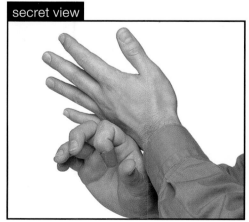

10 This view from the back shows the thimble being recovered.

11 Finish by displaying the thimble back on the fingertip against the palm of the left hand.

thimble from silk

A thimble is produced from a silk, ready to be used for other amazing tricks such as Thimble through Silk. Even though you might not think *this is a startling piece of magic, it is a nice visual way to introduce a thimble; better than simply pulling a thimble out of a pocket.*

secret view

1 Hold a thimble in the right-hand Thumb Clip position. Display a silk handkerchief, stretching it between the two top corners with both hands.

2 From the front, all the fingers and the entire silk can be seen, and the thimble remains completely hidden.

3 Cross your arms to show the back of the silk, then uncross your arms again.

secret view

4 Hold the silk by a corner in the left hand. Your right hand reaches under the silk and retrieves the thimble from the Thumb Clip.

5 Drape the silk momentarily over your right first finger.

6 Whip away the silk to display a thimble on your fingertip.

thimble through silk

A thimble is placed under a silk and visibly melts through the fabric. This trick is the perfect follow-up to Thimble from Silk. Although it is not easy to learn or perform, it is beautiful to watch when performed well. Use a thimble that contrasts with the colour of the silk.

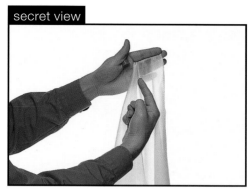

secret view

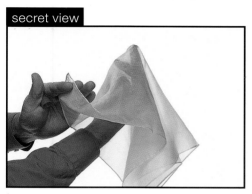

secret view

1 Hold a silk handkerchief with your left hand. It should be clipped between the first and second fingers, draping down the inside of the hand. The right hand displays a thimble on the first fingertip.

2 Hold the silk about chest level and start to move the thimble under the silk. As it passes the left hand, the thimble is secretly placed into the left-hand Thumb Clip position.

3 Without hesitation, continue to move the finger under the silk to a position in the centre. Under cover of the silk, extend your second finger and bend your first finger backwards. This can be seen here through the silk for ease of explanation.

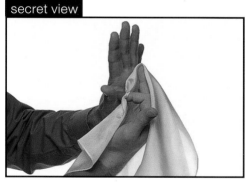

secret view

4 Make a gesture with your left hand, which positions itself directly behind the right hand.

5 During this gesture, push the thimble from the Thumb Clip on to the first finger through the silk. In this view, the silk is lifted for ease of explanation.

secret view

6 The first finger straightens behind the second finger. Care must be taken to keep the thimble hidden.

7 From the front, the thimble remains totally unseen.

8 With a shake of the hand, lower the second finger so that the thimble pops into view.

paper magic

A most versatile material, paper is easily available and comes in a wide variety of shapes, colours, sizes and thicknesses. Of the many tricks that use paper, a few are given here which are simple to prepare, and very enjoyable to watch. Cut and Restored Newspaper, together with Snowstorm in China, are perfect for a platform or stage show because they can be seen from a distance.

telekinetic paper

A small piece of paper is folded and stood upright on a table. Apparently using nothing but the power of the human mind, the paper is made to fall over. Is this a true demonstration of telekinesis? No, but it certainly looks like it!

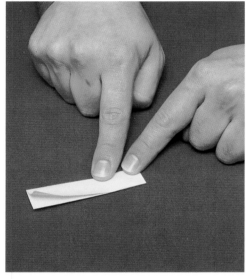

1 For this trick, you will need a small piece of paper, approximately 6 x 3cm (2¼ x 1¼in). The exact size is unimportant but the success of this trick depends on the height of the paper being sufficiently more than the width. Fold the paper in half along its length.

2 Open up the fold to form a "V" shape and position the paper about arm's length in front of you. Due to the height of the paper, it is relatively easy to secretly offset its balance and make it fall over. Rub your first and second finger on your arm, explaining that you are harnessing some static electricity.

3 Gently swing your arm to a position directly in front of the paper but about 15cm (6in) away. As your arm swings around, the air will move and cause the paper to become unstable. As you are a little distance away, the change in air current will take one or two seconds to reach the paper – this will also help to disguise the method to this trick.

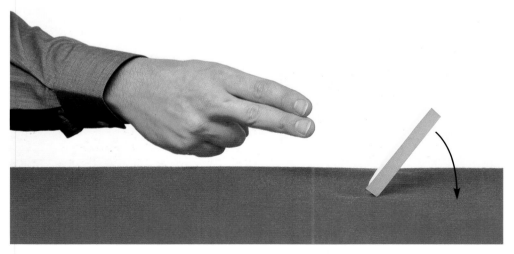

4 The paper will fall to the table. Try experimenting with the distance you place between your fingers and the paper. The further away you are, the better the illusion looks. Despite the fact that the method is very simple, the trick itself is extremely baffling – as you will see when you try this out for yourself.

cut and restored newspaper

A strip of newspaper is unmistakably snipped into two pieces, yet is instantly shown to be restored. This is an ideal trick for a larger audience. It can be performed for a group of children or adults with equal success.

To add to the presentation, invite a member of the audience up on to the stage with you. Give them a pair of scissors and a normal strip of newspaper and ask them to follow your actions carefully. You will always succeed and they will always fail. This can be very comical.

If you plan your moves carefully, after a few demonstrations you could switch your strip with theirs and have the spectator "unexpectedly" succeed. This would be a great finish to the routine.

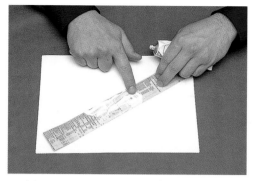

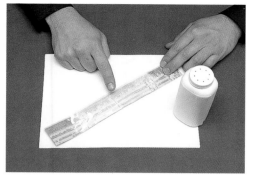

1 To prepare, cut a strip of newspaper from the financial section. The content of such a page will help to camouflage the join. Place the newspaper on top of a scrap of paper to protect the table. Apply a thin layer of rubber cement glue to the middle section of the strip, as shown here.

2 Wait for the glue to dry completely, then apply some talcum powder to the covered area. This will stop the glued surface of the strip prematurely sticking at the wrong moment. Blow any excess powder off the newspaper so that everything looks normal.

3 The final piece of preparation is to fold the strip in half with a sharp crease.

4 To begin the performance, display the strip of newspaper in one hand and the scissors in the other.

5 Fold the strip in half along the crease and clearly snip off about 1cm (½in) from the centre. Try to make the cut as straight as possible. Because of the rubber cement glue, the two separate pieces will be glued back together at the join.

6 Open the strip and the paper will have magically restored itself. You can stop here or repeat the cutting and restoring process. It all depends how much of the strip you covered in glue.

7 Instead of cutting the paper straight, experiment by cutting it at a right angle. You can also place the glue at strategically placed points on the strip of newspaper so that you can begin by actually cutting the strip into two pieces. Then place the two pieces together, cutting again to re-join them.

snowstorm in china

Several sheets of tissue paper are displayed and torn into strips. They are soaked in a glass of water and squeezed dry. An ornamental Chinese fan is used to aid the drying process and the paper begins to turn into confetti, creating a mini snowstorm that fills the air and covers the stage. This is a spectacular closing effect for a show.

There are several versions of this traditional trick. The following method is the invention of a wonderful Hungarian magician, the Great Kovari. We graciously thank him for allowing us to share his method with you. Many top professional magicians feature versions of this trick in their act.

1 To prepare, cut a strip of flexible plastic, approximately 1 x 10cm (½ x 4in). Pierce a small hole in the centre with a sharp point.

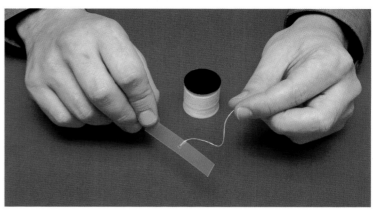

2 Attach a short length of thread to the plastic strip by tying it in a knot through the hole.

3 Use adhesive tape to attach the thread to the back of a fan so that the plastic strip hangs down behind the centre.

4 Make a hole in the top of an egg and empty the inside. Wash it out and let it dry completely before continuing.

5 Cut some coloured tissue paper into confetti-size pieces. Carefully pack them into the egg.

6 Bend the plastic strip in half, then place it carefully into the hole in the egg so that when the strip expands it grips the sides of the egg securely.

secret view

7 Cut two notches into the sides of a box. These will function as a display stand for the fan, as well as a secret holder for the wet tissue.

8 Set a table with the fan displayed in the box, a glass of water to the left and some tissue paper sheets at the back of the box. From the back, you can also see the egg hanging from the fan.

9 From the front, there is a pretty display of props and the egg remains hidden behind the fan.

10 To perform, display the various coloured sheets of tissue paper and clearly tear them into shreds. ▶

11 Roll up the shreds into a ball and drop it into the glass, soaking the paper thoroughly.

12 Replace the glass on the table and display the wet ball of paper in your right fingertips. Squeeze it dry.

13 Now make a fake transfer into your left hand. Place the ball of paper against the fingers of your open left hand and close it as your right hand comes away with the ball hidden behind the fingers.

secret view

14 This close-up view shows the position of the hands as they come together. Your body movement should suggest that the ball of paper is really in the left hand.

secret view

15 The right hand drops the wad of soggy paper into the box as it reaches for the fan.

16 This view from the back shows the paper being dropped as the hand reaches for the bottom of the fan.

17 Hold the fan up with the left hand hidden behind it. Say that you are going to dry the paper by fanning it.

secret view

18 With the left hand, secretly pull the egg off the plastic strip. The fan provides a great deal of cover for this.

19 Squeeze the egg tightly, breaking the shell, as you rapidly wave the fan to distribute the confetti pieces as far and wide as possible. The broken eggshell will drop to the floor with the paper, and the evidence will not be noticed. All that is left to do is tidy up!

money
magic

Money is the one thing that most people carry with them at all times. The following pages reveal some wonderful magic tricks for you to perform. Have you ever dreamed of making money appear from nowhere at your fingertips, or of being able to change a blank piece of paper into a banknote? If so, your dreams are about to come true – or so your audience will believe!

- easy money tricks
- basic coin techniques
- coin vanishes
- more money tricks

introduction

Rightly or wrongly, the one thing most people desire in their lives, along with health and happiness, is money. If we could really perform magic, we would make money appear so that we could live the life of our dreams and help others live theirs. The idea of producing money out of thin air was born a long time ago. There cannot be many children who have never had a coin pulled from behind their ear.

Towards the end of the nineteenth century, one of the most skilled coin manipulators of all time created an act entitled "The Miser's Dream". His name was Thomas Nelson Downs and he billed himself as the "King of Koins". The act is said to have lasted about 30 minutes and contained only coin magic. His act was so popular that he left his American homeland in 1899 and travelled throughout Europe, where he found further fame and success. Part of his act involved showing his hands completely empty, removing his hat, showing that empty too, then producing coin after coin after coin. Each coin was thrown into the hat until it was full of money. "The Ariel Treasury", as it was then called, is now better known by magicians as "The Miser's Dream", in remembrance of the late, great T. Nelson Downs. It is still being performed regularly today, and is received as well now as it was then.

For general coin tricks and coin manipulation you can use any coins that may be to hand, but magicians favour the American half-dollar for its size, weight and

Above: You too can learn how to produce money at your fingertips from out of thin air!

Left: An early poster publicizing the master coin manipulator Thomas Nelson Downs (1867–1938), also known as the "King of Koins". Many theatres and agents were dubious about booking an act comprising only coin tricks, thinking that it would be too monotonous and that the coins would not be seen easily in a large theatre. However, Downs proved the sceptics wrong when his performances caused a sensation wherever he worked.

Above: Magicians all over the world have been performing magic with coins for centuries. Coins are available in all shapes, sizes and colours, and they are easy to find at any time.

Above: No matter where you are in the world, you will always be prepared to amaze and amuse with a few banknotes and a little knowledge of the secrets in this book.

gripping qualities. The milled edge makes it relatively easy to palm and manipulate. Try to choose shiny coins to maximize their visibility. Old coin shops are often a great source for a variety of different coins in all manner of shapes, sizes and colours. Introducing such items to your audiences will cause interest. You may even be able to build a presentation around the existence of the coin. Where does it originate from? How did you come to possess it?

The following pages reveal how to make banknotes and coins appear and disappear (Appearing Money, Handkerchief Coin Vanish), how to cause coins to change places (Switcheroo) and bend (Bending Coin, Versions 1 and 2), and even how to turn a piece of blank paper into a banknote (Paper to Money). Basic sleight of hand is explained, and with the knowledge of a few of these routines you will always be able to perform a trick or two.

Above: Make a coin melt through the centre of a silk handkerchief without any damage whatsoever.

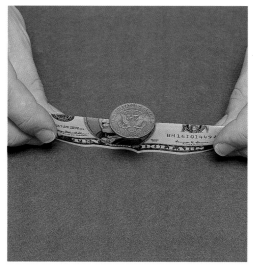

Above: Challenge your friends to balance a coin on the edge of a banknote.

Above: Make a banknote defy gravity by floating it above your hand. No strings attached!

easy money tricks

All of the tricks described in this chapter require money. Thankfully, the only thing you will actually have to invest is your time in order to learn the tricks described. The first few tricks are easy to learn and

perform. They fall into the area of impromptu magic, since they require no special set-up or gimmicks. You can perform these easy money tricks at the drop of a hat.

linking paper clips

Two paperclips and a rubber band are hooked on to a banknote. The three separate objects instantly link together! This is an old classic of

magic and only requires everyday objects, so is ideal for those occasions when you are suddenly asked to perform unprepared.

1 Fold one-third of a banknote under itself and attach a paperclip at the edge.

2 Place a rubber band over the note, at approximately the centre, as shown here.

3 Fold the other side of the note in the opposite direction to the first fold. Using a second paperclip, clip this edge to the top layer of the fold made earlier.

4 Grip both sides of the banknote and gently pull your hands apart until the banknote is stretched out flat.

5 The result is a rubber band with two paperclips linked together, hanging from a banknote. It seems impossible. The three items link so quickly that it will take your spectators completely by surprise.

bending coin (version 1)

A coin is examined and then held in the fingertips. The magician creates an optical illusion which makes the coin look as if it is bending like rubber. This effect can be followed by Version 2, which appears *later in this chapter. To accompany the trick, you could explain that although a coin is made of metal and therefore solid, the magical warmth of your hands can cause it to melt!*

1 Hold a coin with both hands, thumbs on the back of the coin, first and second fingers on the front. Allow as much of the coin's surface as possible to be seen by pushing the thumbs forward and pulling the edges of the coin back.

2 This is the view from above, and it can be seen that a good deal of the front surface of the coin is visible.

3 Move both hands inwards so that the backs of your hands move towards each other. The thumbs maintain contact with the coin at all times. Move your hands back to the position shown in step 2 and repeat the motion five or six times.

heads I win!

A pocket full of change is emptied on to the table and a small selection of coins chosen. While the magician looks away (or leaves the room) the spectator is instructed to turn over two coins at a time, as many *times as desired. Finally they are asked to hide one of the coins under their hand before the magician returns. The magician is able to reveal, with absolute accuracy, whether the hidden coin is heads up or tails up!*

1 Throw some change on to a table. You can use any number of coins, but six or seven is perfect. Note whether there are an even or odd number of coins facing heads up. In our example, there are three heads up so we simply remember "Heads are odd".

2 Turn your back and instruct the spectator to turn over two coins at a time, as many times as desired. All the while, keep remembering "Heads are odd". Ask for any one of the coins to be covered before you turn around.

3 Glance at the uncovered coins on the table to see how many coins are now heads up. In our example, there are three. Remember "Heads are odd"? If there are an odd number left, then the hidden coin must be tails up. If there were an even number remaining heads up, then the hidden coin would also be heads up.

4 Assume a hypnotic state, or pretend to receive psychic vibes, then reveal the orientation of the hidden coin. If your instructions have been followed correctly, Heads I Win! will work every single time. Most people carry small change with them, so you can perform this trick at a moment's notice.

explanation *The reason this trick works is because the coins are turned over two at a time, so if there are an odd number* *of heads facing up at the beginning there will be an odd number of heads facing up at the end, and vice versa.*

impossible coin balance

This is a perfect way to win a drink! Challenge your friends to balance a coin on the edge of a banknote. The chances are, no matter *how hard they try or how many different ways they attempt to tackle the problem, they will not succeed unless they know the secret.*

1 The success of this stunt relies on the use of a crisp banknote. Fold and sharply crease the note in half, along its length.

2 Fold the note in half again, this time along the width. Ensure that the creases are sharp and neat.

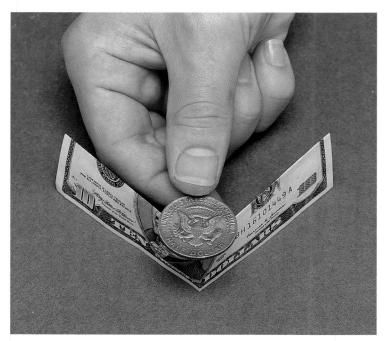

3 Place the note on a table so that the folded edge is pointing upwards. Position a coin on top of the "V" shape. You may even amaze yourself with the next part!

4 Slowly and gently pull both edges of the note away from each other, straightening the paper. The coin will always find its centre of balance and will remain on the folded edge of the note, in an apparently impossible position.

explanation
In reality, the short crease is never pulled completely flat and the tiny kink in the paper is enough to *stop the coin from falling off. Once the banknote is stretched flat, a steady hand is vital for the success of this trick.*

floating banknote

A banknote is held in the fingertips and caused to float away from the hand without any visible means of support. There are many versions of this trick, and nearly all of them are difficult to master.

However, this particular version is surprisingly easy to learn and can be performed at the drop of a hat with only a few seconds of preparation before you begin.

1 To prepare, take a piece of reusable adhesive and attach it to the centre of a banknote.

2 To begin the performance, pick up the note so that the adhesive sticks to your right second fingertip.

3 Rub the note between the palms of both hands, explaining that you are generating static electricity.

secret view

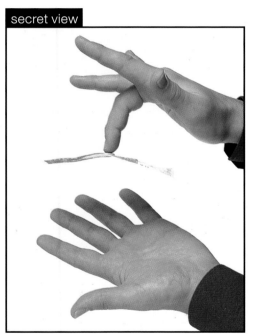

4 Slowly remove your left hand, showing the banknote adhering to your right fingers. Begin to spread the right fingers, simultaneously bending your second finger inwards, which will move the note away from the palm of the hand. From the front, it appears as if the note is floating away from the hand and hovering in mid-air. Watch this in a mirror to see how good it looks.

5 When your second finger is fully extended, the note seems to be floating quite a long way in front of the hand.

6 This view from above shows what is really happening. To finish, slowly bring both hands together again as in step 3, then put the note in your pocket or secretly remove the adhesive and hand out the banknote for examination.

basic coin techniques

Now that you have learnt some easy money tricks, it is time to learn a few sleight-of-hand techniques that will enable you to perform some even more amazing magic. Many of these techniques will take *time and practice to master, but the outcome is most rewarding. As suggested earlier in the book, practising in a mirror will make it much easier for you to correct your own mistakes.*

finger palm and production

The Finger Palm is an essential grip in coin magic, allowing you to secretly hold and therefore hide a coin (or any small object) in your *hand. The coin can then be made to appear from anywhere, using the Finger Palm Production (for example, from behind a child's ear).*

secret view

1 Position the coin at the base of your right second and third fingers. It is held in place by the creases in your skin and by your fingers curling in to hold it. Try to forget that you are holding a coin – look in a mirror to see if you can hold your hand naturally by your side. Your hand should not look as though it were holding anything.

2 You can produce the coin in many different ways. One way is to pretend that you have spotted something floating in the air in front of you. Point it out with the hand that is secretly holding the coin.

3 As you reach for the invisible "something", use your thumb to push the coin from its position at the base of your fingers to the fingertips.

4 Try to allow as much of the coin to be seen as possible. The coin seems to appear during the movement between pointing at the floating object and you reaching for it.

5 From the front, it looks just as if you have plucked a coin from thin air.

thumb clip

This is another technique for gripping a coin secretly in your hand. It can also be used to "vanish" a coin. The beauty of this grip is that *it allows wide movement of the fingers, while convincingly keeping the coin out of sight.*

secret view

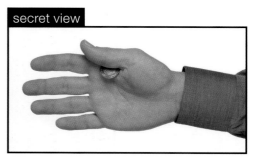
secret view

1 Begin by resting the coin on the right fingers. It should lie flat, in the middle of the first and second fingers.

2 Close the fingers into a fist. The coin almost automatically ends in a position which can be clipped by the thumb.

3 With the hand open, the coin remains hidden from the front. This exposed view shows the Thumb-Clipped coin.

classic palm

This is one of the most useful sleights to learn. It enables the performer to hide any small object (in this case a coin) in the palm of the hand, without its presence being detected. The most important aspect of any Palm is that the hand must appear natural, so do not hold your hand in an awkward position or move in a way which attracts attention. A common problem is that both the thumb and fourth finger will try to flare out at an unnatural angle, but this will happen less as you learn to relax your hand. After enough practice, your hand will develop tiny muscles that will help you to palm. A palmed object should not be gripped tightly; a gentle touch is all that is required.

1 Place a coin on your outstretched hand. It should lie flat on the tips of the second and third fingers.

2 Keep the fingers parallel to the ground as you turn your hand palm down. The coin should be directly below the palm of your hand.

3 Push the coin into your palm with your second and third fingertips. The exact position of the coin is crucial to success. You may have to move it about a few times and try the coin in slightly different areas of the palm until you feel comfortable.

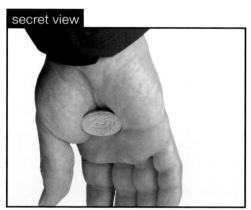

secret view

4 Remove the second and third fingers from the coin, trapping the coin in the palm by gently squeezing the edges between the fleshy pad of the thumb and the area of skin at the opposite edge of the coin.

secret view

5 This view shows the correct position of the coin. The coin need not be pinched hard. Only a gentle pressure is needed to stop the coin from falling.

6 The coin can be held in the Classic Palm without detection, however it must look natural.

7 In this example, the distortion of the hand is totally unnatural and therefore a clear sign that it hides something.

secret view

8 Continue your everyday activities (such as writing, typing and eating) with a coin palmed, and you will soon learn to forget it is there.

downs palm

The Downs Palm is named after the nineteenth-century American magician Thomas Nelson Downs, who is still recognized as one of the finest manipulators of coins ever. This grip is very deceptive as you can show both the front and back of the hand empty before producing a coin. There are angle problems, however, and anyone viewing from too high or too low may glimpse the hidden coin. Practise and check your movements in the mirror – before long you will develop an instinct as to whether or not the coin can be seen.

Performed well, this creates a beautiful effect. The coin can be plucked from the air or from any suitable location.

1 Grip the coin between the tips of the right first and second fingers.

2 As the hand closes, the coin should naturally position itself in the crotch of the thumb.

secret view

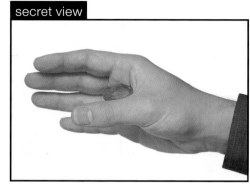

3 Open the fingers, leaving the coin gripped in the web between the thumb and the first finger.

4 You can show your hand from both front and back without the coin being seen, as long as you keep the correct angle in relation to the audience.

downs palm production

1 To produce the coin, reverse the above moves. Close your hand, ensuring that the edge of the coin becomes gripped between the tips of the first and second fingers, as seen here.

2 Open your hand, bringing the tip of your thumb on to the edge of the coin and keeping this contact as your hand continues to open.

3 Finally, pinch the coin between your thumb and second finger. Steps 1, 2 and 3 should happen together in one seamless movement.

bobo switch

This is a method of switching one coin for another. It was invented by French magician J.B. Bobo in about 1900, and is still used widely today. The switch is not used as a trick by itself, but being able to switch your coin for a spectator's is an invaluable tool. Bending Coin (Version 2) is an example of the use of the Bobo Switch. Study the following explanation carefully and it will not take too long to learn.

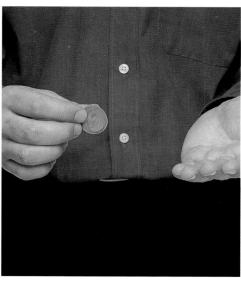

secret view

1 Hold the coin to be switched in the right-hand Finger Palm position. Borrow a coin from a spectator and hold it clearly displayed in the right fingertips. Hold the left hand out flat.

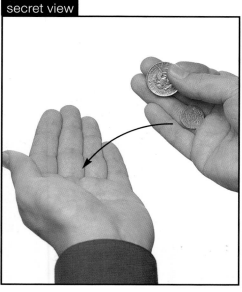

2 From the front, the secret coin is completely hidden in the right palm.

secret view

3 The switch occurs as the right hand tosses the borrowed coin into the left hand. It goes unnoticed because the coin is in motion the entire time. The right second and third fingers extend to cover the coin and the secret coin is allowed to fall from the Finger Palm position to the outstretched left hand.

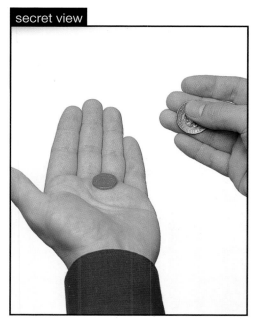

secret view

4 Without hesitation, the right thumb pulls the borrowed coin into the Finger Palm position, and the left hand closes around the switched coin.

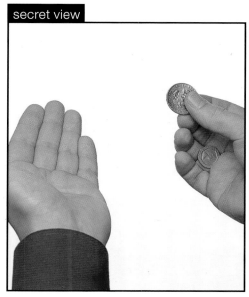

5 From the front, the action of tossing the coin from one hand to the other looks very natural and should not arouse any suspicion from your audience.

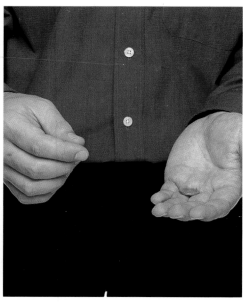

6 Slowly open your left hand to show that the coin has been switched.

coin roll

This flourish is a well-known favourite with audiences worldwide. A coin is rolled across the knuckles in a flourish which looks as magical as it is beautiful. The Coin Roll is a wonderful example of digital dexterity; it is also one of the most difficult things you will

learn in this book. You can practise it while you are watching television. Once you have mastered it, try learning it with the other hand and perform two Coin Rolls simultaneously! It is possible to perform the Coin Roll with four coins, each coin rotating ahead of the next.

1 Close your hand into a loose fist. Your knuckles should be parallel with the floor. Begin by balancing a coin on the tip of your thumb.

2 Pinch your thumb against the side of your first finger so that the coin flips on to its edge.

3 Loosen your thumb's grip on the coin so that it balances on the back of the first finger. At the same time, raise your second, third and fourth fingers just enough to clip the coin's edge between the first and second fingers.

4 Raise your first and third fingers while lowering the second finger. This allows you to roll the coin across the back of the second finger.

5 Lower the third finger and raise the second and fourth fingers. The coin will roll across the back of the third finger. Allow the coin to flip over and rest on the side of your fourth finger.

6 Move your thumb under your hand, towards the coin.

7 The coin is transferred to the tip of the thumb, which carries it back under the hand to the start position.

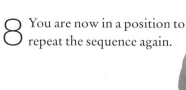

8 You are now in a position to repeat the sequence again.

coin vanishes

There are countless ways to make a coin vanish. The French Drop, Fake Take and Thumb Clip Vanish are all sleight-of-hand methods and generally should not be used as tricks in their own right. As you *become more experienced, you will find that you can incorporate the coin's disappearance into a longer sequence, which can be extra mystifying and a lot of fun.*

french drop

This is one of the oldest and best-known techniques used to "vanish" a coin or any other small object. The coin is held in the fingertips of the left hand and supposedly taken by the right hand. In reality, the coin is secretly retained in the left hand. This move should not be shown as a trick on its own, but as a way of "vanishing" a coin within another trick.

1 Display a coin by holding it high in the left fingertips. As much as possible of the surface of the coin should be seen.

2 The right hand approaches the left to supposedly take the coin. The thumb goes under it while the fingers go over it.

3 As soon as the fingers close around the coin and it is out of view, let the coin fall into the left hand.

secret view

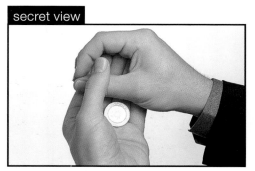

4 The coin falls between the right thumb and the back of the left fingers, almost in Finger Palm position.

5 From the front, it looks as though you pinch the coin with your right fingers and thumb. Watch the coin yourself and actually believe that you are taking the coin.

6 Move the right hand up and to your right, at the same time allowing the left hand (with the coin) to drop naturally to your side. Follow your right hand with your eyes. Your hand should look as though it is actually holding a coin.

7 Squeeze your right hand slowly, supposedly shrinking the coin. Open the fingers wide and show the coin is no longer there.

tip *To make the move more convincing, place a pencil on a table, off to your left-hand side. Hold the coin in the start position. Execute the French Drop, then immediately use your left hand to pick up the pencil. Tap your right hand with the pencil, then show that the coin has vanished. Using the pencil like a wand provides a reason for taking the coin with your right hand – it is more natural to pick up the pencil using your left hand than to reach across your body with your right hand. When executing a sleight, it is very important to justify moves which may look strange if made without a reason.*

thumb clip vanish

This creates the illusion of placing a coin in your left hand while you secretly retain it in your right hand. It makes use of the technique in magic known as "time misdirection". If you leave enough time between secretly retaining the coin and showing that it has *"vanished", the audience will not be able to remember the last time they actually saw the coin or in which hand they saw it. This makes it very difficult for them to reconstruct the method. "Time misdirection" can be applied to many other secret moves and routines.*

1 Display a coin on your right fingertips in preparation for the Thumb Clip.

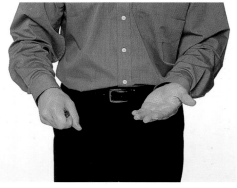

2 Display your open left hand at waist level. Move the left hand up. At the same time begin to close the right hand, placing the coin into the Thumb Clip.

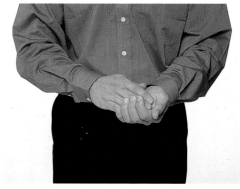

3 Supposedly place the coin on to the fingertips of the left hand, but secretly retain the coin in your right hand.

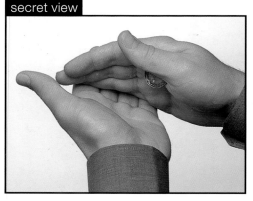

secret view

4 This view from behind shows what is happening.

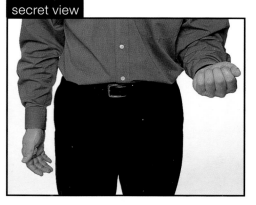

secret view

5 As the right hand moves away from the left and drops to your side, the left fingers close around the "coin". Your eyes must follow your left hand and your body language should suggest that the coin really is in this hand. This exposed view shows the coin in the right hand; in performance it would be hidden in the Thumb Clip or would be allowed to drop into the Finger Palm position.

6 The left hand moves away from your body, to the left. Open the hand and show that the coin has disappeared.

7 To make the move look more natural, give your right hand something to do after it leaves the left hand. Pick up a pencil with the coin in the Thumb Clip. Tap your left hand with the pencil, then show that the coin has gone. Even better, have the pencil in your right pocket and, as you take out the pencil, leave the coin in your pocket.

fake take

Like the French Drop and the Thumb Clip Vanish, the Fake Take enables you to secretly retain an object in one hand while supposedly taking it in the other hand. Try to provide a reason for taking the coin in the right hand – for example, to pick something up with the other hand. This type of sleight should not be used as a trick in its own right, but as part of a longer routine. In some routines the French Drop or Thumb Clip Vanish will be more suitable than the Fake Take. However, it is important to learn several ways to achieve a similar result so that you can choose which looks best. It will not necessarily be the same technique every time.

1 Display a coin on the outstretched fingers of your left hand at about waist height. The coin should be in a position ready for a Finger Palm.

2 The right hand approaches the left hand, supposedly to take the coin. The right fingers lie flat on top of the coin.

secret view

3 The left hand begins to close as the right hand feigns pinching the coin with the thumb against the fingers. This view from behind shows that in reality the coin remains in exactly the same position, ready to be finger-palmed by the left hand.

4 The right hand swings to the right (with the back towards the audience) as the left hand drops to your left side, supposedly empty, holding the coin in a Finger Palm.

5 As the right hand moves across your body, watch it as you would if the coin was really there. Your body language should suggest that the coin really is in your right hand.

6 Slowly open your right hand to show that the coin has vanished.

sleeving a coin

Magicians are always accused of using their sleeves to secretly hide objects. In fact very few tricks rely on this method, known as "sleeving". There are many different sleeving techniques. If you perfect this method, you will be able to make a coin disappear instantly without the need for any gimmicks. The only requirement is that you wear a jacket with loose-fitting sleeves. The trick will take lots of practice to perfect, and many people give up too soon. If you persevere, you will be rewarded handsomely with a baffling quick trick which will amaze all who see it. Sometimes, even when you know how a trick is done, it still looks magical. Such is the case here.

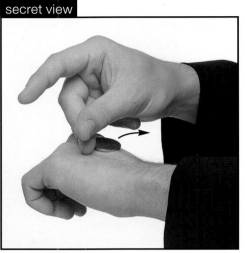
secret view

1 Close your left fingers into a fist. Place a coin on the back of your hand. The coin must be parallel with the ground, otherwise it may fall off.

2 Hold your right fingers above the coin. Snap your fingers. As your right second finger snaps off the thumb, it strikes the coin. With practice, if you strike the coin correctly it will automatically sail through the air and up your right sleeve.

3 As soon as the sound of the snap is heard, the coin seems to melt away. Try to keep your left hand perfectly still and as soon as the coin disappears, freeze, so that your spectator doesn't think you tried to sneak the coin away with your right hand.

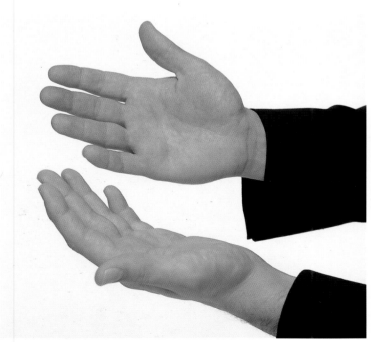

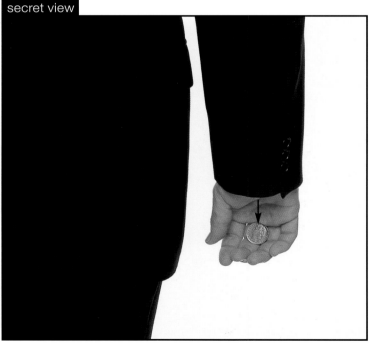
secret view

4 Show both hands back and front. They are unmistakably empty. Keep the right arm slightly bent and be careful not to let the coin fall out of your sleeve.

5 You can retrieve the coin by allowing your right arm to hang by your side. The coin will fall from your sleeve and you can catch it in the Finger Palm position.

coin in elbow

You hold a coin in your fingertips and rub it against your elbow. After several apparently unsuccessful attempts the coin seems to *dissolve into your elbow, disappearing completely. This is another good example of how "misdirection" works.*

1 This is best performed sitting at a table, although you could perform it standing if you alter the handling slightly. Hold a coin in your right fingertips and bend your left arm. (Your left hand should be in a position next to your left ear.) Rub the coin against your elbow. After a few seconds, let the coin fall to the table.

2 Pick up the coin with your left hand and display it on the fingers as you explain that you will try again. Pick up the coin from the left fingers with the right hand. This should be done to look identical to the Fake Take described earlier, which is the move you will be performing later in the trick.

3 Once again repeat the rubbing sequence, only to let the coin fall to the table again. Your audience will become accustomed to these moves, which will help you to accomplish what happens next.

4 Just as before, go to pick up the coin with your left hand and display it in the left fingertips. However, as the right hand approaches to take the coin from the left, execute a Fake Take. Briefly the right fingers mime taking the coin while the left hand returns to a position near the left ear.

secret view

7 Display both hands to complete the "vanish". The coin can be recovered later. It will either stay under your collar or fall down your back. Make sure your shirt is tucked in, or the coin may fall out!

5 This exposed view shows the coin in the left hand. Secretly slip the coin under the back of your shirt collar to dispose of it. Plenty of "misdirection" is caused by the movement of the right hand, which furiously rubs the supposed coin into the elbow.

6 After a few more seconds of rubbing, show that the right hand is empty. The coin has apparently been absorbed into your arm.

handkerchief coin vanish

A coin is placed under a handkerchief and held by a spectator. The handkerchief is shaken out and the coin seems to melt away. A specially prepared handkerchief is required. Cut a corner from

a duplicate handkerchief. Stitch it neatly into one of the corners of the handkerchief along three sides. Before stitching the final side, drop a coin into the secret pocket.

1 Show the coin held in the right fingertips. The handkerchief is opened and held by both hands. The special corner is held in the right hand together with the coin. Your right fingers hide the secret pocket.

2 As you move the coin under the handkerchief (aim for the centre), take the hidden coin with it. Ask a spectator to hold the coin through the fabric. They will assume they are holding the one shown originally, but it is really the duplicate coin sewn into the corner.

3 Allow the loose coin to fall into the Finger Palm position, then remove your hand from the handkerchief in a natural manner.

4 Hold one corner of the handkerchief in each hand and ask the spectator to drop the coin on your command. Count to three and say "Let go!"

5 As they do so, the coin seems to melt away and the handkerchief can be displayed completely empty. You can finish by folding it up and putting it back in your pocket.

clever coin vanish

A coin is placed under a handkerchief and held by a spectator. When the handkerchief is shaken out, the coin melts away. The effect is the same as in Handkerchief Coin Vanish, but the method is very different. This is true of many tricks: there are, for example, dozens of ways of sawing a woman in half! Next time you think you know how a trick is done, take a closer look and see if you really do.

1 To prepare, secretly place a coin into the lining of your tie so that it lies down by the tip.

2 To begin the performance, show another coin in your right hand and an opaque handkerchief in your left.

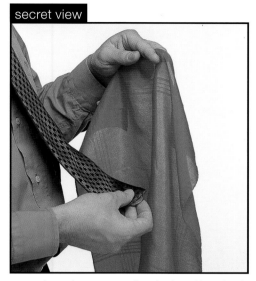

secret view

3 Place this coin under the handkerchief, taking the tip of your tie with it. Practise this in front of a mirror.

secret view

4 Hold the handkerchief at approximately waist height and close to your body so that your tie continues to hang naturally. If you lift your tie too high, your audience will see what you are doing.

5 Ask a spectator to hold the coin, which is really the one in the tie. As in Handkerchief Coin Vanish, allow the other coin to fall into the Finger Palm position, then casually remove your hand.

6 Hold one corner of the handkerchief in each hand and ask the spectator to let go. Display the handkerchief completely empty and hand it to the spectator for examination. They will find nothing.

tip *For a complete "vanish", simply hide the coin in the lining of your tie as you place it under the handkerchief. This way you will not have to palm anything. The use of your tie is so subtle that the method will never be guessed by your spectators.*

coin wrap

A coin is wrapped in a piece of paper. It can be seen and even felt until the final moment when the paper is torn into pieces and the coin seems to have vanished without a trace. This is an ideal way to "vanish" a

marked, borrowed coin, which can then be made to appear in another trick later on in your act (for example, Coin in Egg and Coin in Bread Roll). This is a baffling "any time" coin trick worth learning.

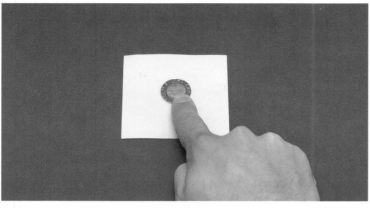

1 You will require an opaque piece of paper approximately 9cm (3½in) square. Place a coin into the centre of the paper.

2 Fold the paper upwards against the bottom of the coin with a sharp crease.

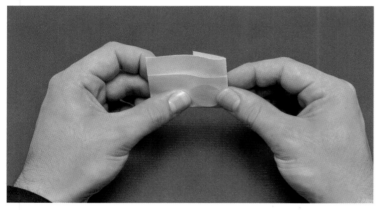

3 Fold the paper to the right and back, behind the coin. Make the creases as sharp as possible.

4 Repeat with the left side of the paper. Be careful not to wrap the coin too tightly, as this will hinder the secret move.

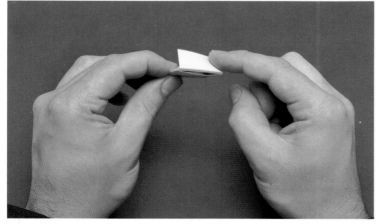

5 Fold the top flap back, at the edge of the paper. It seems as if the coin is trapped, but in reality it can escape from the top of the paper where a gap has been left.

6 Press the coin against the paper with your thumbs, turning the package end over end as you do so. This will position the opening of the packet towards the bottom, while creating an impression of the coin on the paper, proving its presence.

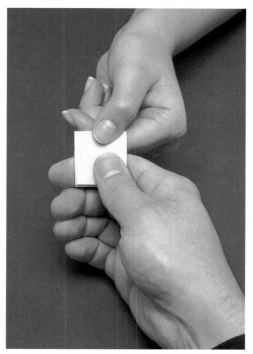

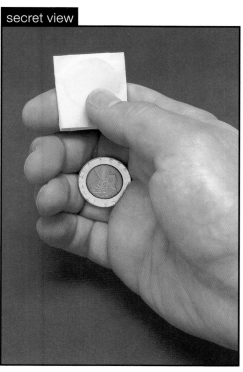

7 Have a spectator verify that the coin is still there. Carefully note the position of the paper at this point.

8 Release your thumb's grip, allowing the coin to fall from the paper. The back of your right hand provides a good deal of cover.

9 The coin lands in the right-hand Finger Palm position. It should fall easily from the paper. If not, your folds at steps 3 and 4 may have been too tight.

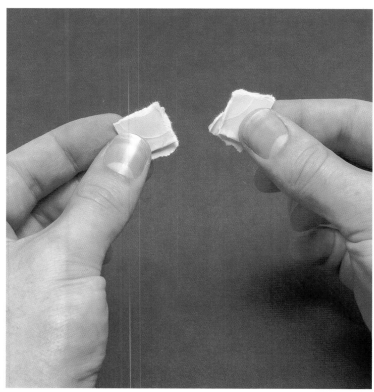

10 Tear the paper in half, then into quarters. The coin remains hidden in the Finger Palm.

11 Toss the pieces of paper on to the table to complete the "vanish". Make the coin reappear in a place of your choice (*see* More Money Tricks for ideas).

coin vanish from matchbox

A coin is placed inside an empty matchbox. The box is shaken to prove the contents are still there, but moments later the box is shown empty. You can then choose any method you like to make the coin reappear.

You could also adapt the method used in Vanishing Box of Matches (see Match Magic) to add to this routine, enhancing the illusion of the coin being in the box even after it has gone.

1 Open the drawer of an empty matchbox. Insert a coin and display it clearly.

2 Hold the matchbox in your left hand and close the drawer, trapping the coin.

3 Transfer the box to your palm-down right hand.

4 Shake the box by turning your right hand over and back several times. The coin will rattle, proving its presence.

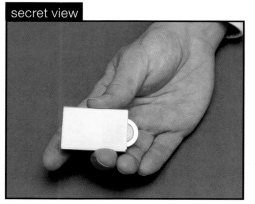

secret view

5 Rattle the box again, but as the hand turns palm up, squeeze the sides of the box so that the top of the box bows open just enough to let the coin slip out into your right hand. This secret move can be disguised by tilting the hand upwards and towards you slightly.

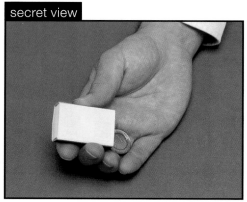

secret view

6 The coin is secretly retained in the Finger Palm position.

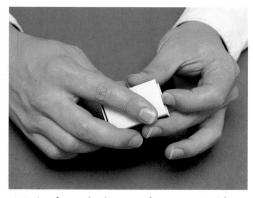

7 As the wrist is turned over again, the box is transferred back into the left hand. The left hand holds the box between the thumb and second finger.

8 The left first finger pushes open the drawer to show that the coin has vanished. The box can be dismantled and checked by the audience. There will be nothing to find.

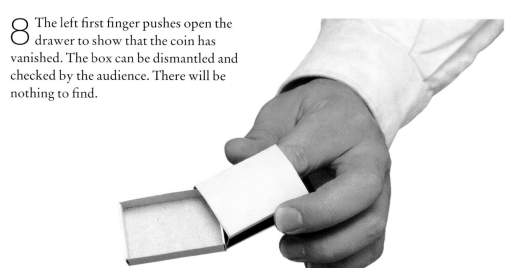

pencil and coin vanish

A coin is held in the fingertips and tapped three times with a pencil. Unexpectedly, the pencil disappears and is found behind the magician's ear! The coin is tapped again and vanishes completely. This routine can be performed at any time, anywhere. Instead of a coin, you can use anything small enough to hide in your hand. This routine is a practical example of how "misdirection" works. It is also a "sucker" trick in that your audience thinks they are let into the secret when in reality you still manage to amaze them.

1 Hold a coin on the outstretched palm of your left hand. Hold a pencil in your right hand. Stand with the left side of your body towards the audience.

2 Tell everyone to watch carefully. Tap the coin three times, each time bringing the pencil up towards your right ear.

secret view

3 On the third tap, without any hesitation, leave the pencil behind your ear. The first two taps are made to build the expectation that the coin is going to vanish.

4 As your hand descends to tap the coin, open it wide and look amazed as you seem to realize at the same time as your audience that the pencil is no longer there.

5 Explain that you should never reveal the secret to a magic trick, but that you are going to break that rule. Turn your body so that your right side is now towards your audience. Point out the pencil behind your ear.

secret view

6 As you do this, secretly place the coin into your left trouser pocket.

7 Explain that you will do the trick again. Return to the position you were in before, with your left side to the audience. Your left hand should be closed as if it holds the coin. Tap your hand three times with the pencil, then open it to show that this time the coin really has gone.

tip *The success of this trick relies on the spectators convincing themselves that the coin is going to vanish. They will be so focused on watching the coin that they will fail to watch the pencil!*

more money tricks

This section explains the methods to various tricks that require some of the knowledge learnt so far. Coin in Egg uses the Coin Wrap vanish and Bending Coin (Version 2) utilizes the Bobo Switch, while several use palming techniques. The final magic trick in the book, Paper to Money, does not require difficult sleight of hand, but is a very strong, visual illusion which you can perform at any time.

switcheroo

In this trick you introduce a game of hand-eye co-ordination. A coin is held on the outstretched palm of a spectator. You explain that you are going to try to grab it before the spectator can close their hand.

You manage to grab the coin twice, but fail on the third attempt. When the spectator opens their hand, they see you have not only removed the coin, but have replaced it with a different coin!

1 For this trick, you will need two different coins. Place one coin on the palm of a spectator's hand.

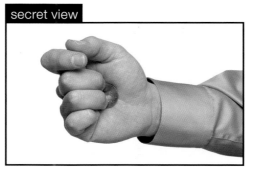
secret view

2 Hold the second coin classic-palmed in your right hand. Details regarding the Classic Palm can be found in Basic Coin Techniques.

3 Explain that you will try to grab the coin before the spectator closes their hand, and that they are not allowed to move until you do. Your fingers should be curled in except for your thumb and first finger, which will act like a pair of pincers.

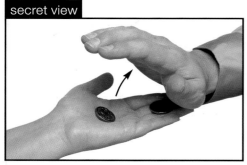
secret view

4 As the right hand descends, open it fully so that the hidden coin is brought down on to the spectator's fingertips. The force of this motion will bounce the coin in their palm up in the air.

5 Grab the coin as it bounces, and the spectator will close their hand around the second coin. This occurs so fast it that is impossible for them to feel or see what has happened.

6 The spectator will think you failed, but when they open their hand, they will see that you have switched the coin!

tip *This is a genuine act of sleight of hand, which relies on fast movement and precision timing. With practice you will be able to perform it successfully nearly every time, but it doesn't matter if it takes more than one attempt, because it is not a trick but an example of your dexterity. In order to build a little routine, begin by simply taking the spectator's coin, without performing the switch. It is not as difficult as you might think. Explain that you want to try again and repeat it. The third time, execute the switch.*

coin through table

This quick trick will catch people off guard. A coin is made to pass straight through the centre of a table. Once you understand the *workings of the trick, try using three or four coins and making each coin pass through the table using a different method.*

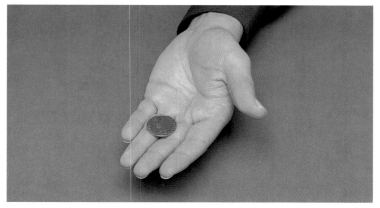

1 With your left hand, tap a coin on the surface of a table at random points, explaining that every table has a particular "soft spot". Display the coin in your left hand in readiness for a Fake Take.

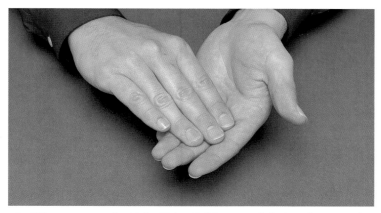

2 Now execute the Fake Take. With your right hand, pretend to pick up the coin. In reality the coin never moves from the left hand.

3 The right hand moves away, pretending to hold the coin in the fingertips. At the same time, the left hand drops below the table to a position directly under the right hand.

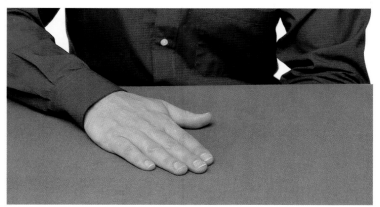

4 Slap the right hand flat on the table, and just at the same moment slap the coin on the underside of the table with your left hand. The result will be a sound which will make the spectators believe that the coin is under your right hand.

5 Pause for a few seconds and then slowly lift your right hand to show that the coin is no longer there.

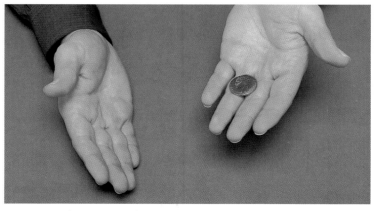

6 Bring the coin out from below the table on the outstretched palm of your left hand.

coin through handkerchief

A coin is placed under the centre of a silk handkerchief. A layer of silk is lifted to confirm to the audience that the coin really is underneath. Very slowly the coin begins to melt visibly through the fabric. The silk is unfolded to show the absence of any holes.

secret view

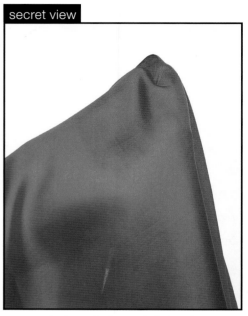

1 Hold a silk handkerchief by its edge in the left hand and display a coin in the fingertips of the right hand.

2 Drape the silk over the coin, positioning it directly in the centre, as shown here.

3 With the aid of your left hand, obtain a pinch of cloth between the back of the coin and your right thumb.

4 Lift the silk with your left hand to display the coin still held by the fingertips. Note how it is lifted back directly over the arm and above the other half of the silk.

5 Let go with your left hand and flick your wrist down so that both layers of the silk fall forward over the coin. The coin is now outside the silk, hidden under the pinch held by your thumb.

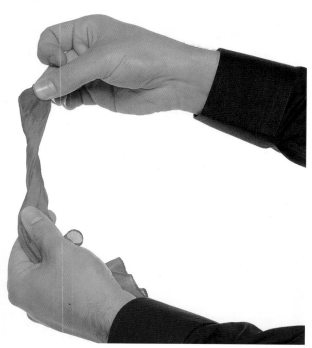

6 Wrap and twist the silk so that the shape of the coin is clearly visible through the fabric. Be careful not to expose the coin accidentally.

7 In this view from behind, you can see that the coin is being held by the fingers and the fabric that surrounds it. Begin to pull the coin up and into view.

8 From the front, the coin appears to be slowly melting through the silk. With practice, you will be able to make the coin look as if it penetrates on its own by simply pinching your left fingers together and using your right hand to support the coin as it emerges.

9 Remove the coin completely. Display both the coin and the silk – you can safely hand them to the audience for examination.

coin in egg

This is one of the many methods that exist for producing a coin from nowhere. These can either be used independently, perhaps to introduce a coin that you will proceed to use in another trick, or can follow on from a "disappearing" trick, to make a coin reappear.

In this trick, the mystery is increased by vanishing a marked coin borrowed from a spectator. The marked coin is then found inside an egg chosen at random by the spectator. With a little thought, there are many other places that you can make the coin appear from.

1 Borrow a coin from a spectator and ask for it to be marked with a permanent marker pen for later identification.

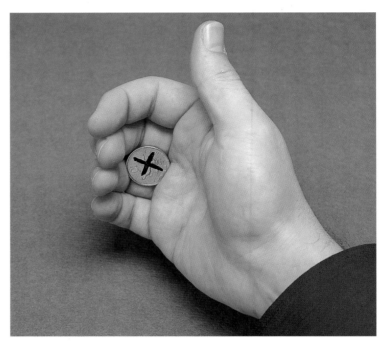

2 Vanish the coin using any of the methods described earlier. The coin should end up in Finger Palm position. The Coin Wrap would work well here.

3 Display a box of eggs and ask someone to point to any one at random. Lift and display the egg with your left hand.

4 Transfer the egg to the right hand, placing it directly on top of the finger-palmed coin. The coin should remain completely hidden from view.

5 The left hand brings a glass to the centre of the table and the right hand taps the egg on the side of the glass, breaking the shell. The eggshell is opened with one hand so that the contents of the egg fall into the glass. Simultaneously allow the finger-palmed coin to drop into the glass with the egg. If timed correctly, it looks just as if the coin falls from the centre of the egg.

6 Scoop the coin from the glass with a spoon and have the mark verified as that which the spectator made a few minutes before. Have a napkin ready to wipe the coin dry. Using a similar method, you could also make the coin appear inside other impossible places, such an unopened can of food held by a spectator throughout the trick. The possibilities are endless.

coin in bread roll

In this trick, after "vanishing" a coin, you find it seconds later inside a bread roll that has been sitting on the table the entire time! To make this effect more astonishing, ask someone to mark the coin with *a pen so that when they see it again they can be sure that it is the same coin. You could also ask them to choose from a selection of rolls, adding an extra dimension of mystery to the presentation.*

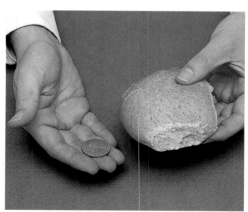

secret view

1 Make a coin disappear, using one of the methods described earlier. Finish with the coin secretly hidden in your right hand. Ask someone to pass you a bread roll. Hold it with both hands so that the coin is hidden on the bottom. This view shows the right hand a split second before the roll is placed on top of the coin.

2 Bend both sides of the roll up so that the bottom splits open. With your fingers, begin to push the coin into the split. This exposed view shows the coin entering the roll. In performance, the bottom of the roll must be pointing down towards the table to hide these actions.

3 Bend the roll in the opposite direction with both hands so that the top cracks open. As it does so, the split at the bottom closes up and the coin appears to come from the centre! Ask the spectator to remove the marked coin and verify that it was the one they marked a few moments earlier.

coin through pocket

A coin is held against the outside of the trouser pocket and caused to pass through the fabric into the pocket! This quick routine makes use of the Finger Palm. It is quite easy to perfect and makes a good impromptu trick to remember for those times when you are stuck without props. Try to enhance the illusion by using the biggest, shiniest coin you can find.

1 Display a coin held against your right thigh, in line with the bottom of your pocket.

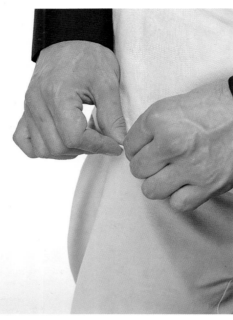

2 With both hands, pinch the fabric underneath the coin. Turn over the coin, simultaneously covering it from view with the fabric.

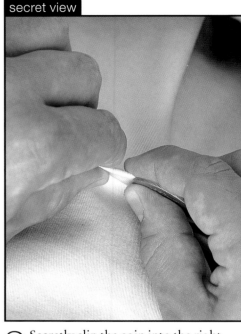

secret view

3 Secretly slip the coin into the right-hand Finger Palm position, using your thumb. This is unseen from the front. The photograph here shows your view.

4 With the coin still hidden in the Finger Palm, hold on to the top of the fold with your right first finger. Position your left first finger and thumb under the right and pinch a small piece of fabric.

5 Pull the fabric flat and show that the coin has vanished.

6 Reach into your right trouser pocket. Remove your hand with the coin displayed clearly at its fingertips.

bending coin (version 2)

Earlier in the book, Bending Coin (Version 1) showed how to create the illusion of a coin bending. You will now have learnt the necessary skill to perform a similar type of illusion, which is *the perfect follow-up. The amazing thing about this trick is that at the end you give the lender their coin back in its bent condition – a souvenir they can keep forever!*

secret view

1 To prepare, you need to bend a coin. First cover it with a cloth so that you do not mark it. Use a pair of pliers to hold the coin, then bend it with another pair of pliers. The result will be a coin that looks like the one shown here.

2 Before you begin, hide the bent coin in the right-hand Finger Palm position. Begin the performance by borrowing a coin which matches yours, and hold it in your fingertips as shown. Perform Bending Coin (Version 1) as described earlier.

3 At the end, hold your left hand out flat with the coin held in the right fingertips. You now apparently toss the coin from your right hand into the left. In reality, you perform the Bobo Switch, as described earlier.

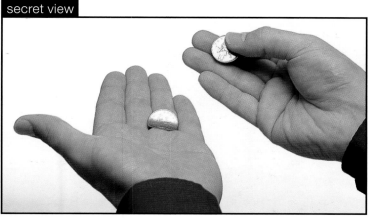

secret view

4 This exposed view shows the bent coin lying on your left hand and the right coin about to be placed in the Finger Palm position. There should be no hesitation in your actions.

5 As the coin touches the left hand, it closes immediately into a fist so that the bend remains hidden. Squeeze the coin hard as if you are squashing it.

6 Open your left fingers wide to show that the coin really does have a bend in it. Give it back to the spectator, who will treasure the curiosity and think about it long after the event. As mentioned earlier, Bending Coin (Version 1) is a great prelude to this trick, and together they make a nice, memorable routine.

appearing money

Imagine reaching up into the air and producing real money. You would never have to work again! Your audience doesn't have to know the money was yours to start with. This is one of the best

impromptu tricks you can perform. If you set up the trick prior to receiving your bill or check at the end of a meal, you can magically produce a tip for your waiter.

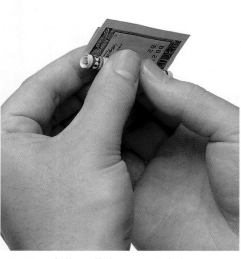

1 To perform this trick, you will need to wear a long-sleeved shirt. Take a banknote and fold it in half, widthways, down the middle.

2 Carefully roll the note tightly into a cigarette shape, starting at the fold, as shown here.

3 Place the rolled-up note into the crook of your left elbow. Fold over the fabric to hide the note and to keep it in place. Keep your arm bent to prevent the note from falling out.

4 Show your right hand empty, simultaneously pulling your sleeve up with your left hand. This should look very natural, and will make your audience less suspicious when you repeat it.

5 Repeat the motion with your left hand. However, as the right hand tugs the sleeve, it secretly grasps the rolled-up note from the crook of your elbow.

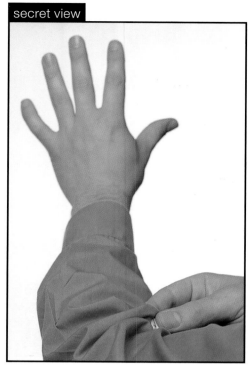

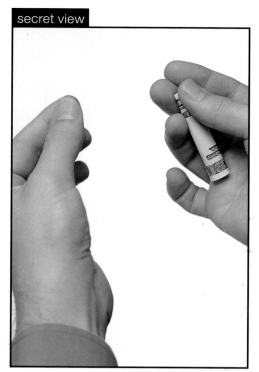

6 The exposed view shows how the left hand creates enough misdirection for this to happen. The right hand secretly retrieves the note, while the audience are focused on making sure that your left hand is empty.

7 Bring both hands to a position in front of you, at about chest level. The rolled-up note is held hidden in the right hand. The top end is pinched between the thumb, first and second fingers. These fingers pull the rest of the note back and out of sight.

8 From the front, both hands still look completely empty. This is a very convincing illusion.

10 Snap open the note.

9 Bring your fingers together and, without pausing, use your right thumb to pivot the note into a position that allows both hands to grip an edge each.

paper to money

A piece of blank, white paper is shown on both sides. It is folded several times and then unfolded again. It instantly changes into a banknote! The larger the value of the note, the more impressive the effect is. Try this out and you won't be disappointed. The success of the trick depends on the gimmick being made perfectly so that it operates easily and smoothly.

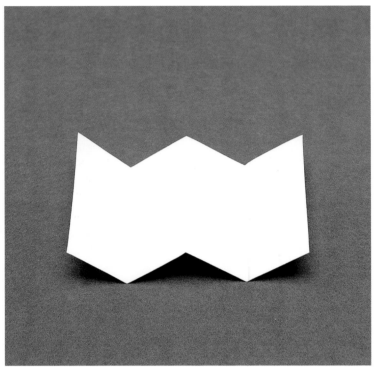

1 To prepare, cut a piece of paper exactly the same size as the banknote. Fold it neatly in half precisely down the middle.

2 Unfold the paper, turn it over and fold each side in half again, creasing the paper sharply and neatly.

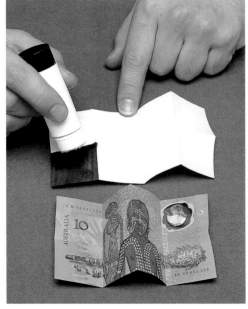

3 Fold the paper along the creases, concertina-style, ensuring that the ends of the paper are to your right. Fold it up and towards you, making one final sharp crease directly down the centre.

4 Unfold the paper and repeat exactly the same procedure with the banknote. It is vital to the success of this trick that the creasing and folding is as neat and accurate as possible.

5 Apply glue to the upper right corner of the paper. (This section is marked in black for ease of explanation.)

6 Attach the glued corner of the paper behind the lower right corner of the banknote. Check that the edges match up exactly and that both pieces are perfectly aligned. Check the photograph here to ensure that you have orientated the papers correctly.

7 Fold the banknote along its creases so that you finish with it folded neatly at the top right corner of the white paper. If the edges of the banknote extend beyond the edges of the paper, the handling will be hindered.

8 Turn over the paper and hold it so that your right fingers cover the banknote, which is now positioned under the bottom right corner of the paper. This is how you should hold the paper when you begin the performance. The gimmick can be kept in a wallet or pocket until needed.

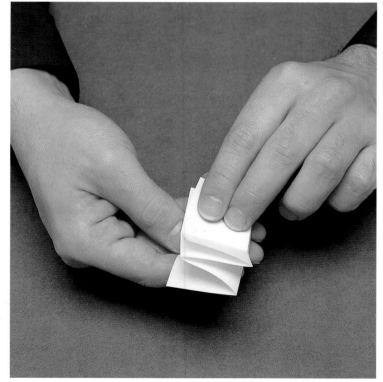

9 In performance, hold the paper with both hands, thumbs on top, fingers below. Quickly display the paper front and back by turning both wrists. When the back is seen, the banknote is hidden under the right fingers. Explain that money is printed on very special paper and that you have managed to find a piece.

10 With the front of the paper facing up once more, begin to fold the paper from left to right concertina-style, along the creases, with your left fingers. ▶

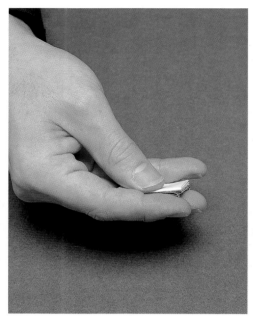

11 Fold the paper back towards you, still using the creases made previously. (Notice how the right hand stays in the same position throughout.)

12 Lift the right thumb and clip the package between the thumb and first finger. Then quickly lift the right third finger, clipping the paper between the right third and second fingers.

13 Squeeze these fingers together, flipping the package up at right angles to the fingers.

14 Your right thumb helps to turn the paper end over end. These steps are all done in one quick movement with a shake of the wrist, and take only a second.

15 The crease in the banknote will open slightly under its own tension. This enables the right thumb to push open the first fold without fumbling.

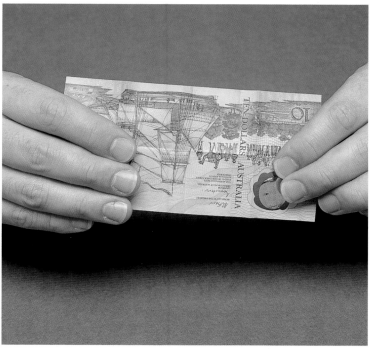

16 Immediately, the left fingers open the banknote out completely flat.

17 Turn your wrists, showing the back of the note exactly as you did at the start of the routine. This time it is the paper that is hidden under the right fingers.

18 Finish by displaying the front of the banknote again, then quickly put it away in your pocket or wallet.

tip *Make sure that you have a duplicate banknote (with similar crease lines) in your pocket or wallet so that if somebody asks to examine it, you can give them the duplicate note instead.*

glossary

There are many specialist words used within the magic fraternity, and their meanings may not be immediately obvious to a novice. The meaning of some of the most common terms are explained here.

Book test
A word or words chosen at random from a book which are revealed by the magician either as a prediction or through thought transference.

Cabaret magic
A stand-up act, generally viewed from at least three sides and for a large crowd of people.

Card control
The technique of keeping track of one or several cards and secretly shifting them to another position in the deck.

Close-up magic
The performance of magic shown very close to the audience, often using small everyday items.

Deck
Another name for a pack of playing cards.

Double lift
The showing of two cards held as one.

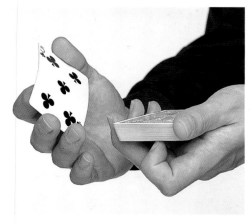

Above: Double Lift – two cards are in the right hand.

Effect
A description of the overall trick.

False cut
The appearance of a regular cut which leaves the deck or part of the deck in exactly the same order as at the beginning.

False shuffle
A shuffle that does not change the order of one or more cards. Also used to reposition particular cards to other locations in the deck.

Finger break
A small gap between the cards held by a finger (or thumb), often, but not exclusively, used to keep control of a certain card or packet of cards in the deck.

Flourish
A showy and often attractive display of skill.

Force
The action of influencing a spectator's choice, often pertaining to cards. The spectator believes that their choice was fair.

Gimmick
Sometimes known as a "fake". A secret tool employed, often unseen, to cause the trick to work.

Glimpse
To take a secret look at a card in the deck.

Illusion
Generally refers to large-scale magic tricks designed for a large audience.

Key card
A card used to help locate a selected card.

Above: Lapping a glass to make it disappear.

Lapping
A technique used to secretly ditch objects in the lap. Always performed at a table and often used as a method for the disappearance of an object.

Manipulation
Any form of manual skill, but usually associated with the highly skilful performance of sleight of hand on stage, such as the production of playing cards.

Mentalist
The name given to a performer who specializes in mind-reading and other psychic effects.

Method
The secret workings of a trick.

Misdirection
The skill of focusing the minds or eyes of the audience on a particular point while secretly doing something else.

Optical illusion
An image that is distorted to create an untrue picture of what is being viewed, thus deceiving the eye. The impossibility of the optical illusion leads people to disbelieve or misinterpret what their eyes are showing them.

Packet

A small group of cards that is often, but not always, separated from the main section of the deck.

Palming

The secretion of an object in the hand. There are several different palms (Back Palm, Classic Palm, Finger Palm, etc). They do not necessarily use the palm of the hand itself.

Patter

The banter that accompanies the performance of a trick. This is a very important aid to "misdirection".

Practice

The rehearsal required to make a performance appear slick and without mistakes.

Presentation

The overall term describing the trick, patter and style given to a routine.

Routine

One whole trick or a series of tricks which lead from one to another.

Short card

A card trimmed slightly shorter than the others so that it can be located immediately. Often used as a key card.

Above: Trimming an Ace to make a short card.

Silk

A piece of silk, or a silk handkerchief, fine enough to be folded and squeezed into a small space and thus easily hidden. Silks come in all shapes, sizes and colours.

Sleeving

The secret action of hiding an object in the sleeve.

Sleight of hand

The secret manipulation of an object. Often associated with close-up magic, but also very relevant to larger acts.

Stage magic

An act performed on stage for a large audience, often using large props and illusions. Similar to cabaret magic, which was a development of stage magic after the closure of many music halls and theatres at the end of the vaudeville era.

Stooge

A secret confederate in the audience who helps to make the magic happen.

Sucker trick

An effect that seems to let the audience in on the secret and then turns the tables at the last second. Also refers to a trick that appears to have gone wrong but is later proved to be part of the routine.

Time misdirection

The term given to the technique of leaving time in between a secret move and the subsequent moment of magic. It is an additional way to hide the method to a trick.

Vanish

To make an object disappear.

acknowledgements

The author would like to thank the following (past and present), who assisted in the process of writing this book: Aaron Barrie, Milbourne Christopher, Davenports, Edwin A. Dawes, Joanne Einhorn, John Fisher, Walter Gibson, Ian Keeble, George Kovari, Peter Laine, The Magic Circle and Christopher Pratt.

The playing cards used throughout the book are Bicycle cards. Bicycle, the Bicycle logo and the Bicycle Rider Back Design are all registered trademarks of The United States Playing Card Company and are used with permission.

Thank you to the following, who provided props for photography: Carta Mundi (tarot cards), Ann Childers (money), Betty Davenport (antique box of tricks), Tim Ellerby (antique books), Jennifer Schofield (ring, money), Sarah See (money) and Amanda Wood (napkins, money).

Picture credits

The publisher would like to thank the following for the use of their pictures in the book (l=left, r=right, t=top, b=bottom). *Colin Rose*: 136r; *Edwin A. Dawes Collection*: 7b, 14t, b, 15t, b, 16tl, tr, 17b, 19t, b, 21, 22, 23b, 24bl, 25t, b, 28t, b, 29t, 32t, 112, 113tl, 151br, 168b; *The Fortean Picture Library*: 18t, b, 20t, 150t, b, 151t, 169tr, 188b; *Graham P. Jolley*: 169tl; *Hulton Archive*: 151bl; *The Image Bank*: 6; *Mary Evans Picture Library*: 136l; *Popperfoto/Reuters*: 27; *Rex Features Limited*: 29b (photo by Jean Catuffe); *Stone*: 7t, 9; *Telegraph Colour Library*: 8; *Vin Mag*: 16b, 17t, 23tl, tr.

suppliers

There are hundreds of magic shops all over the world that you may wish to visit in person or on the Internet. If your area is not listed below, take a look in your local business directory. Please note that the following details are correct at the time of publication, but it is advised that you contact the shops prior to your visit in order to avoid disappointment.

Australia
Bernard's Magic Shop
211 Elizabeth Street
Melbourne, Victoria
www.bernardsmagic.com.au

Hey-Presto Magic
Shop P34, Imperial Arcade
Pitt Street Mall
Sydney, New South Wales
www.hey-presto.com.au

Taylor's Magic Shop
Shop 1, The Interchange
432 Victoria Ave
Chatswood, New South Wales
www.taylorsmagicshop.com.au

Belgium
Mephisto Magic
(The Magic Hands)
Brugsesteenweeg 166b
B-8520 Kuurne

Select Magic
CV Slachthuisstraat 21 8500
Kortrijk

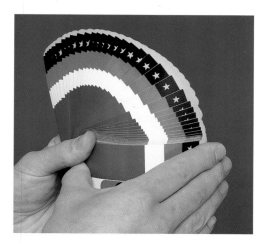

Canada
Browsers Den Of Magic
875 Eglinton Ave. W. #10
Toronto
www.browsersden.com

Magie Spectram Magic
1592 Jean-Talon est
Montréal
www.spectram.com

Morrissey Magic
2477 Dufferin Street
Toronto
www.morrisseymagic.com

Le Palais de la Magie
312 St-André Street
Gatineau
Québec
www.palaisdelamagie.com

Tony's Trick & Joke Shop
688 Broughton Street
Victoria
www.magictrick.com

Denmark
A & Z Magic
Ålekistevej 203 (basement)
2720 Vanløse
azmagic.net

France
Magic Productions
1 rue Froment, 75011
Paris

Mayette Magie Moderne
8 rue des Carmes, 75005
Paris
www.mayette.com

Germany
Astor Magie-Studio
Postfach 220 121D-42371
Wuppertal

Freer's Zauberladen
Greifswalder Str. 197
10405 Berlin

India
Electro Fun
9E Sandel Street, Calcutta 700016
www.electrofunmagic.com

Italy
La Porta Magica
Viale Etiopia 18, 00199
Roma
www.laportamagica.it

Japan
Magic Land
Tokyo
www.magicland-jp.com/Home/
LandMap.html

The Netherlands
Arjan's Show-Biz Centre
Bogerd 25
2922 EA Krimpen a/d Yssel
(By appointment only)
www.show-bizcentre.com

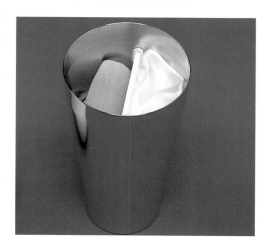

Dynamite Magic
Akkerwinde 7
5941 JP Velden
(By appointment only)
www.dynamitemagic.nl

Jan Monnikendam
Gedempte Raamgracht 5-7-9, 2011
WE Haarlem
www.monnikendam.nl

Spain
Magia Cadabra
Calle Navarros 7
Seville
www.magiacadabra.com

El Ray De La Magia
Calle Princesa 11
Barcelona

Selecciones Magicas
Calle Enamorandos 124
Barcelona

Switzerland
ZauberLaden Zürich
Hoerbi Kull
Rieterstr. 102
CH 8002
Zürich
www.zauberladen.com

Thailand
A & Z Magic
To find your nearest stockist, visit:
azmagic.net

UK
Davenports
7 Charing Cross Underground Arcade
The Strand, London
WC2N 4HZ
www.davenportsmagic.co.uk

International Magic
89 Clerkenwell Road
London
EC1R 5BX
www.internationalmagic.com

J.B. Magic
226 Lytham Road
Blackpool
Lancashire
FY1 6EX
www.jokeboxmagic.co.uk

Kaymar Magic
189a St Mary's Lane
Upminster
Essex
RM14 3BU
www.kaymarmagic.co.uk

USA
Abracadabra Magic
125 Lincoln Blvd
Middlesex, NJ
www.abra4magic.com

Daytona Magic
136 South Beach Street
Daytona Beach, FL
www.daytonamagic.com

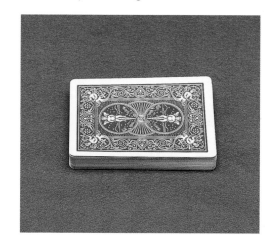

Denny & Lee Magic Studio
325 South Marlyn Avenue
Baltimore, MD
www.dennymagic.com

Hank Lee's Magic Factory
112 South Street
Boston, MA
www.magicfact.com

Hocus Pocus
2311 E. McKinley
Fresno, CA
www.hocus-pocus.com

Hollywood Magic Inc
6614 Hollywood Blvd
Hollywood, CA
www.hollywoodmagicshop.com

Houdini's Magic Shops
Las Vegas, NV
www.houdini.com

Louis Tannen Inc
24 West 25th Street, 2nd Floor
New York, NY
www.tannenmagic.com

Stevens Magic Emporium
2520 E. Douglas
Wichita, KS
www.stevensmagic.com

Worldwide
Marvin's Magic
www.marvinsmagic.com

index

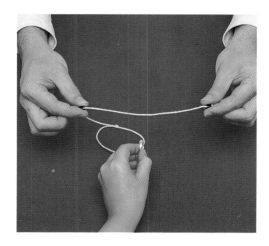

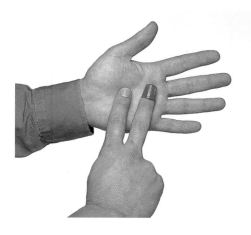

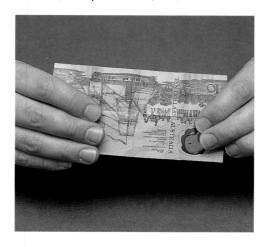